THE ADVENTURES OF JOHN WETHERELL

THE ADVENTURES *of* JOHN WETHERELL

Edited & with an Introduction by

C. S. FORESTER

MICHAEL JOSEPH
LONDON

MICHAEL JOSEPH LTD

Published by the Penguin Group
27 Wrights Lane, London w8 5tz
Viking Penguin Inc., 375 Hudson Street, New York, New York 10014, USA
Penguin Books Australia Ltd, Ringwood, Victoria, Australia
Penguin Books Canada Ltd, 10 Alcorn Avenue, Toronto, Ontario, Canada m4v 3b2
Penguin Books (NZ) Ltd, 182–190 Wairau Road, Auckland 10, New Zealand

Penguin Books Ltd, Registered Offices: Harmondsworth, Middlesex, England

First published in Great Britain 1954
First published in this paperback edition 1994

Printed in England by Clays Ltd, St Ives plc

ISBN 0 7181 3844 9

INTRODUCTION TO

John Porritt Wetherell's Adventures

by C. S. FORESTER

JOHN WETHERELL was a native of Whitby, one of the thirteen children of Nathan Wetherell, a whaling captain. He was born in 1780, and his father died in 1789—killed, according to Wetherell, in a skirmish with Eskimos in Davis Strait. Wetherell himself died, probably in New York, sometime after 1834. He left behind him an autobiography, in three volumes of manuscript amounting altogether to a thousand pages. It had been the object of a fruitless search by students of the period until, a few years ago, Mrs Anne Klein of New York, an enthusiastic collector of rare nautical books, discovered it at the New York auction of the library of the late Gabriel Wells. There can be no doubt about its genuineness; the paper, the script, and the ink help to bear it out, even if the internal evidence was not conclusive. The water colours with which he illustrated his work, some of which, quite charming in their simplicity, are reproduced in this volume, could only have been painted by a seaman of the time.

There can be no doubt about the genuineness of the document, but unfortunately there is room for doubt about the truth of many of the passages contained in it. It purports to be a diary, but on the face of it the manuscript is at best a fair copy made from the original documents—that is obvious from the uniformity of paper, ink, and handwriting, and the absence of erasures or corrections. And a very brief further analysis shows that there is considerable variation in the value of different parts of the book. Wetherell was shipwrecked over and over again, a dozen

times in all, and on more than one occasion he was the
sole survivor, escaping with nothing more than his life and
most certainly without the current volume of his diary. Later on
he reconstructed the lost passages from memory—his memory
was clearly very tenacious of names and dates—but then he
never could resist the temptation to embroider his narrative.
Some of the reconstructed passages are absurd, and some are
demonstrably false, which is a great pity. For instance, there
can be no doubt that he was an eyewitness of the Battle of the
Nile, being present as one of the crew of a hired storeship, and
if he had stuck to the truth in his account he might have made
a decided contribution to history; but what he wrote about the
Nile is so coloured by newspaper accounts (the style can be
detected) and so distorted by faulty memory as to be value-
less.

Yet on the other hand there are long passages in the book
which are obviously quite genuine, an exact reproduction of his
original diary, unretouched even in transcription. It calls for
only a brief examination to determine that these passages
represent the portions of his diary which he was able to bring
home to his relations in Yorkshire on the occasions when he
completed a voyage without being shipwrecked or was able to
save his belongings if he was. The quality of these passages is
enormously higher than that of the other material. The style is
more natural and there is no attempt to touch up the truth.
The longest and most interesting of these passages deals with
Wetherell's service in H.M.S. *Hussar* and his captivity in France,
and that is the passage that has been selected for reproduction
in this book. In length it is between a quarter and a third of
the original manuscript, and it shows Wetherell at his best,
patient and resourceful, simple and yet observant.

Wetherell had served his time as an apprentice in the British
merchant navy, having narrowly escaped (by his own efforts)
from being apprenticed to a baker. His articles dated from March
1793 (England was just entering into the long war with revolu-
tionary France), and the ships in which he served were all North
Country owned, from Whitby and South Shields and Hull. He
made voyages—several of them, as has been said, abruptly terminated by shipwreck—to the Mediterranean and the Baltic, and

one in an auxiliary vessel which took part in the successful British amphibious attack at the Helder. Much of his time, however, was spent in the Newcastle coal trade, the most instructive and exacting school of seamanship to be found at that time. Cook the circumnavigator learned his seamanship half a century earlier in the same school. Winter and summer, but especially in winter with its gales and fogs, the collier brigs made their way up and down the treacherous east coast of England where aids to navigation hardly existed, bringing the coal of Newcastle to London (sea coal, it was called, because of the way it was transported) in thick weather or clear; the tricky tides complicated the problem of picking their way through the sands of the Thames Estuary; the easterly gales of winter always found them with a dangerous shore to leeward; and the more usual westerly winds imposed upon them the necessity of working to windward into the Thames or the Tyne.

It was hard work and dangerous work, but nowhere in his account of his adventures does Wetherell bewail his lot, and most certainly never does he allow himself to dwell for one moment on the possibility that he might have grown up into a journeyman baker safe on shore. His articles of apprenticeship expired in 1803, the original seven years having been prolonged by the periods when he was not in his masters' employ through shipwreck and through transfer to another vessel. Up to this moment he had been protected from the press gang by the fact of his apprenticeship, for the Royal Navy did not press apprentices. This was partly because the Navy rightly considered apprenticeship as the best school in which to train young men for the highly skilled profession of handling sailing ships (the sailing masters and master's mates of the Royal Navy were mostly drawn from the merchant navy), but also because there was a conscientious objection to interfering with the rights of private property—for a shipowner it was a definite investment to train an apprentice.

Wetherell's indentures terminated at an unfortunate time for him, just when the uneasy Treaty of Amiens was ending and England was mobilising afresh for war. The Navy had to be hurriedly expanded to ten times its peacetime strength, and skilled seamen had to be found. Landsmen were useful, and could eventually be trained, but the men who were needed were men who could 'hand, reef and steer,' men already possessed of the myriad skills that were necessary to the sailor, and without such men a ship was helpless. They could only be found in the merchant navy, and quite legally they could be drawn from there, on the principle that the men so seized could be replaced by landsmen who could be trained for life at sea in conditions less exacting than in the fighting service. As a principle, it was entirely sound, but it was applied clumsily and with a good deal of friction. A naval officer, captain of an unmanned ship and anxious to get to sea—with his professional reputation largely dependent on his ability to man his ship—was not likely to observe rules and regulations too closely, especially as once he had his men on board, subject to the Mutiny Act and safely at sea, there was not much chance of protests reaching any influential quarter for a long time if at all.

Wetherell was on the threshold of his career. He had been offered the position of mate in a ship engaged in the West Indian trade, plying out of London. If he should survive the West Indian diseases as well as the hazards of the sea he could look forward to steady promotion and even to acquiring a respectable competence. But his ship was not ready, and while she was fitting he had returned to Yorkshire to say good-bye to his family and friends; he was at this moment betrothed to a girl, number three or four on the list of seven or eight to whom he lost his heart, according to his own account. The farewells made, the question arose as to whether he should return to London by road or by sea. To travel by road was slow, difficult, and expensive, and Wetherell elected to go by sea. British ships of war were watching the mouth of the Thames—much more than half of England's sea-borne trade came up London river—and Wetherell was seized, among others, and found himself a sailor of King George, on board H.M.'s frigate *Hussar*, Captain Philip Wilkinson.

She was one of a small squadron under Sir Sydney Smith (the man who had defended Acre and made Napoleon 'miss his destiny'), stationed for the very purpose of seizing men from the merchant shipping. For the authorities the situation was

desperate. Immediately after the Treaty of Amiens had been concluded a most rigorous regime of economy had set in, under the
direction of St. Vincent, and the number of men on the perma-
nent establishment of the Navy had been reduced to the lowest
possible figure. There were a few half-manned ships, and the
rest of the Navy had been laid up under the smallest care and
maintenance parties. In a day or two, not more, the French
privateers would be out, and in hardly longer Napoleon would
have his fleets at sea, and it was his boast that he only needed
command of the Channel for twenty-four hours to be able to
dictate peace on English soil. It was of the most pressing im-
portance to reman the Navy, and every rule and regulation
went by the board. Wetherell had provided himself with a
'protection' as a carpenter, which in the previous war would
have been sufficient to keep him out of the hands of the press
gang, but as it was, it only served to mark him out as the first
man to be seized.

All the merchant ships that could be caught were denuded
of their crews, to such an extent that they were unable to go
on up to London. To deal with this situation the regularly enlisted men of the Navy (the Lord Mayor's men, in Wetherell's
term, who could be more trusted not to desert) were put on
board to sail the vessels up to London, whence the men could
be returned to their ships via the guard ship. To the guard ships
also were despatched the men in excess of the number necessary
to complete the crews of the squadron; as Wetherell points
out, the captains naturally retained all the best men for themselves. The distinction between the pressed men and those
regularly enlisted was rigidly maintained; boats for the shore
were manned only by 'Lord Mayor's men,' and the fact that
even this precaution might not prevent desertion was proved
by the nearly successful conspiracy of Wetherell and his friends
to desert with the *Hussar's* boat with the first lieutenant on
board. But it was noticeable—more than one naval writer of the
period has remarked on the phenomenon—that the pressed
men played their part with zest when it came to pressing other
men, perhaps because misery loves company.

At this time, with the war only just beginning, there was a
difference in status between the men who 'entered' and the men

who were pressed. The former were considered as voluntary enlisting, and theoretically they had certain rights. They had entered for service in one particular ship and could expect, when the ship was paid off, at the end of the voyage or for refitting, to be released from service, as at the termination of a contract. Subsequent events were to show that any such implied contract was unavailing, and men who had entered, and men who were pressed, were indiscriminately turned over from ship to ship without chance of liberty. But that was not foreseen at present, and pressure was applied to induce the men to 'enter'; the credit of the captain rose the higher with the number of these apparently voluntary enlistments. Wetherell's motives in refusing were twofold. He had no wish to serve under Wilkinson—and, as a pressed man, he might be transferred out of the *Hussar*—while at the same time he hoped that his friends at home might secure his release, which would be impossible if he had entered into a contract.

Harwich was raided, as Wetherell describes, and every available man there was swept off into the Navy. The men were ceaselessly exercised at their new duties—Wetherell complains about this without allowing for the anxieties of the captains, who might at any moment find themselves alongside a well-manned French ship of war in a battle where life, liberty, and honour would be at stake—and eventually the *Hussar* was sent off to join the squadron blockading Brest; she paid a brief call at Plymouth on the way, where Wetherell gives us an insight into the arrangements made for the entertainment of women on board the ships whose crews were never allowed to set foot on land, and then she began the dangerous and tedious service which resulted eventually in her loss.

Philip Wilkinson, her captain, was a brute, even making allowance for the strong prejudice Wetherell bore against him. He undoubtedly had previously been captain of the *Hermione*, as Wetherell says, but whether he was really responsible for the mutiny that took place under her next captain, Pigott, as Wetherell alleges, cannot be determined now; there is no doubt that Pigott was a brute too, and a most unpleasant one. The mutiny, to which Wetherell continually alludes, was famous, or rather notorious, in British naval annals. The crew of the *Hermione*, driven frantic by Pigott's treatment of them, rose during the night and murdered their officers. Pigott, badly wounded, was dropped overboard (in the evidence at one of the courts-martial there is a graphic account by an eyewitness of hearing Pigott's last words as he fell into the water), and the mutineers brought the ship into Spanish waters in the West Indies and handed her over to Spanish authorities. For many years after this event British naval records are studded with accounts of the courts-martial of the mutineers as they fell into the hands of the naval authorities. Quite a number of the muti-neers could not endure their self-imposed exile and drifted, homesick, back to England. Most sailors of that day were unfitted for any shore employment, and they took to the sea again, and either they were pressed from merchant service or even, pathetically, enlisted direct into the Navy, where sooner or later they were, inevitably, recognized, tried, and mostly hanged. The *Hermione* was subsequently recaptured with a Spanish crew on board in one of the most daring cutting-out expeditions ever recorded, and incidentally the captain respon-sible, Edward Hamilton, years later was reprimanded by a court-martial for cruelty to members of his ship's company.

Cruelty was common enough. Flogging was frequent, severe, and practically unregulated, but before the practice is unre-servedly condemned it is worthy of some little analysis. Even a conservative organization like a fighting service does not cling long to institutions that are actually deleterious. The first point to be borne in mind is that flogging was still a common and a legal punishment in ordinary life. While civilians were still being publicly flogged it would be Utopian to hope that soldiers and sailors could be made exempt. There was still an enduring superstition, surviving from the Middle Ages, that corporal punishment had some sort of intrinsic reformative effect on the victim, and it occurred to no one to question the effect it had on the person who inflicted it. But there was a more practical side as well. The sailor led a hard life; when the existence of a nation was at stake—its freedom, its institutions— the men of the fighting services had to submit to hardships pushed to the limit of human endurance, just as they have had to in every war save those of limited objectives. The sailors stayed at sea literally for years without a moment on shore, and they had to endure the consequent hardships of bad food and unhealthy living conditions. Life was as hard as it possibly could be, and in that case what was to be done with the recalcitrant, the lazy, or the rebellious? If a man shirked his work, how was he to be treated? To turn out to reef topsails on a wild night, to make one's way up rigging slippery with ice, whipped by a howling gale, in pitch darkness, in a ship rolling fantastically and unpredictably, was unpleasant as well as highly dangerous. What could be done with the skulker? Lock him up? The skulker would welcome any prison as an alternative to his present duty. Cut down his rations? He only had enough now to keep him in health, if that. Stop his pay? He could see no opportunity of spending his meagre pay for years to come. Hang him? Then his services were lost anyway. The only solution was to find a punishment that made life even worse than the hell on earth that he was already enduring, and the cat-o'-nine-tails was the answer in those days.

The problem has endured to this present day; let that be understood. Soldiers and sailors still endure hell on earth. When conditions grow too bad for mortals to endure for long, something even more horrible must be devised to compel them to submit to those conditions. What could be more horrible than Passchendaele, to quote no nearer example? Something had to be devised, something even more horrible than self-mutilation, with its agony and danger and shame, something worse than death. So in these modern days there are secrets and dreadful places which are whispered about among the ranks and the ratings—Bull Rings and Glass Houses and so on—and which inevitably are revealed in the end, to become the subject of Congressional or Parliamentary inquiry, and to be thought about with shame by the nations that unknowingly maintained them and that nurtured the men who staffed them. But the shame should not be felt, as long as total war exists, for those things are necessary to total war, and the war into which England was about to enter, and in which Wetherell was reluctantly to bear a part, was a total war, in that the existence of England as a free country depended on her victory over the tyrant.

Yet it is quite obvious that in the Royal Navy of that period the power to flog—on which ultimately efficiency and discipline depended—was frequently and shamefully abused, so that often —the *Hermione* being the most vivid example—it defeated its own object. There were captains and subordinate officers who were sadistic brutes and who enjoyed the infliction of punishment, and their appetite for it grew with indulgence. There were also unimaginative officers, and stupid officers, and timid officers, who could think of no alternative to physical punishment or who were afraid not to employ it. Captains with powers of leadership, who could inspire their men with their own devotion and patriotism, seldom or never had to use the lash. There were many ships where flogging was unknown for months or even years at a time. In those days of long voyages and poor communications much had to be left to the discretion of the captains, and with seven hundred ships of war at sea—one ship to every fourteen thousand of the population—it was impossible to find enough discreet captains, and it would have been even if the methods of selection for promotion had been less imperfect than they were.

This leads to the consideration of one of Wetherell's most serious grievances against his captain, the fact that Wilkinson was of ignoble birth. It is a curious cause of complaint. Wetherell himself came from good middle-class stock, but he rose from poverty to the eventual command of a ship by his own efforts, and it is hard to understand why he should bear a grudge against Wilkinson for doing exactly the same. The distinguished naval officers of the British service have always been drawn from the most diverse strata of society; Cochrane inherited a peerage; Nelson was the son of a poor country parson (and so were many of his colleagues); but there were plenty of officers whose parentage was quite obscure besides Wilkinson—Westcott, the British captain who was killed at the Nile, was the son of a baker. But there was long a prejudice (which has not yet quite died out) among the lower ranks of the British services in favour of being commanded by gentlemen—that indefinable term being interpreted according to the standards of the lower ranks themselves. It might be said on the one hand that the men expected more sympathy and justice, straightforward dealing, and ingrained leadership from a gentleman; on the other hand it might be suggested cynically that the lower ranks feared that an officer who had arisen from among them knew too much about them and was not as susceptible to having the wool pulled over his eyes. Edgar Lee Masters warned against the man who rises to power from one suspender; Wetherell felt that fear a century before Masters wrote those words. The officer who proved himself could rely on the devotion of his men whatever his origin, but at least until recently if he came from the lower orders of society the proof he had to offer was far more exacting, even if the prejudice or superstition of his men was quite baseless.

Wilkinson offered no proof, but it can hardly be believed he was such a poltroon as Wetherell makes him out to be. When the *Hussar* went aground on the French coast and Wetherell was made a prisoner of war, the only boat that escaped to the British forces was the one commanded by Wilkinson, and the reader can form his own opinion as to whether or not this was due to Wilkinson's superior ability, but the Admiralty's opinion of him can be guessed at from Wilkinson's subsequent career. In the absence of all competent witnesses except Wilkinson himself the court of inquiry into the loss of the *Hussar* could reach no conclusion, but Wilkinson was only rarely employed again. Most of his time was spent on half pay; in the records we find a mention of his marriage; occasionally he was appointed acting captain to fill a gap caused by death or illness, but that was all. Before the war was ended he had risen by seniority to the top of the captains' list, received his automatic promotion to flag rank, and was 'yellowed'—left in retirement and never employed further.

During the year in which the *Hussar* was part of Cornwallis's squadron off Brest she had taken an active part. Her boats shared in the cutting out of the *Faisan*—a brilliant achievement—and in the attack on the *Revenge*, which ended in a bloody repulse, in which Wetherell was wounded. Cruising in what even at that time were called the Western Approaches, she intercepted a good many would-be blockade runners. She carried messages, and she played her part in harassing 'Johnny Croppoe' as Wetherell calls him—Jean Crapaud, in other words; to the Englishman of that day the fact that Frenchmen occasionally ate frogs' legs was the most astonishing thing about them.

Perhaps a word of explanation is necessary regarding the *Hussar*'s visits to Ferrol and Corunna. At this time Spain was a neutral in the struggle, but a neutral decidedly benevolent towards France. Secretly she paid a million francs a month to Napoleon from her bankrupt treasury (much to the easing of Napoleon's complicated finances), but openly she made her ports free to French ships of war. A French squadron had taken refuge in Ferrol and was blockaded there by Commodore Sir Edward Pellew with his pendant in the *Malta*, 80. The Spaniards could hardly deny the British the ordinary privileges of neutrals (especially as Spain was deliberately temporizing in order to get her treasure ships in from the Indies before declaring war), so that British officers with telescopes sat on hilltops round the harbours ready to report to Pellew any preparations the French might make to escape, and Pellew continually sent in for fresh provisions and water. Wine and brandy were cheap in Corunna, and tobacco was dear. It was only natural for the men who manned the boats to smuggle tobacco on shore and exchange it for liquor, and the men whose funds were too low to allow them to buy ship's tobacco parted with their shirts on their backs—literally—for something to drink. Wetherell describes how he was detected by the Spanish authorities in the act of smuggling; it is hard to believe there is any truth whatever in Wetherell's hint that he was smuggling on the captain's behalf. Wilkinson certainly would not have put himself in that manner into Wetherell's power—he had plenty of toadies to execute such a commission for him—and it is to be feared that when Wetherell speaks about the 'captain's tobacco' he means tobacco that had once belonged to the captain and had been removed from the captain's possession without the captain's agreement. It is a thousand pities that no research has been able to establish the truth or falsity of Wetherell's statement that Pellew himself obtained Wetherell's freedom by his threat to burn the town. Undoubtedly Pellew made energetic representations, and after that incident one can hardly blame Wilkinson (although Wetherell does; nothing Wilkinson did could ever meet Wetherell's approval) for mustering his ship's company, going through their kits, and punishing the men who were short of necessary clothing.

But that was very nearly the last of Wilkinson's official acts as captain of the *Hussar*, for shortly afterwards she was ordered back to Cornwallis's squadron, and was lost on the Saints' Islands. The ship's company, taken prisoner at the very beginning of a long war, languished in prison for many years. Wetherell himself was sent to Givet, a fortress originally planned to defend France on her Belgian frontier, and now, with the steady extension of the Empire, more nearly in its centre than on its border. A word of explanation may not be out of place regarding his method of going there and his delightful journey back again. Our minds have grown so accustomed to other means of transportation that it is hard for us to realise now that during the Napoleonic Wars every soldier who went anywhere, the conscript on his way to the depot, the recruit going to join his unit, the convalescent returning from hospital and the fortunate man who was granted leave, went on his own two feet, taking with him no more than he could carry on his back. Very rarely indeed fighting units were moved for some vital manœuvre by waggon and diligence (like Maunoury's taxi-borne Paris army in 1914), but all the continual to-and-fro movements of detachments and drafts were made on foot. During the feverish military activity of the Empire, France was thronged with parties of soldiers going this way and that, and a system had been evolved which took care of the details efficiently enough. The soldier, or the noncommissioned officer in charge of a party, was given his marching orders—in French his *'feuille de route'*—telling him where he was to go and what was to be the first day's march. Off he went, and at the end of the day he reported to the authority there. With the centralized French Government he could be quite certain to find a representative of the Emperor there; if not a military commandant or a prefect, then most certainly a mayor. The local authority endorsed his *feuille de route* and marked the next stage on it. Also he allotted him a billet for the night. Sometimes it would be in barracks, sometimes even in a building (often a disused church or a warehouse) specially devoted to the needs of transient soldiery, but most usually it was an order on a named householder to provide the bearer with a night's lodging—food, lights, and floor space to sleep on, all on a well-defined scale. This the householder was bound to provide, willy-nilly, and if he was a French citizen he could recover payment for it from the local authority, and the local authority from the central government; if the transaction took place in a satellite or subject country, it was only too unfortunate for the householder; for many years Napoleon maintained a large proportion of his army at other people's expense. But in France the system worked well enough, and private persons became accustomed, and even reconciled, to hearing a knock on their door and finding they had to receive a soldier or two as lodgers for the night. In humdrum provincial life it was one way to hear news and gossip, and a new face was not particularly unwelcome, particularly as most households had sons who were serving somewhere in the Empire.

In the morning the soldier set off again, bearing in his haversack the unconsumed portion of his day's rations to sustain him on his day's march of fourteen miles or more; in each town experience had long shown what was the most convenient next stage in whatever direction the soldier was taking, to Poland or Spain or Italy. So he went on, day by day, sometimes going for hundreds of miles—he could even, when his meagre pay fell due, draw that from the local authority as well. In many of the hundreds of military memoirs of the Empire the remark is to be found that those carefree days spent on the way to join one's unit were the happiest part of the military life, despite homesickness and footsoreness.

With prisoners of war the system applied with hardly any variation. There was a military, or at least a police, escort to the party, with an officer or noncommissioned officer in charge, and every member of the party had to be accounted for at each halt, but that was equally the case with parties of Napoleon's reluctant conscripts. Treatment was considerably more variable; on the credit side was the provision of waggons to carry the party's baggage. The application to the mayor for billets was a dip into a lucky bag containing more widely assorted possibilities than for a soldier, for there was always the chance that the party might be housed in the local gaol, to be overcrowded and underfed, attacked by vermin and blackmailed by an unscrupulous gaoler. But it was always in the cards that they might be given billets in private houses, unlikely as that may appear to us, and there they could usually expect, prisoners of war though they were, good treatment from their compulsory hosts. National enmity, and even resentment at the violation of domestic privacy, usually died away at personal contact, in face of the deeper appeal to charity and hospitality; Hitler's slave labour sometimes had the same experience despite the Fuehrer's savage edicts, and so did German and Italian prisoners of war who volunteered to work for the Allies. Moreover, in those unenlightened days Frenchmen with friends or interests in England did not hesitate to show their sympathy towards the prisoners of war.

In this introduction no explanation can be offered for Wetherell's claims to have witnessed an exhibition of public and judicial torture in Amiens; it seems more like a complete fabrication than an exaggeration, but it is hard to imagine what suggested the story to Wetherell. The judicial procedure of the Consulate certainly did not permit of torture. It may be suggested that Wetherell actually did see what he claimed to see, and that he was a witness of one of the last survivals of the methods of the old regime before the new criminal code was established, but it seems flatly impossible. Wetherell as yet knew no French, and there was some misunderstanding if there was no deliberate lying.

From Amiens, Wetherell went on through towns whose names have a different significance nowadays—Bapaume; Cambrai; he spent a night in the church at Albert, under the statue of the Virgin which a century later was to be watched by the soldiers of four nations as it hung head downwards from its spire and whose fall was—incorrectly—predicted to come with the end of the war. It was a march of seven and a half weeks until he reached his destined prison in Givet, the distance from Brest being nearly seven hundred miles—not very severe marching, but not too easy.

Wetherell was a prisoner for eleven years, and the account he gives of his imprisonment is very like accounts by prisoners in many prisons in many countries—the hopes and the disappointments, the weariness and the synthetic amusements, the riots, the escapes, the treachery, the infiltration of news. He was by no means badly treated; materially, as regards food and housing, he was probably better off than he would have been while serving in a British ship of war, and it is to be feared that he lived better than the prisoners in England lived. Yet already there was one marked difference apparent from the amenities of the eighteenth century. There was almost no attempt to exchange prisoners, although even in the last war there had been frequent exchanges; Wetherell himself had already been a prisoner once, after shipwreck on the coast of Flanders, and had been exchanged after only a brief confinement in Valenciennes. Bonaparte now had reason to believe that his resources in manpower were greater than those of England, and refused to contemplate exchanges in consequence. He had already taken the unprecedented step of arresting, at the outbreak of war, all British civilians in his domain, and he kept most of them prisoner during the eleven years of war; in Wetherell's notes we find allusions to these prisoners, most of whom lived on parole near Verdun.

Wetherell like a sensible man kept himself occupied, learning French and navigation and music, and later on had frequent cause to be thankful for all three. Like the prisoners of 1914–18, and 1939–45, he learned of the victories of his captors through their bulletins, and of their defeats only from new prisoners. Austerlitz was balanced by Trafalgar, Wagram by Talavera. Givet was on the road to one of the principal crossings of the Rhine at Mainz, and time and again he saw the Grand Army pouring forward to fresh victories. Then at last came the issue of the famous 29th Bulletin, when Wetherell, like the French Empire, first heard of the magnitude of the disaster in Russia. It was a moment of cold common sense on the part of Bonaparte, unlike Hitler's reaction to the news of the surrender of Paulus at Stalingrad. Wetherell knew the Empire was tottering, but he had another year to wait—a year during which he saw a new Grand Army thronging forward to the Rhine and the battered wrecks of it falling back.

With the arrival of the Allies on the frontiers of France itself the prisoner of war camps at Givet had to be evacuated; there were many similar incidents in 1945, but they were attended with a dreadful horror that was almost entirely missing in

Wetherell's experience. Bonaparte was as much a megalo-
maniac as Hitler, and both those potentates fought it out to the
last gasp because admission of defeat could only mean giving up
all power, but Bonaparte to the end retained some sanity and
some clarity of vision, and he ruled a people and had delegated
power to subordinates who retained, or regained, their common
sense with the approach of disaster. There were few atrocities,
and on the other hand there were remarkable displays of kindness towards the marching prisoners; Wetherell and his party
completed half the circuit of France, first at a moment of total
mobilization, and then at a moment of total collapse, with few
hardships and many experiences that involved something quite
the opposite. There is something oddly appealing in the picture
of the well-rehearsed band marching into the little French provincial towns playing catchy tunes and the townspeople gathering
round them as they gave their concert in the *place*. France had
been a dreary place for the last year or two, with every man of
military age caught up into the Army, with news almost entirely
lacking, with an impending sense of disaster, and with taxation
and regimentation pushed to what in those days seemed the
uttermost extreme. Here came Wetherell and his fellow instru-
mentalists, youth and music and fun. They brought news, the
townspeople could learn about Salamanca and Vittoria—battles
of which they had never heard—from the lips of men who had
actually fought there. And they brought the promise of the end
of the regime, and they were living proofs that the conquerors of
France would not be the undisciplined horde of savages that
Bonaparte had threatened them with. And they brought spring
with them, too, the lovely first budding of the coming summer,
into the Loire Valley that Rabelais loved. Small wonder that
the girls lost their hearts and the rich men opened their purses.

France was being assailed on two sides at once, as was
Germany in 1945. While Russians and Prussians and Swedes
and Austrians advanced across the Rhine, Wellington and his
ever victorious army had burst in over the Pyrenees and was
pressing into the fairest provinces of France. Toulouse and
Bordeaux fell to him, and the prisoners who had been hurried
in one direction to avoid recapture by the Russians were turned
about to avoid recapture by the British.

The present editor has confined his editorial efforts to an endeavour to make the book easily read. Wetherell's style is unaffected and good, and his spelling is of a remarkably high standard, but he knew nothing whatever of punctuation. Periods and exclamation marks and colons and quotation marks are dotted about lavishly with almost no reference to the sense, making the matter difficult to read; there are some passages in the original that have had to be puzzled over before their sense can be extracted. But with the punctuation supplied remarkably little more needed to be done. Occasional redundant words had to be removed and some necessary conjunctions supplied, but in no case has the sense of the original been varied.

Wetherell wrote a great deal of doggerel verse. Most of it was remarkably poor, and most of it has been eliminated, only enough being retained to show what the rest was like. The reader is assured that he has lost nothing of consequence.

C. S. Forester.

CHAPTER

I

FEBRUARY *28, 1803.* Our time rolled round and the Ship Jane was shortly expected to be ready for Sailing, her crew partly engaged, her cargo nearly all on board, My things all ready to take on board any time required.

The great mistake found out by being protected Carpenter

March 8, 1803. We had a rumour that set all Shields in an uproar. The ship Desdemona came in with the woful newse that two large Frigates lay in the Swin impressing ev'ry man protected or not. This was a bitter pill but I had to swallow it. Away to my dear Girl I directly ran with those cursed tidings. We consulted what course to take. Whether to go by land or water to London. Father wish'd me to go over to My Owner and have his advice, which accordingly I did. Mr. Makepeace advised me to take the Carpenter's Affadavit for the Ship as she always protected one and gave me a letter to the Captain. I returned to Shields and gave my Father and his Daughter my Answer from Mr. Makepeace. I told father I thought to go up to London by land; however he and Betsey both thought My offer in the Ship was best. I took the birth, bid adieu to my greatest pride and on the 11th of March left Shields with wind N.W. We had light winds and on the 19th at day light in the morning clearly saw two Frigates and several boats making towards us. Shortly after one of the Boats fired at us. We hove too, they came on board, gave orders to send every body aft. A grim looking fellow took up the ships Articles. Turning to

Nicholson 'Where is your carpenter?' 'There Sir, at the helm.' 'Relieve him and put his things in the Boat.' 'WHY SIR, HE IS PROTECTED.' 'That is the reason we want him in our carpenters' crew. Come, make haste. Coxwain bundle his things in the boat.' 'All ready Sir.' 'Here, drag this fellow along and bundle him in the boat.' This was all in five minutes transacted, away they bore me on board the Hussar Frigate. In a little while Capt Nicholson Anchord the ship and came on board after me but it was all in vain; he had to return to his ship and leave me. I was called aft to be stationed and told truth that I was no carpenter; they put me in the top.

The Golden rule on board the British Navy

In a little time gave me to understand that I was now entering on my first adventures and must consider myself under the Martial laws of My Country and must use ev'ry means to obey My Superiors, attend to my duty, all calls and Orders, to be sober, Silent and Submissive, and above all to curb your tongue and temper was what I soon found a golden rule. Another great comfort attends a young man on board one of those inquisition Bastile prisons; that is, not to have any learning whatsoever: and only very little knowledge, if you have the luck to be born dumb and have quick ears, and eyes, you are the boy for those sort of destructive engines . . . however here I am therefore must make my time as light as Master Mates Boatswains Mates and Ship mates will permit me. A boy comes to me. 'What is your name? Sir Wm. Smithson desired me to enquire.' I informed the Boy what was my name and the place of my birth Vc. [et cetera]. Mr. Smithson was a native of Stamford and acquainted with all my family. He was verry friendly to me and did me many little favours. I took his coat up and down, hung it up Vc. In his letters to Stamford he mentioned me and often has said it would be a great pleasure to him to be transferred to any other Ship and many other things which I shall not relate at the present. However night drawing on apace the hammacks were piped down and being on the gang way with mine, on the word being given pipe down, the crowd made a rush and drove me and my hammack headlong into the waste of the Ship. Obrian a Master's Mate flew at me and in great triumph dragged me and my dunnage aft under the Centry's charge to wait the hammacks being all off the deck.

> *This horrid 19th day of March from Pole to Pole*
> *does for me search*

After the bustle was over I was order'd aft on the quarter deck as an unruly villain. However the Midshipman of the main deck proved to be my friend Smithson; he came up and said he saw me drove down off the gangway with my bedding in my arms. The Boats. Mate of the deck also came up and spoke in my behalf and by those two friends to humanity I had the good fortune to escape at least two dozen I was set at liberty and felt verry happy at so narrow an escape. I thanked both my friends for their humane kindness and turned in. Next morning wash decks Vc., loose sails and exercise them, up and down top galt yards. Our first Lieut. would smile and say, 'Those North country carpenters are the verry boys fitting for H.M. Navy. They are mechanical Mariners and we must not let one go past us.' Yet he was much mistaken; to my own certain knowledge many of my acquaintance went past.

On board the British Frigate Hussar

March 19. Mr. Wallace the first Lieutenant smiling at me says you collier Carpenters are the verry boys we want on our tops, as we were all convinced yesterday by Barney Appleby. This Appleby had sailed on board the Defiance of 74 guns with the gunner and Boatswain only 15 months back. He was carpenter of the Neptune of Shields, and the Gunner being in the boat when they boarded the Neptune finding Barney Carpenter and knowing him perfectly well he steps up to him. 'Well old ship mate,' says he, 'you have been verry Smart in learning your trade since we were paid off, however the Hussar is a fine Ship and you have not quite forgot old times, so put your dunnage in the Boat.' Thus it was that thro' Barney the first Man called for at first boarding was the poor unfortunate fellow who had the misfortune to be protected Carpenter (and thus it was Capt. Wilkinson used to say he could work his top

with Mechanicks equal to any Ship with their able Seamen).
Our topmen were Mostly young men from the Northward. In
the Main top out of 36 Men 24 were imprest from those unfortunate affadavits which in the late War was the strongest protection granted. We shall leave them inventing some other
trap for poor Men.

March 21.   This day HBMS Antelope commanded by Sir
Sidney Smith joined us and anchored in Horsley Bay. Made
a signal for our Boat. Also the Athelion Frigate's boat, she being
the frigate in company with our frigate, the Hussar, as before
reported.

Our boats at this time had all been mann'd with imprest
Men and were called sea boats crew's, and the old peace
established crew's the land or harbour boats crews. Our boat
was mann'd to answer the signal with our sea boats crew, it
was my lot to be one of the number. Ran down to the commodore, lay along side some time, spoke to several acquaintances
had shared the same fate as myself, got our instructions
returned back and hoist in boats all well. Several sail of colliers in sight, out all our boats and board them. Caught a
number of three year servants all young men. It happened
that the newse reached the north concerning carpenters. This
made them try three years indentures which equally prov'd
as great a trap as the Carpenters' protection.

March 29.   In the course of this day the three ships tore
away from the fleet in passing near 150 Men. Sent their Lord
Mayor's men on board of those vessels they had distressed by
taking their hands, to assist them up to the Nore, and there
they must be deliver'd on board the guard Ship. Their Manner of picking their crew on board the Hussar was thus . .
on the first entrance on board a man was questioned, how long
he had followed the sea in what employ Vc. He was then
stationed and told where he had to do his duty and to start the
moment he heard his part of the ship call'd or all hands Vcc.
In fine weather loose and furld Sails two or three times per
day, up and down top galt and royal yards, Morning noon and
night. Exercise guns every day at four Bells at the same time
the Capt. and Officers were marking every man they took a
fancy to and the rest was sent up to the Nore.

The horrid outrage in Harwich

April 1, 1803. In this manner they obtain'd their ships crews. On the first of April early in the morning our orders were to have our boats ready to go on Shore after breakfast, harbour boats crews; accordingly three boats from our Ship, three from the Athelion, and four from the Antelope all started for the Shore, having orders to fetch ev'ry man on board that was able to Serve his King and country. They laid under the land till evening and then in great pomp made their landing good in Harwich. They commenced their Man plunder as I term it. The Market house was to be their prison, where a lieutenant was station'd with a guard of Marines and before daylight next morning their prison was full of all denominations, from the Parish Priest to the farmer in his frock and wooden Shoes. Even the poor Blacksmith cobler taylor barber baker fisherman and doctor were all drag'd from their homes that night and without the least timely notice as on former meetings. All assembled in private to hold a nightly meeting in the Market house. The assembly started round in terror and confusion at the sight of their President and Lieutenant and his attendants the marines. 'What means all this fun?' says one; 'Holy Father!' cries the Parson. 'We are all enchanted,' says the Blacksmith; 'Why, the Devil never wears arms,' says the cobler; 'I think,' says the barber, 'there has been some invading enemy or some Algerine landed on the coast and intends to drag us all from our families and our homes and use us as their Slaves.' 'I should like to take a stitch in him,' says the taylor; 'he is certainly a Magician; dont you see those red fiends all round him?'

Barker the Governor of Harwich

Poor Jack chanced to be taken in the same Snare. For some time he sat pensively listening to their various tales. At last he hail'd the quarter deck as he term'd it. 'Yo hoy . . . you scab necks do you mean to keep a poor fellow here and give us no grog?' 'Stop, My Man,' Says Lieutenant Barker, 'till you go on board then you will get your grog twice ev'ry day.'

Barker then addresses his hearers as follows. 'My friends, you must understand it is orders from Government to man a fleet immediately against our inveterate enemy France, therefore to murmur is in vain. Be of good courage; you will soon be questioned and regulated. Those that are entitled to be set at liberty will be released, and those fit to serve their country and rush their threatening invader must fly to their Standard and like true patriots protect that small garden, the residence of our first parents. Besides there is reason to believe this present dispute between us and France will be decided in a month or six weeks. It cannot be otherwise; we are all certain France has no Navy at this moment and her Merchant Ships are mostly out at her colonies in the west Indies. This will be a grand opportunity for our Seamen; they will fall in with them on their return to France, so cheer up my boys, this is the time you may make your fortunes and gain great laurels.' In midst of this lecture all attention was paid to Barker's oration; daylight made its way thro' the shatter'd roof and once intended windows of the Market house. A crowd of Women soon assembled round the prison and their business was quickly made known. Wives demanded their husbands, children their Fathers, and aged parents their Son perhaps their only support.

The Siege and bombardment of Barker's Castle Harwich

April 2. The first salute was a shower of stones at the door and roof of Lieutenant Barker's Castle. All the other officers at this moment were in their glory outside the town.

Why should one man differ from another both holding one office

Some of them, good disposed men, sat down and eat their breakfast with the peasants and disdained to put them to the least trouble or allarm. Others full of self presumption took ev'ry harsh unfeeling means to perplex and terify ev'ry living soul in their direction, dragging away Fathers and Children and sending them down to the Market house under a convoy of Marines. Lieutenant Barker finding his castle surrounded by an inveterate enemy and having a verry poor guard was in a pitiful state and after a little reflection came to a parley, putting his head out thro' a hole formerly a window verry mildly addressed his besiegers in the following style: 'My good people, you no doubt feel greatly allarm'd at this unexpected visit we have paid your town and its vicinity, a visit to you verry rare and to us verry unpleasant but as our orders are from the Admirality we dare not refuse to obey their command. However, good people, I will give my word and honour that by this day noon your husbands Fathers and Children shall be restored to your Arms again, only such as are entitled to serve their king owing to their being able Seamen or gain their living by the Salt water such as Fishermen Vc. Every other will be liberated as soon as the rest of My brother Officers can all meet here, which I know must be shortly. Such is their particular orders, to assemble here at noon.' This short story of our trembling son of Mars caused the besiegers to cease firing and for a little while the castle remained unmolested.

The Governor's happy deliverance and reinforcement

At last the wish'd for visitors began to muster from their various stations; a most welcome message to the Besieged governor, he verry seriously made known the serious attact that had been made against his castle and the determination of the foe was to release all prisoners under his charge. He also related his parley with them from his observatory and the articles agreed on between him and his adversaries Vc Vc.

Being all assembled and the Marine officers gave in report of all their men being present, Lieutenant Leftwidge of the Commodore's ship gave orders to embark all imprest men on board the Boats under the guard of marines, and should any person make the least objection or attempt by any means to effect their escape on their way from the Market house towards the boats, or from the boats after having embarked, with intent to gain the shore, that Man was to be fired at by the Marines there present, and any Marine refusing to obey such orders was to be tried by the Martial laws of his country, and thus by parties of 12 or 15 they marched all those unfortunate men down to the Boats and left the shore crowded with hart broken wives and parents. One brave Young Man, William Wright, the Fisherman, whose courage was daring sprang from the boat as she left the strand and ran with the swiftness of a deer pursued by a number of marines firing at him most furiously but all in vain; he crossed a mud bank and gain'd the other bank of a large inlet where he stood and wav'd his hat in defiance. Thus he was once more at his own liberty on Shore. The marines and officers return'd to the boats all mud and dirt, swearing vengeance against the next Man that made attempt to desert.

The boats leave Harwich with their prey

April 3. Having all embarked again orders were to make the best of our way for the Antelope, Sir Sidney's Ship, which we gained by sunset; lodged all our strangers on board that night and all boats return'd to their respective Ships. Next day was appointed as regulating day on board the commodore, the Monkey Brig and a Small cutter, to attend orders and receive on board such as were pronounced able to serve by Sea. All such were cram'd on board the Monkey and set up to the Nore there sent on board the Guard Ship and by the Sloop Cutter. Those not able to serve were sent directly back to the Shore, thus we past our time. Old Andrew McCarthy can not be forgot by me he was aged and made cooks mate being a lord mayors man as we term it; enter'd on the peace establishment, drinking a little ships beer or pursers swipes rather freely; after his work was done some enemy reported him to the quarter deck. He was taken aft put in irons all night to ruminate on his past frolic.

An electric shaking, a certain cure for the spring fever

At daylight next morning this unfortunate mortal was called on deck and order'd to be lash'd up in the forerigging and salt water to be poured down his throat thro' the help of a funnel, which was done and repeated several times, untill the water passed through him as clear as when administered. He was then left in the rigging way they termed a spread Eagle. This proved to be one of those cold sleety mornings quite frequent in the North Sea accompanied with a N.W. wind and verry severe. After remaining in this horrid situation nearly two hours orders came to cut him down and make him scrub the coppers ev'ry morning for one month. When placed on the deck he was nearly at death's door being nearly chill'd to the heart his messmates took him below and nursed him up so that in a little while he returned to his duty. As the treatment on board this noble Ship proves at present to strike my memory more strongly than in general I will make it my present study.

Bob Moody had the misfortune to taste pursers' swipes rather freely. Being made warm and quite palatable it is a common practice on board Men of War while in harbour; ev'ry ev'ning numbers meet in the Galley and make what they call hot nog, and over this they relate old stories and sometimes chance to have the misfortune to make too free and perhaps one looses his master; his doom is the Brig (the irons), another makes too much noise, go in the Brig. Others begin to dispute and fight.

A purgative Ametic of salt water verry good for the blood

However we can not forget Bob Moody; it was in some of those Galley Meetings poor Bob was led too far, and was sent on board the Brig reported drunk next day he was made fast to the Spanker boom by his hands his feet placed in buckets and Salt water administred to him thro the aid of a funnel untill passing thro' him. The buckets prevented any wet falling on the deck. Glorious good Usage.

April 21. John Markins, another patient, had to pass thro' the mill. Not pleasing Dennis Obriant the Master's Mate while at work washing decks, Dennis calls old Cole the boatswains mate, order'd him to take Markins forward and give him a good starting.[1] At this time Mrs. Markins was on board with her husband, and before Cole commenced his exercise poor Jack set up a horrid roar. This in one moment brought Sally on deck, and seeing her husband takeing those nausious bitters, knowing by his grinning and dancing they were not pleasant, Sally flys to the Cabin door Squalling out, 'Captain they are killing my husband.' The centeniel drove her away not untill she had roused the great Mogul who sent for the Officer of the deck, learnt the whole, and gave orders to put Markins in irons. This done at seven bells, 'all hands to witness punishment.' Markins was brought forth order'd to strip down his pantaloons, and then lash'd him to a gun. Made Sally stand by his side untill he had Six dozen lashes on his bare posteriors. Great.

The origan and dignity of our audacious commander

April 27. The first Lieutenant Mr. Wallace, a poor little diminitive creature, but considering himself sprung from the race of Cornwallis, was by far the largest man on board H B M S Hussar.

Should any person produce a Tyrant there is a Coward

On the 27th of April in the morning being nearly calm our Brave and Bold commander desired the Barge to be got ready to convey his grace on Shore to Harwich the place of his nativity. His Father kept a small Barbar's Shop in the town known by old Wilkinson the Barber. This great Brave tyranical cross unfeeling Coward was his son and heir SIR PHILIP WILKINSON CAPTAIN OF H.B.M. FRIGATE HUSSAR OF 38 GUNS. The Captain now being on Shore the command must fall into the hands of our Undaunted Wallace. His first attempt was what he most delighted in, impressment. After breakfast down Boats and let them be manned with the Sea Boats crews. The

[1] 'Starting' was a hasty and unofficial corporal punishment, often administered with the first thing that came handy, such as a rope's end, but many petty officers habitually carried a 'starter' about with them—a two-foot length of line with a knot at the end. Starting had no legal warrant whatever, and perhaps in consequence long survived flogging in the Navy.

weather being moderate numbers of vessels were in the Swin, colliers coasters fishing smacks and numbers of Dutch Galliotts Vc.

If Wives and Children thou distress thou art
a beast in human dress

Away goes our expedition a man hunting and sea robbing, distressing parents, robbing Wives, and Making Widows and Fatherless children. It was on one of those inhuman acts our hero sent his young blood hounds (Midshipmen) to rob over-haul and drag away. In the course of the day several unfor-tunate men were drag'd on board and had silently to bear such treatment . . . We shall refer to a circumstance both inhuman savage and horrid, on a young lad they took from one of the Harwich smacks. This boy was about 17 Years of age (and at this time we had a small tender used to attend our Ship from the Shore with letters Beer soft Bread Water Vc). The master of this smack or tender was a neighbour to the Mother of the Boy we refer to; this old fellows name was Lan-caster and as the tender was to lay all night anchor'd near us this unfortunate boy thought if he could get on board of old Lancaster he would be conveyed safe to his dear old Mother he being her only support.

The briny flood this youth did brave and refuge sought
his life to save

His resolution was fixed and some time in the night he made his escape overboard and swam to the tender being convinced when there he was safe. Poor Boy. To his astonishment on gaining the vessel his only supposed friend Lancaster put him in irons and on the following morning took him back on board the Hussar. His young Sighs tears and lamentations were all unheard by Lancaster; he was taken on board the Frigate, put both legs in irons to wait the return of the grand judge Sir Phillip Oh . . . this was the moment, revenge sparkled on the brow of each friend to humanity, . ah, , Lancaster had we dared to show our feelings, that day had been thy last!

April 30.   This evening our Captain returned on board and the verry planks appeard oerladen with his wretched frame; his weight of abominations were enough to Sink him Ship and crew all in the boundless deep. Sodom and Gomoro were destroy'd for their wickedness and Wilkinson ought to have been in the midst of them . . .

Hail Liberty thy smiles are sweet. We venture life
with them to meet.

He was not long on board before his prime minister informed him what had transpired during his absence, and on the following morning this boy was brought forth to suffer for attempting to gain that liberty that ev'ry imprest seaman strives to enjoy either in his mind or actions. All hands were called to be once more agravated to take revenge. The Marines all placed on the gangways and front of the quarter deck all under arms to protect the Bloodthirsty monster in his bar- barous tortures. However, let him proceed to work. Old douse-the-glim[1] presented himself to the altar of pollution (the quarter deck) reporting the prisoner ready. 'Seize him up,' answered the son of thunder; 'and as for you boatswains mates do your duty or I will see your back bones. So go on.' Another boatswains mate. 'Go on.' 'Oh Captain for the sake of my poor Mother have Mercy on me and forgive me.' 'No Sir, if I forgive you I hope God will never forgive me. Go on Boatswains Mate.'

Had not tyranny been guarded by numbers his
kingdom had fell

'Master at arms how many has he had?' 'One dozen and five Sir' 'Go on Boats[n] Mate'—he faints. 'Stop!' says the doctor 'no Sir he is only acting. Go on, I say' / / / He lay as still as any dead man. Poor fellow, that was the time ev'ry heart not made of Stone whisper'd revenge: and had not the Antelope and Athelion both laid so near our Ship, vengeance would have rose its horrid head and dash'd the standard of

[1] 'Douse-the-glim' was the ship's master-at-arms, head of the ship's police and responsible for the details of the administration of discipline. The last words the sailor would hear at night before going to sleep would be those of the master-at- arms ordering lights to be extinguished.

cruel tyranny under foot, and in its stead planted the conquering flag of generous humanity. No, that blessed moment was not yet at hand . . . We had to grin and bear it may the Almighty direct us in what he thinks best.

What tortures we to mortals are all reveng'd
by heav'ns just laws

By this time he had received two dozen, another Boatsⁿ Mate had orders to go on—not any signs of life was to be seen in him. The Doctor felt his pulse and ordered him not to have any more lashes at present, he being entirely unsensable of what was transacting. 'Well Sir,' says Wilkinson, 'Your orders shall be obey'd in that respect, by mine shall in another. Mr. Hill (the master-at-arms) take that fellow forward, and you Boatswains Mates Make him fast with a rope and heave him overboard. I know how to bring him to his sences again.' Accordingly his orders were obey'd. They hove him three times over board and then hove him on the deck, not any signs of life in him. Doctor Graham order'd him below and to be wrapped up in a blanket. In the course of an hour they let blood from him, he began to groan, and afterwards cry out for his Mother. On the following day he with some more unfortunate men was sent on board the Monkey and up to the Nore. On board the Guard ship this was the last account we had of poor Henry Wilson.

That evening Lieutenant Barker or in other words the bold Jack of Clubs made a visit on board the Athelion. As we had just arrived alongside with the Barge, Wilkinson order'd the Barge to attend on Mr. Barker. In he tumbled, half drunk as usual. Away we go helter skelter, got on board, had our orders to wait alongside; we accordingly left a boatkeeper in her and the rest of us went on board the Athelion.

A man of words and not of deeds to slaughter
many a hero leads

At last eight o'clock; set the watch and lights Vc. We sat down on the forecastle with some acquaintances we found on board, found a little grog to kill grief; we then related different

acts of cruelty committed on board the Hussar every day . . .
says one, 'I cannot bear it much longer.' 'Nor either will I,'
says another. 'Well, but,' says a third, 'we have to bear it
all, and by what I understand of his usage to the crew of the
Hermione we shall grow worse and no better . . .' 'Well what
is best to be done?' says Jack Waddell, a wild daring fellow.
'I dont know,' says one. 'Nor I,' says another.

Since Man to Man proves so unjust Man cannot tell
what man to trust

Thus the consultation passed around in private amongst us.
(At this time not one of us twelve had enter'd nor would we
although made the sea boat's crew.) 'Well, my boys,' says
Waddell, 'our only way to make our escape is a verry quick
one. Requires a firm resolution and to be done courage sin-
cerity and to be bound on the sacred Bible to stand true to
each other.' 'What way do you mean?' was ev'ry mans desire.
'Brothers,' says Waddell, 'will you all swear on this holy
Book never to reveal my proposals if you do not like to unite
in with us in search of Liberty?' We then all swore to be true
to each other, to use our utmost exertions in endeavouring to
effect our excape and to defend each other as long as we
were able to stand. All being duly swore and resolved to proceed Waddell observed to us, 'Now men all we have to do
must be done privately and in haste. We must endeavour to
accomplish our design without taking life.

After all our secret discourse a Snake lay lurking by

'Our only means at present to escape from that cursed Ship
is on our return back with the Lieutenant. The night is dark
and will answer our design to a tittle, and we are sure Barker
is drunk and most likely will fall asleep in the Boat. Therefore our first care must be not to give any suspicion before
we are out of sight from the Athelion, and not then should
he not prove to be asleep. We must have a signal; that must
be to heave the bow oar fore and aft over all the rest, and
then if he is awake make him fast and tye a handkerchief

round his mouth, threatning him at the same time if he make the least noise that moment he shall be hove overboard. This all done then the Coxswain take charge of him and the rest of us take our oars and as it is flood tide we will make the best of our way on shore to the Naze, land him there where there is no house near, and he will not be able to give the allarm for some time. At the same time we will pull up Swin to Maldon, there sink the Boat, and either go on board a collier or take our land tacks on board in different directions.' 'A Most noble plan' was ev'ry man's answer.

In Antient days was Judas found. His poison spread
the globe around

May 7, 1803. At this moment a boatswains mad mate roar'd out for the Hussars barge to be manned; we quickly were ev'ry one in his station, ready to receive our death or liberty as we then term'd him . . . Over the side comes two lanthorns and sides men. Then bold Barker roars out, 'Are you all in the Boat coxswain?' 'Yes,' was the answer, 'Sir.' Down he crawls as drunk as any porter and was Seated wished a good night ; ; ; and away we row'd for our Ship. She have a lanthorn hoist as a mark for us, the Ships lay nearly two miles apart and we were at some distance from the Athelion, when young Haswell being the bowman (finding by Barkers noise he was awake) hove his Oar fore and aft over the top of all the others, that was the critical moment . . . death or liberty . . . whisper'd in most of our minds . . . when the Coxswain roars out, 'You bowman, why don't you pull away? what do you mean Sir? Out with your oar this instant; you stop all hands from pulling.' A dead silence for a moment prevail'd and horror seized us all at the same time, we saw the cowardly spirit of the coxswain, betraying us all, , , when Barker thunders out, 'You damn'd Grass combers, why dont you pull?' 'It is only the bowman Sir, that is taken short and his oar has confused us for a moment.' 'Damn' you all,' says the coxswain. 'That is no excuse. Mind what you do or say . . . I tell you all to pull away.'

A coward would Father and Brother betray

Oh, Wretch, what canst thou think thus to betray the undaunted sons of liberty even thine own brother when only an hour hence thou on thy bended knees with the holy Bible in they hands in the name of thy redeemer and in the presence of us all? Wretch thou didst swear to be true in our present adventures, and to stand firm and render ev'ry assistance in thy power to gain that sweet liberty, for which we have all left our lives to the mercy of a traitor. As that title is by far too good for thee, thou whose heart is not so large as that of a fly go hide thy face lay down and die. Die. Die. We got all our oars out again and with dreadful apprehensions made the best of our way on board. We wanted to speak to each other but durst not utter a word. What our feelings were at such a disappointment any man of rational reason can plainly understand. However arrived on board the Hussar boat, hoist in, and all quiet. We had an oportunity to speak to each other and that verry circumspectfully. Having liberty for half an hour's light we drank our grog and turned in. I shall give you all the Names of our Barges crew at this time, Coxswain Tho. Haswell. after oar John Waddell and next Richd Wilson. Next John Wetherell. James Boatfield Jos^h Andrews, Ja. Burchel, Richd Lindle cap^t top John Patterson Ja. Potter William Smith Robt Sadler Richd Haswell brother to the coxswain bowman. Those are the names of us poor misguided young men that signed the Athelion convention.

May he nee'r close his eyes in peace . . . but die in
torments neer to cease

We were now left to the mercy of this Judas Iscariot as we used afterwards to term him in our discourse, he being a Captain of the Top and we all station'd in the tops left us under his eyes or ears continually, caused us to be constantly on our guard, and, as the old word goes, we had to take our words and look at them before we spoke. To speak plainly we even were in dread of giving him the smallest offence least he might in his unmanly manner, discover our plot and turn

kings evidence. We are now and have to remain in dread of
this Monster whose sight we dread worse than the sight of
Bonaparte the hero of Europe. Our Corporal of Marines
Rich[d] Wright another of Sir Phillips followers had his wife on
board, a fine young woman. She took sick and died on board.
The Boat was order'd to be mann'd next morning, her body
put in a shell made by the ships joiner taken out to sea and
sunk, at the same time the ship lay within three miles of Harwich . . . inhumane Monster to one of the trusty Officers.

May 12.   This morning several of our Married men's wives
left the ship and went on board the tender and landed in the
evening at Harwich. They would not remain on board where
such an unfeeling Monster commanded. One morning the
little tender came off and the post man with the letters came
on board as usual. My name was called. A letter from London.
Take the welcome Messenger and perused it, found it from
Mr. Faith and my Brother George, in it I was informed that
Governor Nuemburg and my uncle Adams in Stamford had
undertaken in behalf of my Mother to have me clear by
paying for a substitute and informed me my papers were
signed by the Admiralty and forwarded down to Captain
Wilkinson, therefore I might rest happy because my liberty
was at hand. This was the greatest blessing, as I consider'd at
this moment, could be bestowed on me . . . My mind was fixed
one minute at home, another at Shields or London, other
times anticipating in my simple mind the result of my intended
voyage to Jamaica, not dreaming of the numerous changes
might take place even at that verry moment to rob me of my
imaginary happiness. However what leisure time I had was
all employ'd in composeing a letter to my sole intended partner
in So. Shields. Having at last got a copy to my liking I got
paper ink and pens and in a verry loving manner, as I thought,
reveal'd the Secrets of my throbbing heart, gave ev'ry particular of my letter from London and my daily expectations to
be discharged. I then wrote to my dear Mother informing her
of my promiseing good fortune and my determinations in
regard to making the best of my way to London Vc.

A humane shape and heart of Stone Should die
an Exile all alone

I then sent my letters on shore by the Cutter and on the following day as I sat on my chest foreward being the day to wash and holy stone the lower deck I heard Fotheringham the Boatsⁿ Mate thund'ring out, 'Pass the word for John Wetherell.' I ran towards him. 'Sir!' says I. 'Away aft, sir, on the Quarter deck (there I suppose I shall have the pleasure of knocking some of the coal dust out of your hide),' says he smileing. Aft on the quarter deck I went and there Stood his Worship and his clerk at his elbow, turning towards me with one of his leering grins. 'What is your name? Where does your parents live?' I told him correctly, 'Have you any relations in town? Their names and ocupations?' He then asked me if I would not enter for the Hussar Vc. My answer was 'No Sir.' He then said he had learnt that I had been taking private means to gain my discharge in producing a substitute which my friend in London had in some measure obtain'd, having got the permission from the Admirality's Office to have my discharge by finding an able Seaman to serve. 'Ah, ah,' says his worship, 'damn your blood, you son of a whore. In spite of you and all the interest of your damn'd tribe of grass-combing relations I will let you know you shall remain on board the Hussar, and wait my pleasure. That will be at the close of the ensueing campaign. Therefore start off and go to your duty Sir, make yourself contented, and rest assured your discharge shall be kept safe for you untill England no longer wants your service. Therefore take my advice, enter for the ship, and you will enjoy the privileges same as the rest of the crew.' I made my obedience and retired in a most horrid state of mind being nearly on the brink of leaping overboard to terminate my cruel treatment, at one moment death would have been a welcome visitant; at another I wish'd to live and see the result of all those trials I was at this time oerwhelmed in. However I sat down on my chest and began to reflect in my mind; I am not the only man on board, I have numbers of companions suffering here, suffering the cruel treatment of this tyranical savage. His feelings are far below the uncevilized race of Canibals on the coast of Malabar; they in their ignorant savage state take delight in masacreeing a white Man for the simple purpose of gaining his shining buttons or any glittering bauble he may have about his person, and afterwards devour his carcase. Those unfortunate beings are ignorant and know not the least sentence of the gospel; therefore we can excuse them owing to want of knowledge, but not this destroyer of Man, brought up in an enlightned age surrounded by the laws of christianty. His laws in their purity are good, founded on the principals of Justice, reason, truth, and equity, but under the administration of such arbitary lawbreakers, who make their own laws and trample down the laws of God and Man, and thus it is hard with mankind in general when it is in the power of those arbitary rulers to say damn such laws and the country govern'd by them

Those birds were too cunning to be taken in Sir Phils snare

May 24. One morning after breakfast a thund'ring roar came from the quarter deck. 'Send all those fellows aft, those that have not enter'd for the ship!" Up we all goes. There stood the terrible ruler and his clerk with the ships books open, our names were called to pass one by one and answer enter or not enter . . . 'No Sir' was each mans answer. Sir Phillip spoke up. 'My men you had better enter. It will be to your advantage as the ship is ordered round to Portsmouth and will sail shortly. On arriving there you shall enjoy the same liberty on shore as the rest of the crew.' This to us was all music. Our determinations were never to enter for him but any other of H.M. Ships we would enter on board with pleasure, as we were all anxious to defend our country's cause against all those who dare oppose our nation and its righteous laws. Wilkinson finding our determination were not to be persuaded by him turns round . . . 'Go forward you damn stubborn rascalls to your duty, and you shall be sorry for your conduct before many days. Take care of your selves I shall look out for you.'

May 25, 26, 27. On the 25 of May in the morning orders were to weigh the best bower and ride by a single anchor. At 10 A.M. orders were to weigh anchor and make Sail to Join the

Antelope, Sir Sidney the Commodore, in Osley Bay. In a short time our ship was under a crowd of sail accompanied by the Athelion. A smart gale at N.W. In a little while we joined the Commodore in the bay and made sail to the eastward, passed outside of the sands into the North Sea where we passed away two days Exerciseing. This was Exerciseing Officers, , , Men, , , Ships, , , Sails, , , Guns, , , Yards Washing, , , holystoning, , , Small arms, , , Mustering bags. Reefing in two minutes, , , punishment, , , Up and down hammocks, , , Stow them, , , Scrub hammocks. Up all chests and bags, , , , Sprinkle and scrub, , , Serve out pursers Slops and tobacco, , , Serve grog, , , Turn all hands up to skylarking, , , Set the Watch. All those little changes were transacted in the course of two days cruise in the North Sea.

CHAPTER

2

MAY *28, 29, 1803.* Returning to our old anchorage in the Swin we Anchor'd, furld sails, took on board beer and water, stores Vc., and on the following morning sail'd thro' the Queen's channel bound to Spithead, wind West N.W. At 12 Mer made the North foreland light, winds inclinable to calm. At 4 PM struck on the Goodwin Sands having caught a fresh air of wind from the ENE. 'What ho, she comes!—Take in the royals topgallantsails and all the light-sails. Brace the yards to the wind. Out Boats. Fire signal guns for assistance. Be smart my brave fellows, exert yourselves to get the Ship afloat. Run away the Stream Anchor to the S.E. Well done my brave boys. Now man the barrs and heave away the Cabstern. Drummer beat up and fifer play a merry tune to give the men life to heave the ship afloat . . .' Such was the language of this terrified tyrant to his men when he thought his honour was in danger, and in one minute after she was afloat, 'Silence, damn you all!' was the first salute of his honour the Moment he found the Ship was afloat.

May 30. I shall give the credit to three boats from the Shore which on seeing our dangerous situation boldly ventur'd off to us and knowing the channel took an Anchor out, weigh'd the one we already had ran out, and by their directions in a little while our Ship was safe in the Downs, came to an Anchor and lay till Morning, and next day you now have an instance of Wilkinsons generosity . . . Those Men in the Deal boats that were the only means of saving the Ship came off to the ship to beg his honour to sign a paper which is customary So that they may deliver it to the custom house and receive a sallary allowed them for assisting H.M. Ships in distress, this is as an encouragement to those brave fellows for their courage and perseverance. Wilkinson took the Capt. from each boat and would have kept them had not the Admiral order'd them on Shore.

The Admiral on Shore having ordered Wilkinson to grant the Boatmen their certificate as their due and then restore ev'ry man of them on Shore without the least delay as he (the Admiral) was commander in the Downs at present and would be obey'd in what was consistant with reason. Wilkinson reluctantly obey'd his orders, and on their landing on the beach our Signal was made to weigh and proceed directly for the harbour of Plymouth, the Athelion being order'd to Portsmouth in our place. Our boats returned on board, up anchor, made Sail and arrived in Plymouth Sound on the first of June. Moored Ship Vc. In the course of an hour the ship was surrounded with shore boats. First the Married men had liberty to take their wives on board then the young Men had their girls came off and took them on board, a curious sight to see boats crowded with blooming young girls all for sale. Our crew were mostly young men and caused the boatmen to have a quick dispatch or as we usually term it a ready market; this business over, nothing particular ocurred that day. Next morning it was found that there was two more women than men on board . . . a mighty Jovial crew ·616 Souls on board. We took on Stores provisions and Water, and on the 4th orders were to send all the girls on shore except one woman to each mess and the married women certainly to have the preference. This all settled at 12 Mer., fired a salute weighed and made sail; our orders were to join the Grand fleet off Ushant. On the 6th in the morning made the fleet, and deliver'd our dispatches and letters on board the Ville de paris, Admiral Cornwallis. We remained with the fleet two days, then were order'd into Brest Bay as look out ship to watch the motions of the French.

June 12.   We remained on this station some time, and used to have pretty rough usuage from the batteries on shore when we chanced to be taken in a calm when close under the land. They used to give us pretty heavy doses of both shot and Shell; on one of those affairs we were beating close up to the narrows with a smart breeze blowing directly from the land and standing rather too far over to the south shore when we were becalmed and the ship was some time before we could get her head off shore. The land being verry high took the wind out of our sails and the French at this time were not idle in the forts; they were not at all sparing of powder Shot nor Shell before we got our Boats out and the Ships head tow'd round off shore.

A French Bombadier made too free on the gun room table

Johney croppi had measured his distance pretty well for they hove a Shell that burst over the Ship split the Mizen topsail cut away some of the rigging and a piece of Shell weighing 18 pound fall on the Quarter deck and past through close to the foot of Captain Wilkinson, and stuck fast on the gun room table where dinner was ready to sit down. It made itself more free than welcome, breaking dishes and scareing waiters and Stewards into the officers cabins. However with the assistance of our boats we got round and caught the breeze just at the moment where another Shell fell close under our stern. Had we not caught the light air and got head way the shell was intended to fall on board and then burst, which might have been a serious consequence. Wilkinson was quite offended at the French Bombadier for sending such a ragged piece of iron so near him while doing his duty, and we were quite on the contrary—we were angry with the Frenchman that he did not make better use of his shell by sending it in contact with a Shell that we dreaded more than that hove by the Frenchman. The Dragon 74 being one of the inshore squadron seeing our situation ran close in and sent her boats to our assistance and in a short time we were out of gun shot.

Wilkinson adds another laurel to his victorious brow

June 17. This day we had a severe conflict. Being close under the land at daylight we chanced to fall in with a number of Chasmarie's [*chasses-marées*] or market boats from various parts of the coast bound to Brest and we gave chase. They dispersed in confusion; some ran for the Shore and escaped and others proceeded towards Brest. We fired amongst them in real earnest. At last we brought one of them along side. She was a large craft laden with wine fruit and oil.

A Glorious vict'ry has been won. by Wilkinson
the barbers son.

We took what bold Sir Phillip thought he wanted, took the Captain and his Son prisoners and order'd the rest of the crew to proceed to Brest and inform the French Admiral he had taken a taste of Bowideause [Bordeaux] wine in order to drink his health and had taken the Captain and his Son intending to they shall go to England and taste our beer in return. (How daring a warrior we have to boast of.) A number of such commanders might frighten Many of the small coasting vessels.

July 3, 1803. Having cruised some time and nothing particular took place, excepting feeding goats and hops on sandy Island, smugling brandy in the buckets in the place of Black berries etc. We used to run out to the fleet once or twice per week with our tidings, and our Sea Boats crew being so frequently on board the Ville de Paris we got quite familiar and used, Sailor like, to relate many grievances to each other. There was a number of our own cast on board of her, all colliers boys; they used to perswade us to enter for the Ville, and finding they had such good usage we began to propose to each other what course would be the most prudent for us to gain that privelidge without giving any suspicion to our officers, fearing they might put a stop to our intentions. We had a number of proposals; one thought one thing another thought contrary, generally the case in such proceedings.

Oppress'd beneath this tyrants frown freedom arose
and tore him down

At last our resolutions were to leave the whole Management entirely under the management of three Men, and those three we chose by voices John Waddell. Capt. of the Main top and Midship man John P. W. second captain and Richard Lindle Captain of the forecastle; those three were left to write and do their utmost for the benefit of their fellow sufferers . . . We at present will leave them to their own Judgement and attend to our duty as men. Standing close in to the narrows of Brest we found a Corvette of 22 guns anchor'd in Cranmoran Bay under cover of two heavy forts. We had orders to prepare our boats all in readiness to cut this Ship from her cables and take her out a prise. That night quite dark about 12 Mid off we goes all volunteers, launch Barge and two Cutters all resolutely bent. Our oars mufled and the water still we gave no allarm; the men on board the corvette must have all been asleep because we boarded her on both sides and were nearly all on board before we gave any allarm, and this was by disarming the Marines centeniels at the Cabin door and on the gang ways. We then had a small opposition before we got possession of the Quarter deck however this as well as the forecastle was gain'd without any blood shed. The commander in his cabin was quite loth to give up the command, but however he quickly found lieutenant Leftwidge our second lieut. was acting in his place. We carried that vessel cut her cables tow'd her from under the forts and never fired a gun. She was not discover'd from the forts untill daylight, when she was under sail in company with the Hussar, standing out.

July 20. Our Prize prov'd to be the le Pheasant of 24 guns from Rochelle to Brest to refit for the Isle of France. She had 187 men on board, Mostly cannoniers.[1] After joining our admiral we had orders to mann her and send her into Plymouth under the command of Leftwidge our second lieut. and forty men. We accompanied them within sight of the Ram Head, then returned to the fleet, remain'd with the fleet some time cruiseing round Ushant and at times took a peep into Brest to observe their manovres. Returning from one of our peeping frolics towards the fleet, Wind at S.W., the skies were quickly in confusion, clouds rolling in various directions and thunder rolling nearer, every crash of which pointed out the

---

[1] In order to overcome their chronic shortage of seamen the French had instituted a corps of marine cannoniers, trained to work the guns (or to act as gun captains while landsmen did the physical work) so as to free the seamen of a ship's company to work the ship during action. Cannoniers could be exercised in a ship in harbour or even in establishments ashore, but the system did not prove very effective when tested in battles at sea, as was frequently shown by a comparison of the casualty lists. Wetherell's contemptuous description of the crew of the *Faisan* as 'mostly cannoniers' is a modest depreciation of the brilliance of the achievement in cutting her out.

Approaching Huricane. We shortned sail with all speed, and being close in with Ushant and the wind dead upon the land, ev'ry moment blowing harder, we on a lee shore were forsed to carry sail to avoid the rocks to leeward. The Sea rose dreadfully, and it was some time before we could perceive the ship alter the bearing of Ushant light the least immaginable. It was at this perilous moment, we all expecting the ship to dash on the dreadful rocks to leeward, all in a blaze with the foam breaking over them, it was at this dreadful moment our Main Yard parted by the slings, sprung our foremast main topmast and Mizen Mast. By heaven's decree at that moment a sea struck the ship on her Starboard bow and wore her round the other way—a happy circumstance for all on board as it was impossible she could clear Ushant on the Starboard tacks, and we used ev'ry means in our powers to put her head to the Northward and eastward but ev'ry effort was vain untill the sea managed the affair. We then used our utmost efforts, got what sail we could carry on her, and to our happiness found her clearing the shore fast and by daylight had room to lay to.

July 26. At 8 A.M. more moderate repair'd our damages and that evening made the fleet. Next day were dispatch'd to Plymouth to repair damages, lay in the Sound, took out our foremast, Mizen Mt. and Main Yard, sent them on shore. That night we had a most terrible gale from the S.E. All the small vessels cut or slipt and some got into Catwater some on the Cobler and some on Drakes Island. We rode verry heavy all night in expectations to see our Sheers come tumbling down amongst us. However thro' good fortune no accident happned and next day was quite moderate. Our she messmates came off and we lay quite comfortable untill the New masts came along side. We took them in and next evening were all ready for Sea. On the 29th the women were order'd on shore and on the 30th sailed from Plymouth sound.

The black rock convention hold their private meetings
in Plymouth

August 1, 1803. On the 1st of August joined the fleet, and the first thing we look'd out for to send our letter on board the

Ville de Paris, having during our lay in Plymouth composed three letters or petitions[1] before we could satisfy ourselves. The first was wrote with the three names were chosen to manage the affair signed to it—this would not answer since they were sure to be took for the ringleaders if it should happen that the Admiral might present it to Wilkinson. We then made a second attempt, made some alteration in the language and diction and signed with all our names on one side the petition. This would not do; some were of opinion that the first names on the list would be considered as the heads of the plot.

> *Go on my children persevere nor yet look back*
> *but foreward steer*

We therefore wrote a third, and placed the names in such a manner that if they should pick out any as delegates it would be an entire lottery whose fate it might prove.

August 2, 1803. As I before observed we took the first oportunity to take the paper on board the Commodore, which we found means to effect as all the members of this united society belonged to the Barges sea boats crew . . . And as it was me that wrote the letter of petition to his excellency it was also me that deliver'd it into the hands of the Admirals secretary on board the Ville de paris and return'd on board the Hussar, all then waiting in great anxiety to hear the events, watching ev'ry signal that was made, expecting our Capt. to be call'd for by the Admiral.

---

[1] In writing this petition the men were risking severe punishment and possible death. The British Navy—and the same is true, necessarily, of every armed service in every country—looked with suspicion on any attempt by the men to act in concert. Any single individual was entitled—at least in principle—to air his grievances by request or petition, but when two or three gathered together and discussed their grievances, they came close to laying themselves open to a charge of conspiring to mutiny, and any open action resolved upon at such a meeting could easily be construed as mutiny. The writing and signing of the petition were self-evident proof of both discussion and of action, and any man signing might find himself charged with mutiny. The precautions taken to conceal the identity of the ringleaders, if there were any such, were aimed at making it difficult for the authorities to find any man more guilty than the others, in the hope that they might shrink from punishing the large number of signatories equally.

Man with a quill may soon destroy his freedom peace
and future joy

At last the No 894 was made. 'Now,' says we, 'it will be all decided.' But not yet; the signal was 894—Make sail to the S.W. in chase of a strange sail reported by the Dragon look out ship in the offing. We made all sail and by 8 P.M. were up with a large Ship from Baltimore bound to Nantz laden with flour. We took charge of her, sent an officer on board, and sent her into Plymouth; this all done we haul'd our wind in order to take our station again. The night was blustry and rainy. Wind freshned, we took in two reefs and by 4 A.M. were hove to under close reef topsails and reef foresail.

Thunder may roll and light'nings flash yet more we dread
the tyrants lash

August 3. Lay all those 24 hours, blowing verry hard and the Sea breaking over the ship at a dreadful rate, thunder and lightning was horrid. About 6 P.M. the lightning struck our Ship on the head of the Mainmast, burnt the eyes of the main rigging, and appear'd to burst over the Ship, by a horrible report and sulphurous smell. At the same time we were in the act of taking in and furling our foretopsail when another explosion took place; the men on the topsail yard were some of them struck and made a dreadful noise. The men on deck were all laid flat on the deck and the centeniel at the skuttle butt was burnt on his shoulder and side. Those who were below in hammacks were all upset and hove on the deck. The fluid then exploded with a report like breaking glass and apparently past out thro' one of the ports leaving a strong smell of sulphur. This chanced to happen at the time of my look out on the weather gangway from 6 to 8 P.M. The Boat-swain fell on top of me and we both laid some time in a stupi-fied state. At last I heard the voice of some man saying, 'What shall I do, my eyesight is gone?' 'So is mine,' says the Boat-swain and at that instant another heavy flash passed over the Ship, then after seeing this we were convinced that our eyes were only dazled by the lightning. We got ourselves all gather'd up and the men all safe from aloft without any material injury being done to ship or men. By 12 Mer next day the storm had entirely subsided and the wind shifted round to the Northward; we repair'd our slight damages and made Sail. On the following evening join'd the fleet; they made dreadful complaints of their sufferings during the Hurricane as they term'd it.

The following card will plainly tell. our names and numbers
as they fell

We took our station to leward of the admiral that night and then we began to entertain hopes that Admiral Cornwallis would not pass over our grievances without a farther explanation as we had related every act of cruelty practised on board from our first impressment. Better luck still.

Our thoughts and words kind treatment crave that granted
many lives may save

This shews the form of our letter petition and names as sent to the Hon. William Cornwallis Rear Admiral of England . . . beseeching his Fatherly aid and protection requesting his honour to snatch us from the paws of our tyranical prosecutor. We also beg his honour to accept our volunteer services in his ship or any other of H.M. Ships his Honour may please to appoint '. . . We have inserted our names so that your hon. can demand us at your pleasure. In this act of humanity may heaven add fresh laurels to your honourable brow and crown your days with peaceful blessings, and an eternal crown in the Mansions of bliss is and ever will be the sincere prayers of H. Majesties humble subjects and of Your Honour's Obedient Servants British Seamen,

> done in Plymouth Sound on board H.B.M. Ship the
> Hussar June 15th 1803,
> presented to his honour August 2nd 1803 while cruiseing off Brest on Board the Ville de paris. Commanders
> Sir H. B. Neale
> Captain Charles Jones.'

August 4. The Admiral (as we afterwards understood by one of his signal men on board) after peruseing the letter

Stood some time with the paper in his hand then turning round to Capt. Jones. 'Can it be possible, Jones, that men can suffer this cruel tyranny? Well may our seamen strive to avoid serving their country on board His Majesties Navy when this is the usage they meet with. Abominable! It is a disgrace to the country they are serving! Such men should not be allowed even to set his foot on board any of H.M. Ships. in the Capacity of Capt. of the Mast, more so as Capt. of the vessel. However now I shall not make him acquainted with the affair at this time but will send him out on a cruise; meanwhile we will consider what is best to be done for those brave fellows who crave my protection.' Our signal was made and orders sent on board to cruise between Ushant and Scilly with a letter to take care of his men and treat them well.

Captain Wilkinson has a roving commission one Month

August 6. We made sail and left the fleet with a smart breeze from the N.E. and cruised several days. Nothing particular took place; we fell in with all Nations on the entrance of the channel. One day a Sail was reported; we made sail and with a fresh gale we ran under all we could crowd nearly 12 hours before we got along side. We found her to be the Swallow packet from Jamaica to Falmouth—could not trust our private signals and were jealous of us owing to our having tricolour'd vanes at our mast heads. All things being understood we parted the Swallow for Falmouth and us on our Station. That evening orders were to take in two reefs and that in 2½ minutes. 'All ready! Let go the halyards, trice up and lay out!' Away we fly, helter Skelter. On my passing the top brim I saw the topsail lift jigger was caught under the slide of one of the cannonades [carronades] on the quarter deck, and being in a flusteration, seeing the yard over end, I inadvertently call'd McAlister the Capt of the After guard to clear the fall from the slide.

The British Navy has to boast more Lords than
all proud pharoahs host

Lord George Gordon was Midshipman of the Main top
and as I spoke he kick'd me in the breast with his foot and
order'd me to leave that duty to him. I answered that it was
too bad to be kick'd like a dog when in the act of doing what
I thought was right, and made my way out on the yard arm.
'Walk down Sir in a Moment, you damn'd Mutinous rascall,
and you shall have your desert,' Says my Lord, and down he
goes to the lieutenant on the quarter deck, made his story right
on his side. Down I goes to the tribunal of Justice. First salute
I met was a blow on my head with a speaking trumpet, then
call'd the master at arms and order'd him to put that damn'd
young rascall in irons. This was readily complied with, so
poor Jack was clap't into the Brig as we term it. This chanced
to fall on the 7th of August. Take notice. Next day chased a
Falmouth privateer cutter and took two men out of her with
a pretence that had she hove to without us having to chase her
we would not have taken any of his men. However we kept
them. Next day exercised guns fireing at a Barrel with a flag
on it. Two or three got each 4 dozen thro' this day's amusement
as Wilkinson calls it.

Captains will orders disobey, and for that crime their seamen pay

On the 10th of August chased a large Swedish ship to the
westward. At sunset found out what she was, shortned sail
and let her pursue her course. That night blowing fresh took
in two reefs and that night the Ship rolling heavy by some
accident the main top galt Stud sail boom roll'd out of the
iron and went overboard. This chanced to be the boom on the
yard arm where I was station'd, and next morning it was
mis't and reported. All the main topmen were called up and
the two Captains of the top were called on to strip, John
Waddel the first call'd on. 'Well sir' says the great Sir Phil,
'don't you think yourselves a set of damn'd infernal lubbers to
loose that boom thro' neglect? I mean to go through the whole
of you; therefore I shall begin with you two first . . . strip, Sir.

Quarter Masters ceaze him up. Boatswains mate, go on.' Four dozen was his dow'ry. Next was Rich*d* Lindle. 'Strip Sir and not a word from you. Go on boats*n* Mate, four dozen more there.

How fortunate to be a Captain and have double allowance

'That may be a warning to you both. As you are Capts. of the top I thought you merited double allowance.' John Patterson was next. Two dozens. James Potter, two dozen. Ja. Boatfield, do [ditto]. Wm. Surtees do. Tho. Fostor do. Tho. Green do. Tho. Thompson do. Wm. Ferguson do. 'Now Gentlemen,' says this Monster, 'you all deserve the same but time at present will not allow us the pleasure of fulfilling the laws of our country—it is your country and not me that is chastiseing you. However the first oportunity I shall not forget the rest of you damn'd rascalls. Boatswain, Pipe belay; drummer beat the retreat'—after a small morning's distribution of only thirty dozen. All this time I was listening to hear my name call'd; as they were paying off their debts I felt verry much afraid they were due to me some small accounts. However my expectations were at this moment disappointed; he left me laying in suspence in expectations of being called every time I heard the Boat*s* pipe or the drum—

August 14. This morning we fell in with the Speedy Brig from the fleet bound into Falmouth. She also had orders for us to proceed immediately towards the fleet; accordingly we directed our course for Ushant and next morning were in the centre of the fleet. We hove too under the Ville de Paris' Stern and the Signal was for our Captain. Now methinks I will perhaps be the means of my release one way or another.

His Honours' letter to Sir Phil forbids his useing seamen ill

After our Captain had been on board the Admiral some time he returned with dispatches for England. We took the letters of the fleet and directed our course for Plymouth. After all was Snug and the fleet dropping astern down came the first Lieut. into the Gunroom. 'Damn me,' says he, 'gentlemen, what do you think of those fellows on board that would not enter for the Ship?' 'I dont know,' says one. 'Nor I,' says another. 'Pray Sir what is it?' cries Mad Barker. 'Why, they have wrote to the Admiral informing him with ev'ry thing we do or say on board, and are all going to leave the Ship—old Cornwallis is going to take them all out of the Ship on our return from Plymouth and Capt. Wilkinson has got part of the letter they wrote. Tomorrow we are going to have ev'ry man sign his name and by that means find the damn'd mutinous rascall that wrote such an infernal ditty . . . By God, Barker, he has wrote a cursed well contrived ditty and a good deal of truth can be found in it, but Sir Phillip swears if he can find out who he is God help him for thus exposeing him to the Commander in Chief . . .'

Oh what a horrid bitter Pill Sir Phillip took against his will

All the time of this discourse I being in irons close to the gun room door and the door partly open I had an oportunity to hear ev'ry word. Now, thinks I, you are under a great mistake for if you call me to sign I shall write quite another hand. Therefore this gave me no kind of concern as they unknowingly had given me particular notice. This all past on till next day, then all hands were muster'd aft and called by the Ship's books to sign their names. At last I heard my name call'd. 'In irons,' says the Master at arms. 'Go enquire if he can write.'

August 17. The Master at Arms and Mr. Maxfield the captain's Secretary did me the honour of a visit. I was in readiness. 'Can you write your name Wetherell?' says old douse-the-glim. 'Yes sir' was my reply, 'but I am left handed.' 'What, do you write with your left hand?' says Maxfield. 'Yes sir.' 'Oh damn your crooked disposition; you are not worth the time it will take to release you out of irons to go and sign your name and afterwards clap you in again. Let him remain where he is, Hill, there is no fear of his destroying the nation with his treachrous writings.' Away they goes; my trial was over so far. Barney Appleby, a young man entirely void of learning, could not read his own name—in fact he knew not

his alphabet. This man being a verry ready witted fellow as
we usually say made all the watch on deck amusement thro
the night with his curious stories; he would take a book of any
kind and open it, sometimes upside down, and repeat one of
the Stories of the Arabian Nights, as correct as if he had been
reading it out of the book, and continue every night in the
same manner with a fresh tale every night. The Officers frequently on the first watch would stand all the watch laughing
at Barney. And on this same account when he was called to
write his name and told them he could not write he was called
a liar and they made sure he was the writer of the letter to the
Admiral and on that account would not own to writing at all.
They even accused him of it and told him they knew he wrote
it but if he would only tell them for satisfaction he would not
have any reflections past on him nor yet come to any trouble
. . . His answer still was 'No Sir no, I tell you the truth. I
neither can read nor write.' This was all stuff in their opinions.
Some of the Officers swore he was one of the first readers on
board, they had repeatedly heard him reading and he was the
verry Man that wrote to the Admiral.

August 18.   Therefore no farther enquiry was required; it
was concluded that Barney was the Man. All hands were dismissed. A strange sail reported to windward; haul our wind
and make sail in chase. Found her to be the Heroe lugger
privateer from Guernsey in company with two Brigs she had
captured the night before off St. Maloes, and she was conducting them into Guernsey. We bore away for Plymouth and
at 7 bells all hands for punishment. 'Mr. Hill, the master at
arms, bring forth the prisoner.' Oh my hard fortune, thought
I . . . However up to the gang way goes poor Jack and above
him stood the great distributor of all the tortures hell can
produce. 'Oh,' says he, 'this is one of our ring men. Strip Sir.
You are also one of the damn'd rascally topmen that lost the
studding sail boom. Part of your topmates have already had
their pay and the rest of you will not be forgot. Boatswains
mate give him a dozen.' At this moment I began to inform him
that I had been three or four days in irons when the boom was
lost.

Punishment inflicted according to the patent courtmartial

'Gag the rascal I say, gag him with a pump bolt and stop his damnd lip.' Immediately a pump bolt was introduced into my jaws and tied back of my head. In this manner they gave me four dozen and punished me for a thing that was done three days after I was in irons for what they term'd a crime (my speaking to Gordon was never mentioned nor was I allowed to speak one word in my own behalf).

Dread ruler of the boundless Main release me
from this tyrants chain

After cutting my flesh in a dreadful manner they cast me loose and poor Barney Appleby was called up and order'd to strip. 'For what Sir?' says Barney. 'There is no occassion to Stand spending my breath with this damnd fellow. Gag him.' Those orders were fulfilled and poor fellow had six dozen then was cast loose and him and me both order'd to our duty. Beat to quarter; we were so cut and our backs so stiff and sore we sat still and did not go to our quarter. This was reported and a boatswain Mate was sent to start us up with a ropes end, and made us exercise guns nearly two hours in this Mangled state. God help Sailors.

Old Spanish cruelties on a new patent plan

August 19. At last retreat was beat, and believe me the shirt on my back was like a butchers apron, and so stiff that every time I had to stoop down, it would tear off the bladders of blood and water that were on my poor mangled body ... well may tortures like those cause the unfortunate sufferers to cry out for revenge and have it at the risk of his life. His life did I say? His life is only a burden to him and it is the cause of his long suffering which causes him to be careless how he conducts himself when drove to desperation, and tortures has steeled his once feeling heart so that he no longer being able to govern his bleeding heart, in frenzy he rushes forward to crush his appressor and with vengeance in ev'ry nerve looks for Revenge or Death. This has been the same on board H.M.

Ship the Hermione. and the Dency, , , but we cannot look for much better from Wilkenson. It was the same tyrant that caused so much Blood to be shed on board the Hermione; it was he that wound the crew up to a state of desperation, and revenge was their whole intention. He smelt something of the approaching tempest (and mark his plan to escape the snare he had caused to be laid and lead his Brother blindfold to destruction). At this time the Success Frigate, Captain Picket [Pigott] was ordered home and the Hermione was to remain on the West India station. Captain Picket [Pigott] wishes to remain in the West Indies and Wilkinson thro dread and a guilty conscience was afraid to remain on board the Hermione. It was therefore agreed that they should change ships, which was done the day previous to the Success sailing for England. We must observe that long before this the crew of the Hermione had bound themselves under solemn ties to take the Ship the first time she left Jamaica and revenge themselves on their oppressors and run the Ship down to Laguira [La Guaira] and give her up to the Spaniards as a prize, then enter the Spanish service or lay in prison as long as life existed.

August 20. Those unacquainted with the tale of the Hermione may refer to the history of England time of the French revolution and they will shudder at the name of such a Ship and Commander. This unfortunate circumstance will never be forgot by the Seamen of England . . . thus you have the outlines of this unmercifull Tyrant's proceedings. We will leave him to the pleasure of the great Sovreign of earth and Sea and proceed on our way to Plymouth. That night we made the Eddystone light and having light winds lay nearly becalmed all night. However about 8 AM a light breeze sprung up from the S.E. and by 4 P.M. we anchored in the Sound. Moored Ship, our Boats Vc, landed dispatches and land the ruin of the British Navy. We laid in the sound two or three days. Nothing particular except Wm Kippis a young man fell from the fore rigging and broke his thigh. It had to be cut off. He recover'd and was sent to the Hospital.

3

Remarks in Plymouth

AUGUST *25, 1803.* On the 25th in the morning our boats were order'd to attend a sham fight off the Mew Stone by the Gun Boats from the harbour. All the dock Yard and Navy Boats composed two fleets. Our Boats being order'd to join in the fun the Sea Boats' crews were called and order'd to get ready to go into the Boats. They all muster'd except poor Jack whose back and heart was too sore to partake of any of what young men in that time called a frolic. My name was called but was sick and in the Doctors list and you may believe me was verry desirous to die . . . I shall mention a circumstance of the good effect a few lessons has on the youth that are sent on board the navy to be instructed and made sometimes the Pillars of our Country . . . Those are Mid-ship men, and it was one of those tools of Wilkinson's, Hopkinson by name, a thing not higher than a man's knee, going down into the Boat and not thinking one of the men paid him due respect by moving his hat, Hopkinson looks at him and in great pomp, says, 'Pray Sir, do you know who I am?' James Burchel, the man we allude to, looked at him and laugh'd. 'Yes sir,' says Burchel, 'I believe your name is Pug. Pug I think was what Lieutenant Barker call'd you that night he had a rope round your neck making you dance on the table in the gun room, when he roard out, "Damn you, Pug, hop round," and then he gave you a slap with the rope's end, made you hop Squall and grin—this, Sir, is all the name I know for you.' Burchel at this time was set on the after thoft or seat and Pug stood on the Stern Sheets.

'Damn your blood, sir,' says Pug, 'must I take all this from a rascal like you?' and kick'd Burchel in the mouth with his foot, made the claret fly. 'What, shall it be said Jim Burchel would suffer this from a brat of a boy? No I will die first! Here we go my Boys.' he sprung up, took the Midshipman in his Arms, and overboard plunges head foremost, determin'd to die with him in his ARMS. One of the Men immediately put down the Boat hook and caught Burchel by the back of his Jacket and thus saved him when nearly both strangled. (Burchel has often said since that had it not been for that damnd boat hook he was determin'd to die with him in his arms, as he would rather die than live the life he had to endure on board that infernal Ship.) They were both taken on board verry much exhausted, but in a short time hove up the salt water and were ready again for the next attact, that would be with the prince of devils Wilkinson. Burchel was put in irons and threatn'd to be hung by lieutenants, Midshipmen, and all the combin'd forces of Sir Phillip—he being on shore at this time was not in the tribunal. Several boats were passing the ship at the time the affair took place and one of those being from the Admiral's Ship, the San Salvadore, this newse was soon on board the Admiral, and he came on board the Hussar.

Shortly after the affair the signal was made for Wilkinson. He was on board in a hurry, and meeting the admiral on board, was expecting another of Black rock affairs was going on. However on meeting Admiral Sir Robt Calder on board he soon found the whole concern, and Sir Robt wish'd to have Burchel brought into his presence. After hearing the story from the Midshipman he then heard Burchel, and turning around to the Midshipman. 'You, Sir, that ought to set an example to the men, and placed in this situation by the rulers of your Country who trust you to act with good conduct to protect the laws of your nation which you most outrageously have broken, by takeing that authority on your self to lift your foot with violence against the face of one of our bravest of men, which he has just prov'd in being willing to die with you in his arms rather than suffer such cruel imposition.'

This comic tragic valiant deed. Such are the Subjects
England needs

Sir Robert turning to Wilkinson addressing his honour,
'Capt Wilkinson Sir, it gives me reason to speak, you may perhaps think unreasonably, but I believe not. This present act of
cruelty committed by one of our officers in your Ship and under
your command will cast a stain on you and your Officers for
ever. Our laws are good and will give satisfaction to all parties,
if put into execution, but, Sir, you well know you are placed
here as a lawgiver appointed by your Country, and when you
thus suffer your Midshipmen or Children to raise their hand or
foot against one of H. Majesties Subjects, you set the laws you
are entrusted with, or the power you are invested with, to be
taken out of your hands, and your officers are ruling according
to their own tyranical disposition and set England and her
laws at defiance. And Sorry, Sir Phillip, I am, but it is my duty
to inform you what has been hinted from the Hon. Wm.
Cornwallis concerning your ship and crew. This is a strange
method you have addapted to be placed in your situation as a
father to your Men, to encourage them in what is just and right,
to see them justified and protected against any false charge
brought against them, and on the other hand to teach them
their duty with due obedience to their Superior officers, to
obey every order with due regard, to be sober watchful and
diligent. Use them like men and as I have always found they
will act like men. However Captain Wilkinson I desire the
prisoner to be released and return to his duty and not to be as
is customary in the Hussar for Officers to upbraid a man with
every thing he might have done from his first joining the Ship.
I observe he shall not be abused and upbraided with this circumstance any more and as for that young Gentleman the Midshipman he may prepare to Join the St. Salvadore tomorrow
morning.'

Captain Wilkinson has a severe attack of the gripes

His Honour step'd a little on one side and says to Wilkinson,
'I am sorry to hear that your Men are useing every means to
leave the Hussar and join any other of H. Majesties vessels or

Ships of war and are willing to lay down their lives for their king and country, but it is impossible they can any longer bear with the cruel usage they have on Board the Hussar. Oh, Wilkinson look back to the unfortunate Hermione. You well know my principles Wilkinson. When I commanded a single Ship it was my chief delight to have the goodwill of my men, and I can safely assert ev'ry man under my orders would freely lay down their life to obey me or my commands, and by such means I made my crew both love and fear me. They loved me for my humanity and fear'd to cause my displeasure, and this I found the best school for Seamen. They will fight for you and if required die for you. I have been advised by the honourable William Cornwallis to have a watchful eye on the Hussar while in port. He also informed me of the barbarous methods you practised daily on your crew, and now I am satisfied with the truth of the complaint and will use my interest to put an end to to such base and unchristianly proceedings. Therefore I must wish you a good morning,' and down he goes into the Boat and returned to the Salvadore. That afternoon our Signal was made for the Capt. and he was not long on shore before on board comes lieutenant Pridham with an order for lieut. Wallis to join the Salvadore and Mr. Pridham was appointed first Lieutenant of the Hussar. Wallis gave Pridham a terrible character of the crew but Pridham answer'd him, 'Sir, I am already informed by the hon. Sir Robert Calder what the men are and how they ought to be treated; therefore your recommendations are unnecessary in that or any respect.' Wallace took his baggage and out of the Ship and left us. Thank God one rogue is gone.

August 26. All hands were called and Mr. Pridham was then appointed first lieutenant of the Hussar. He then verry kindly addressed us. 'My Men, I am this day appointed to your Ship as first lieutenant. I have been advised how to proceed with my office by the honourable Robert Calder. Therefore I have only to observe to you that as long as you conduct yourselves as Men, I will make it my chief delight to use you as men should be used, and expects to be used.' We wish'd to give him three cheers with pleasure. 'My Boys,' says he, and off pulls his hat to receive them. We cheer'd him and all hands return'd to their duty. Everything wore a new face and we were all life thinking we had got rid of one of our greatest prosecutors. Next morning the Midshipman left us and went on board the Admiral. The first lieutenant gave one quarter watch liberty to go on Shore 24 hours, on those terms that should any of them break their liberty not any more liberty should be allow'd. However every man return'd within the time, and next day another Watch went on Shore and returned in due time.

We sail on a Cruise off Cape Finisterre

August 28.   Next morning our signal was made to prepare for Sea, and at 2 PM. Capt Wilkinson came off with his orders. In a little while after our Signal was made to weigh which was all performed with activity and life; ev'ry thing went right and no damning of eyes, nor threatning with starting, Stopping grog Vc. We made sail and at Sunset that evening the Eddystone was astern of us some distance. Our orders were to cruise off Cape Finisterre to look out for French vessels returning home from the West Indies. We had a very pleasant run out to the Cape, where we had the misfortune to loose one of our Messenger boys named Tilford. The night being hot he got into the Miz*n* chains, fell asleep, and roll'd overboard; was not heard nor missed until next morning. This happned on the 12th of Sept. 1803.

Captures made off the Cape

September 13, 1803.   This morning the land dipping stood to the westward at 12 Mer. A Sail was reported to the N.W. We made sail having a brisk gale from the southward, and that evening overhaul'd her. She prov'd to be the Le Spark from St. Pierres, Martinique, bound to Havredegrass, a fine vessel richly laden, and a number of passengers returning home to France with their property Vc. Sent her into port, and took care to accompany her part of the way into the Channel. Her Boatswain, a Dane, Wm. Wilson, enter'd for our Ship to Share with the Ships crew in prize money. He informed us there was several more large ships Sailed in company with them from St. Pierres. We directed our course to our cruiseing ground and on the 15th another Ship hove in sight. We boarded her, found her the Le Peace from Port-au-Prince bound to Dunkerque with a valuable cargo on board, man'd her and sent her into port.

Long look'd for found at last dare not approach
he shews his teeth

September 25 to October 7, 1803. Having remained on our station some time and nothing particular occurred on the 25th of Sept. we fell in with the Le Flora from Port Royal Martinique bound to Nantz, another valuable prize. Mann'd her and sent her into Plymouth. We remain'd on our station untill the 29th do., when we fell in with the Active Cutter with orders from England to the Hussar on Station off Cape Finisterre.

The riches of india before us appear Sir Phillip was daunted
and from her did steer

Our orders were to make the best of our way towards St Helena to detain a large Dutch Indiaman that some of our India Ships left laying there repairing her rigging, painting ship Vc, haveing not heard of any war between the two nations. We had every particular description of her, how she was painted with red sides, had her fore top galt. mast on deck, had part of her guns in the hold, was weakly mann'd, her decks all lumber'd up, and would be an easy conquest. This was all great newse; we were on the road to make our fortunes. All was life and glee, we carried on all sail. got hold of the N.E. trades, ran them down untill we began to approach the Equator, and it chanced to happen one fine evening all hands had just been turned up to Skylark when a sail was reported just under the place where the sun had set. The Sky being clear shewd her after the sun was down.

October 7. On hearing the report of a Sail all was in a state of desire hopeing she might prove the Ship we desired to fall inwith. All Sail was quickly crowded on the Ship and just by the close of night we were near enough to make out that she was a large Ship. We then were all in raptures and made sure of our being rewarded for our long Search.

Our Officers were in the same state as the men, all making

sure she was our chap;; but cowardice and tyrany—always united in one body—disappointed all our expectations. That night we had a dead calm and at Sun rise next morning we could just make her out to the N.W., quite a small black speck in the horizon; about 9 AM. the trade wind sprung up and we made towards our grand point and found by 12 Mer. she was a large ship with two tier of Guns or ports and had no fore top galt. mast up. All right, yet by 2 P.M. made out she had red sides and was jogging on under an easy snug sail Dutch fashion. At 5 P.M. we were within one mile; made signals and shew'd our colours to him. He then hoist up a large Dutch ensign. This was all we were looking for . . . 'Now my Boys,' says Pridham, 'she is our own.'

The crew are like the dog crossing the river grasping nothing

October 9, 10. 'I think we are a Set of lucky fellows,' says Robin Gray. 'What do you think Van trump will share amongst us?' Up comes the Capt. Steward. 'Oh . . . men,' says he, 'you are takeing a wrong idea perhaps; as Capt. Wilkinson observed this minute in his cabin she may have all her guns mounted and then should that be the case, the Capt. says she will blow us out of the water.' 'Go to hell you preaching old bugger,' says Waddell; 'we are able to send her to davy Jones in five minutes. You are all always pretending you know how many beans make five and after all know nothing at all, I know develish well She is from Batavia and there I know she would bury half her crew at least, and more than all that She left Amsterdam on the Peace establishment and has neither guns nor Men to lay five minuites along side of our Gallant Hussar.' 'That's right Waddell,' says old Pollard; 'let them lay us along side of her and that old Dutch flag will soon come down.' By this time the breeze fell away with the sun and we were within gun Shot quite becalmed.

Every man knows best how to rule when he has no charge

'Blow up good breeze,' says one. 'Why don't they out boats?' says another. 'What a foolish set of fellows you are,' says McAlister; 'as soon as the breeze springs up we can run along side with the ship and take her without firing a gun.' 'She is all our own my boys,' says the french cook. 'Maybe not,' says his Mate. Thus we debated about her. Mr. Pridham came forward. 'Have patience my boys,' says he; 'when the breeze springs up we will soon be along side and by her appearance she will not make any resistance.' At this Moment she caught a light air and we also began to fell the effects of it. He hove his main topsail to the mast and lower'd his studding-sails down on the booms and lay waiting for us and seemed eager to hear what newse from Europe. They little thought our intentions at the time. As will be seen afterwards the men on board were all busy taking in sail Vc.

The kings adviser in his laws would freely plead
a poor Man's cause

Capt. Wilkinson Says to Mr. Pridham, 'She is too heavy for us and is only waiting her opportunity to give us a whole broad side. I can see them at their quarters all ready for us. She has 64 guns. She is a Dutch 64 and most likely mounts 76 and she is full of troops returning home.

Cowards and Tyrants are never free from horror and dread

'We all know what the Dutch are if they were to subdue us. They are unmerciful enemies; therefore I think it is most prudent to lay with our head to the Eastward all night, keep to our quarters, and be all ready should any thing happen thro' the night. It is now Sun Set and little wind so that the ship is not verry governable. therefore make no delay but let the Ship's head be laid to the Eastward.'

Firm round our Guns like me we stand. Our Captain
dare not us command

'Well Sir, we certainly obey your wise commands with pleasure, but if you will have the goodness to hear my simple opinion and that of all your Officers on board it is that she is weakly mann'd and we cannot make out more than Six guns

mounted on this side next us and we all are of the opinion that
she might be ours without the least resistance.' 'Pho. pho.
pho.' Says the Man hater; 'let my orders be obey'd Sir, immediately,' and verry sternly steps up to the rest of the Officers.
'Gentlemen, you must allow me to have more knowledge in
this undertaking than Any of you; therefore obey my command and lay the Ship the other way while you have a chance.
Perhaps the air of wind may die away and then the Enemy
might fall on board of us.

Wilkinson would rather engage ten of his Officers than one dutchmen

'I know the cruelties of the Dutch. Remember the cruel
Massacre of Amboyna, oh. oh. oh. I know them, I know them,'
and down he goes into his Cabin. For a while ev'ry one stood
in a state of Stagnation; the Officers shook their heads but
said nothing, and as for the Sailors that was the time to hear
Sailors pray in Secret for their fatherly humane feeling tender
harted courageous COMMANDER. ('Damn his Massacre of
Amboyna.' Says one, 'let him look back to the Massacre of
Hermioney and then I think he may keep his cursed mouth
shut and hide his Cain like face.') This was a private prayer,
with numbers more on various acts of his most humane and
tender hearted performances to his crew.

October 11. During this Dramatic Romance I must remark
one instance of secrecy. We had a Midshipman on board
named Matthias, a Jew, Wilkinson's tale bearer. He liv'd in
the cabin with him Vc. Ev'ry word that was spoke worthy of
notice this young imp was encouraged to carry, and as sure as
any person Made any remark or let slip an unguarded word it
was no sooner utter'd than it was in the cabin. Men used to
observe on Seeing him stealing round 'a privateer in sight';
this was their watch word to look out for him. Officers and
crew all were aware of him. To return and proceed with our
duty we put our Ships head to the Eastward and stood in that
direction all night with a light little breeze and all lay by our
quarters according to orders. Officers and crew all grieving but
could not help it; at Sun rise in the morning we could barely

make out the Van Trump to the westward quite down in the horizon. Mr. Pridham went down to inform our Warrior where she was and what was his opinion and his orders Vc.

Lucifer has his agents spread universally and so had Phil

October 12. 'Sir,' Says Wilkinson, 'by what passed amongst you and the rest of the gentlemen on the quarter deck and the damn'd mutinous crew you would soon run his majesties Ship to destruction. You would sacrafise both yourselves and Ship. But, Sir, I let you know I have better knowledge, and finding what a set of unruly Officers and mutinous crew I have to deal with I am afraid with such men—I say I am afraid—to bring H. Majesties ship into Action, and am determined to make the best of my way to England. Go Sir, Make Sail on the Ship, and—wait a minute' (looking at his Chart) 'Steer N1/2E for St. Jago's one of the Cape Verd Islands. At present the Ship is in the Latt of 6..37N and Long..32 24W. and as you are all great men with your tongues Make it appear in your government of the Ship,' and down he lays his skeleton shape.

Her black teeth decayed her lips crimson red
Sir Philip look'd at her and then shook his head

Mr. Pridham came on deck shakeing his head and gave orders, 'All hands make sail.' All hands were at hand in a minute expecting it was to go in pursuit of Van Trump but soon found the mistake.

October 13. Great murmering took place amongst us but the watch word of 'Privateer' we had to observe, as the Jew was always on the look out. Ev'ry one was as much in dread of him as they were of his Prompter. We made sail and stood to the Northward four days with a smart SE trade and on the 15th of October Made St. Jago's. From the time we made sail untill we made the Cape Verd Wilkinson never appear'd on deck nor were any of the Officers invited to dine with him as usual.

When you wish to see a boasting tyrant tremble
fire a great gun

When the land was reported he came on deck and gave orders to continue that course after passing the islands and proceed directly for England. Down he dives like a devil into the lower pits of hell and his heart as full of devils as the whole heard of Swine. May the Prince of the infernal lake be his constant companion may he neither Eat drink nor Sleep without the visitation of Picket [Pigott] and the remorse of a troubled mind. May he be constantly tormented with the Ghostly appearance of the numbers of innocent lives he has caused to be taken.

The Hussar arrives in Plymouth from a fortunate cruise

NOVEMBER *1, 1803.* In the course of 13 days from the Cape Verd islands we made Scilly and on the 1st of November arrived in Plymouth Sound. Wilkinson went on board the Admiral and told a long tale of his falling in with a large Dutch two deck'd Ship full of troops and he thought it most prudent to lay by till morning and see how she might act thro' the night, it being night when we came up to her near enough to Make out her force. However in the Morning nothing in sight, so returned to England according to orders that he might have made another attempt to overhaul her, but there was something he did not like to trust amongst his Officers and crew, therefore for the Safety of H. M. Ship and his own honour he deem'd it the most wise plan to proceed directly to England. 'This, your Honour, Sir Robt., is the heads of my cruise.' We learnt all this afterwards from Sir Robt's Coxswain who heard the whole story and as boats crews will talk and repeat over old stories our Men told them in Sir Robt's Gigg all the particulars of the Dutch Indiaman and of his shewing too many teeth.

Refitting Ship for a most horrid Slaughter

November 2, 1803. This was soon made known to the Admiral and caused many a laugh amongst the Officers of various Ships meeting ours. The word would be 'any country-to cut her Cables, we were struck with astonishment to find her quite ready to oppose us. She was surrounded with boarding nettings which we little suspected, and when we got under her Cable and made the first stroke with the Hatchet. To our great supprise the cable was wormed with chain from the hawse beneath the water, caused fire to fly from the hatchet with the stroke. The boats were all ready for Boarding but dreadfull to relate at that moment a cataract of Fire burst from the Mouth of Strumbolo could not gush from its confin'd regions with greater fury than these infernal engines of destruction vomited death from all parts of the Ship. She was all flames in one moment as it were so that it was instant death to ev'ry man that attempted to mount her side. Those who had gained hold of the Nettings were all either Shot or run thro' with pikes or sabres and fell back into the Boats or the Sea. We never heard of one Man that gain'd her deck. Meeting with such a formidable reception (all hands were in confusion) Muskets roaring over our heads, Officers ordering us to retreat, wounded men groaning, and others dieing, death stared ev'ry survivor in the face. We shall refer to our boat where I was one of the unfortunate crew. Directly after strikeing the Cable, we rec'd a volley from her head and bowsprit, which laid seven of our com'rades dead in the boat, and horrid to relate we the four survivors were all wounded, and as we were endeavouring to bear our boat astern clear of her head, something come in contact with my head. Putting up my hand I found the muzel of a Frenchman's Musket push'd it on one side just as he fired, saved my own life and nearly shot our first lieut. near enough to grase his skull by the flash of the gun. I saw the man in the head that fired it and drawing my Pistol from my belt gave him the contents thro his noodle and laid him in the water under our boat's bow. By this time the Boats that were able had got off and gone astern and we being all four wounded were verry weak thro the loss of blood. Nevertheless we got under her stern and drifted clear of her cursed leaden pills, over our Shoes in blood, and in this state as well as possible followed our companions from the slaughter. Rich*d*. Pridham our first lieut. wounded in the head and right shoulder, John Waddell wounded in his left hip side and right arm, I Wetherell left Shoulder breast bone broke right thigh and left leg, Edw. Carney Marine (a fine fellow) one ball thro his left wrist. We four had to hobble back the boat.

The shatter'd Boats returning from the slaughter

We got under the stern of the Ship and by those means were Shelter'd a little from her constant showers of Musket shot. We found our Boats were all Makeing their best way towards the Hussar but in a verry different order to what we were in when we left her; some boats had four oars and some six, nay even some had only two men that were able to pull the boat back to the Hussar. The day broke soon after we got from along side, and a most wretched appearance we made, some in one direction and some in another, as for our parts we were ready to give up the Ship, being faint and weak thro' the loss of blood, and our having to exert all our efforts at the oars, in order to regain our ship and having our bleeding wounds drest by the Surgeon. About 8 AM. we saw some of the boats gain the Hussar, and at 10 AM we got along side, and I was at that time as happy to get on board her, as I should have been a few days before to have left her, and never to have seen her again. .

Sir Philip sounding his trumpet so loud it burst

Haveing got along side and waiting at the gangway Wilkinson makes his appearance at the entrance of the gangway and Salutes his bleeding partly exausted first lieutenant in this manner 'Well, Pridham, you have had a fine nights diversion. What the devil were you all about to let the damn'd Croppoes give you such an infernal drubbing? Why you must have been all asleep along side her.' 'Capt. Wilkinson,' answered Mr. Pridham, 'Sir, had you been there perhaps you might have done some great exploit, and as for sleeping we are all convinced you would not have found much oportunity to sleep, there was quite the contrary sort of employment.' 'And, sir,' says the first Lieut, of the Villedeparis (having just come up with his launch), 'pray, Capt. Wilkinson, what is your meaning by saying all asleep? I wish to inform you, Sir, there were both Officers and Men in H. M. Boats and those who by their merits have gained laurels and honour to their Country without ever gaining our experience in the Hermione.

Wilkinson attacted again with the Gripes . . . by lieut Boyes

'Sir, we wish you to know that we are all H B M. officers, and have never caused a stain in her Standard, and again we wish you to remember we are all Gentlemen, , (and British Officers prov'd).' Wilkinson left the side and walked aft biteing his finger nails, and says to the Purser, 'Those young upstarts have a great deal of Assurance but I shall have them severely reprimanded for their insolence the Moment I meet the Admiral.' (We are all gentlemen.) 'What I suppose he means is gentlemen enough to exchange gloves with me. I will convince them of their error and let the damn'd Puppies know I am their Superior.' He calls the third lieut. Barker. 'Sir,' says Wilkinson, 'let the Officers come on board the Hussar, and let the boats be passed astern ready for makeing sail on the Ship. Let our Barge be hooked on and hoist up Vc with all speed.' To his Mortification not one of the Officers would enter the Ship but remained in their boats untill they joined their respective Ships, , , Mr. Pridham all this time sitting with us in the Boat (what inhumanity).

The feelings of a tyrant grieves for his boat; ah men men

November 12. Lieutenant Barker obey'd his orders and found the barges crew were not able to hook her on. He ran to the Capt. with the newse. At this his highness struts to the gang way putting his cursed tyrannical head over the side and thus address'd his unfortunate lieut. and three wounded men, 'Pridham, what the devil is the reason you dont see the boat hooked on and you come on board?' 'The reason, Sir, is we are unable to do it; therefore we require help to do it.' 'Mr. Pridham, Sir, you are verry free with your tongue,' Says Wilkinson, 'I have a verry great reason, Sir, for My blood and the rest of my surviving crew had been and is at present flowing verry free,' (a just cause to speak free). 'Well, Sir,

THE *Adventures* OF JOHN WETHERELL   80

please to walk on board and you shall have help to hook on
the boat. Why dam'n my blood, Sir, you have got the Barge
all shatter'd to pieces and all over bedaubed with a parcel of
stinking blood.' Mr. Pridham went on board and then we had
orders to come on board. Some hands were sent down to
Manage the boat and we were sent down to the cockpit and
patched up by the Surgeon.

Joined the fleet and deliver'd up our lame ducks Nov. 15

The Ship took us back to the Grand fleet; she returned the
remaining boats to their respective Ships and remained four
days in company then took on board a number of wounded
men for Plymouth hospital and left the fleet on the 16th of
Nov. 1803. Arrived in Plymouth Sound landed our wounded
men on the 17th, John Waddell John Wetherell and Edw.
Carney were overhaul'd by the Surgeons and thought propper
for them to remain on board their Ship as they were all
recovering fast and they would be fully as well on board On
the 18th took in provisions and water, Stores Vc., and on the
20th of Nov. Sailed with dispatches for the British Squadron
off Ferroll and Corona blockading the French Squadron. Our
orders were to Sir Edward Pelew, at that time a Commodore
with his broad pendant on board the Malta 80 Gun Ship. This
was a great mortification to Sir Phillip having to remain under
the orders of a Commodore——

We had the particular account of the Ship Revenge

November 21. This morning fell in with a French brig
prize to the Warrior. He informed us the Ship that we made
the attempt to cut out he learnt from the Capt. of the Brig,
she being from Brest and gave every particular of our defeat,
he informed us She was the Revenge of 64 guns from Rochfort
to Brest and she had 1500 Troops on board for the fleet in
Brest . . . He also informed us that she had 27 killed and
49 wounded and on the following Morning she weigh'd and
ran into the harbour. Most of her killed and wounded were
from our two launches under her Stern, as not one of the
British ever gaind her deck. The weather being quite calm

Capt. Wilkinson lay by the brig all the evening and the lieutenant of the Warrior being the Prize Master on board was able thro the French Captain to give us all the Particulars. He informed us that they were Sure when the British pursued them the day before under the Forts of St. Mathews and then left them that they would make some attempt either to set the Ship on fire or to cut her out. With those ideas they made ready to recieve them on either point of attact. They worm'd her cables from the hawse under water with Chain. They also got up boarding Nettings round the Ship and all the troops placed round the inside of the nettings with their Muskets loaded, and also a second division to load and the first division to fire. Their orders were not a word to be spoke nor a gun to be fired (Should the British make an attact) untill they were close along side and then on the signal being given to fire as quick as possible thro the Nettings, and the Ships crew to Make use of Cutlasses and pikes at the same time so as to prevent one single souls gaining their deck. This was the account he gave us of that most horrid and bloody Masacree.

The Hussar joins Sir Edward in Ferroll Bay

November 22. Captain Wilkinson having learnt all the particulars of the Ship Revenge parted company and with a light air we stood at the S.W. I wish to observe that by this time John Waddell, Carney and myself were pretty much recovered of our wounds only I was yet unable to go aloft owing to the ball in my right hip. The first lieut. was soon cured of his scalping by the help of a wig Vc. Waddell swore he would never die happy untill he was revenged of the French for depriving him of his chief delight, that was playing the fiddle. Poor Carney was no longer able to shoulder his musket therefore stood centeniel at the Cabin. On the 25th of Nov. we kept up guy faux day exerciseing Guns and small arms and on the 26th exerciseing the gratings and Boatsn cats. 27th field day, wash all clean. Passed Cape Ortegal with a smart NE breeze on the 30th . . . made Ferroll.

Remarks in Ferroll Bay

December 1, 1803. After safe arriving in Ferroll bay, delivering our letters Vc, we were stationed off the harbours mouth to break off all communications between Ferroll and Corona. Sir Edward Pellew and the Squadron lay up the bay, Seven Sail of the line British. The French lay in Ferroll harbour 9 Sail and in Corona one 74 and two frigates. We used to go on shore to market frequently and have fresh beef for all the Squadron at a large town at the extremity of the bay. We carried out great rigs amongst the French and Spanieards on Shore. We also Smugled tobacco for wine and fruit Vc. Got taken with a bag full of tobacco belonging to Sir Phil and had it not been more for fear than love I should have gone to the mines for life. However Sir Edw. set me at liberty. On going on board I sat down and wrote the following Verses . . . mere pastimes

> Escap'd from Spanish slavish chains
> My liberty Pelew regains
> to trade on Shore we thought more fun
> neer saw the risk we had to run
> Our Coxswain leaping on the strand
> Says Weth'rell fetch that in your hand
> we cruised the Market up and down
> then took a peep around the town
> at last our Coxswain found a plan
> And barter'd with a market man
> Gave him tobacco in return
> took oranges and citron
>
> I held the bag between my knees
> two savage Spaniards did me seize
> a guard was call'd of valiant men
> they drag'd me to their horrid den
> few ever escape as people say
> lay there and linger life away
> Sir Edward being on Shore that day
> hastes to the prison where I lay

And like a hero did demand
all Britons under his command
within one hour mind what I say
grant my request or for it pay
if in your cells one briton lay
My fleet shall burn your town this day

down to the Boat they took me then
guarded with Soldiers eight or ten
with orders not to land again
and thus abuse the laws of Spain
Our Capt. heard what was to pay
came strutting down to where we lay
Sir Edward meets him on the Shore
and like a Soldier curs't and swore
he said in all the British fleet
a Smugler ne'er before did meet
who would for such a trif'ling thing
disgrace his country laws and king
return on board. get under way
and cruise the entrance of the bay
he join'd the Ship in furious haste
Swearing we should his vengeance taste
in Barge. then weigh'd and ran outside
More develish mischief to provide

John P. Wetherell

December 19. We had letters by the Dragon for all the squadron, and on the 19th were sent out on a cruise off the cape just to let Wilkinson have his fling for two or three days.

December 21. This day was what we called a grand review. After breakfast the word was passed to muster bags and cloaths. The drum beat to muster in divisions, and a long time we had to stand. A great many were short of their complement and were all put in the Brig to have pay for what was a missing. Some had sold their Shirts some Jackets stockings pantaloons shoes frocks handerchiefs, in fact some had sold all their stock to the Spanish boatmen for Aquadent or wine in Ferroll bay. They, poor fellows, only could say they were sold for fruit Vc.

Muster over then comes on the dreadful time. All hands to punishment, not one of the Blackrock Convention. His Highness on the Quarter deck, his Clerk with a large roll of Paper —articles of Cruelty not of War; those of War are laid on one side, forgot. All the Officers planted round him watching even the motion of his eye. Ev'ry word he spoke to any of them Seemed to have the power of Electricity there was such a perpetual bowing scraping handling hats and presenting papers that the whole group were in motion.

A Scene of horrid tyranical tortures inflicted

Mr. Hill was ordered to bring forth the Prisoners. This was done. Next was 'Quarter Masters rig the grateings.' 'Done'; 'Serjeant, are the marines all according to orders? Let them load their muskets before all hands on the gang ways.' 'Done Sir.' 'Mr. Maxwell have the goodness to read the Articles of War, and let the rascals know it is their Country and not me punishes them.'

> The Clerk proceeds his paper reads
> for ev'ry crime 't is death
> Your words thoughts actions looks and deeds
> all join to stop your breath
> those are your Country's chosen laws
> their Justness no one dare oppose
> So Isaac Brooks strip of your cloaths
> and hear the line beneath
>
> Who shall those orders disobey
> death is their destiny
> to leave a boat or run away
> Shall die for each those three
> to sell what cloaths your laws require
> buy grog and set your brains on fire
> Mischief is then your whole desire
> from death cannot be free[1]

[1] The doggerel here is a paraphrase of the Articles of War for the government of the Navy. The Articles were read aloud in their entirety to every man once a month, and on the occasion of the administration of punishment the relevant

To read the rest is quite in vain
they all know what's behind
Shut that dam'd book it gives me pain
Such ign'rant brutes to find
So Boatswains Mates perform your parts
And thus his cruel torture starts
I will you tame or break your hearts
Compassion there was blind
Obey my Orders right away
no mercy will I have
Six dozen on that rascal lay
his king could not him Save
to some give dozens half a score
Some fainted and could stand no more
Such slaughter ne'er was seen before
While some for Mercy crave

with Savage torture Satisfied
his bloody heart content
the deck with humane gore was dy'd
flesh from the backs was rent
at last he order'd the retreat
went down below and took his Seat
Steward fetch something good to eat
I want some nourishment

December 22–30. By this time it was near Six bells in the Afternoon; went to dinner and a poor dinner it was to many, some thro' pain and others thro' their feelings at such unheard of cruelties. O, England were only one fiftieth part of the cruel sufferings thy subjects endure known to thee, under those chosen by thee, to act as thy faithfull and trusty rulers, when from under thy immediate jurisdiction, I again say did thou but know their cruel treatment to they brave Seamen on the Ocean, thou woulds't Shudder at the verry name of it. And almost be perswaded to say this cannot be true. Yes; it

Article was read in explanation of the course to be taken. Nearly every Article prescribed death as the maximum penalty for violation. Wetherell quotes the Article regarding desertion of a post of duty as well as the one that follows immediately after regarding the felonious sale of government stores.

can be and will be untill that day of revenge put an end to some of the perpetrators of tyranny. . In the Morning of the 23 all hands make Sail and ran close under Cape Finisterre after a lugger that lay close under the land. Found her to be a Jersey privateer, watching a French brig lay in a small harbour South of the Cape. We then Stood out to Sea and on Christmass day had a good Plumb Pudding, and a good piece of beef for dinner, but all this was nothing where contentment was fled; however like true old Philosophers we bore all as patient as possible and of our bad bargain made the best. On the 27th Dec. saw a brig to the NE; we soon made her to be the Ferret brig from the Comodore with orders for us to join the Squadron immediately. On the 30th we arrived in the bay and on the 1st of Jan. Sir Edward gave us orders to Prepare for England with all Speed. He had Orders from the Admirality to dispatch the Hussar home to England with all haste Vc. My friend Mr. Smithson heard the orders and told me all the Particulars. On Wilkinson reading the orders he looks at Matthias. 'I suppose,' says he, 'this is another letter from those damn'd rascalls on board the Ship'; 'Ah, you are dark Sir Phil.'

January 1, 1804. Tyranny returns to his Study again to consult his infernal adviser which would be the most torturing (and to him give the greatest pleasure) and cruel persecutions to inflict on his cursed crew of low bred rascalls. At last his honour's meditations were interrupted by a notice from the quarter deck to inform him the Malta has made a Signal for his grace to wait on Sir Edward immediately. 'Dam those upstart half bred Gentry, they once get preferr'd to office, and take the situation out of our hands that we have gain'd by merit; I say half bred because were they of my brave spirit, they would never wear the broad Pendant of their Country, and give orders to men they are not worthy to sit in the same Cabin with, when H. Majesties service can produce such numbers of us brave undaunted bulwarks of our Nation, to bear the insulting and austere chastisement from such mean Plebians and Seven faced commanders of our british navy.' This was the discourse between Sir Phil and Matthias.

Tyranny tormented in his Sleep by his evil conscience

The barge was manned and his highness was propelled along side the Malta, with his chosen pupil Matthias by his side; otherwise he could not have knowledge of half his transactions as he appear'd half the time like some person deprived of their rest and terrified out of their life. When alone he was often heard (by the centeniel and by his boy Richard) talking in great agony, groaning and saying cut them up make them fear me; knock them down; run them thro'; stop their breath; destroy the whole fraternity of rascalls; leave none to write nor in any manner disturb my happiness, at times would leap from his bed and run to the cabindoor and ask the centeniel who that was in the after Cabin groaning and kicking; the centry reply'd no living soul had past him, nor yet had he heard any thing excepting his honour in his dreaming make a great noise, that was all. 'You lie, Sir,' says this bold Lamma Moore Lion 'I heard some one in the after Cabin and it is some plot to take away my life.' This Lion proved to be a Sheep. This Man Must be a Hermione Lion.

He is on the brink of his carreer and must give way

Sir Edward informed him that all the Stores and provisions could be spared from the Hussar must be left with the Squadron, nothing left on board, only Sufficient for her passage to England, that those were his orders from the Commander in Chief and were to be put into immediate execution. (How droll Some of us has, and always will have the idea, that Sir Phillip on being order'd home, with such strict and immediate dispatch was determined to play them all a trick; and destroy both the Ship, Crew, and himself, rather than undergo the chastisement his tyrannical behaviour had long ere this deserved, which was fully Verified afterwards by the loss of the Ship and then by his wicked design nearly destroy'd the whole of that noble Ships crew; what he left undone in the Ship he nearly accomplished with the Boats—had not kind heavens protected us from his horrid design and safely landed us in the midst of our open enemies, as a place of refuge and deliverance from the hands of oppression, and also to let him know that the Almighty would bear no longer with his infernal abominations, but drove him with his boat in a different direction, and drove him from the Society of those Mens presence he was unworthy ever to Command.)

Captain Wilkinson has orders to sail for England

January 2, 1804. HE RETURNED to the ship and in a few minutes launches were along side to take all our spare Stores and provisions, which was soon done. We then took in a little more water and on the following morning Jan. 3 weighed our best bower and rode by a single anchor. Our appointed hour to Sail was 12 Mer. so that all the ships might have their letters on board by that time. Our Sails loose, boats all on, Anchor a peak, and all ready for the word, when as if nature rose to put a stop to Wilkinson's cruel designs. The Sky was in one entire Sheet of confusion, thunder began to extend his awful grumbling voice; and in the distant S.W. vivid lightning successively followed each awful crash, rain fell in torrents and the wind increased; apparently every peal of thunder brought fresh hands to the bellows, so that by 1 P.M. the gale was tremendous. We furld Sails, let our best bower go, and paid out most of the two cables, then the Sea ran high. The gale was verry heavy all that night, and on the 4th, in the morning more moderate untill about 2 P.M. the wind shifted round to the N.E. and blew with great fury. However being off the land the water was smoother than it had been the day and night before. However we rode thro all this and on the 5th in the morning quite Moderate.

The Hussar sails for England with dispatches Jan 5 1804

JANUARY *5–8, 1804.* At 8 A.M. Sir Edward made the signal for us to weigh and make sail which was done in a short time as we were all in good spirits at the time hopeing on our return to England we should have some overturn in the Ship, either in exchange of Officers, or Men, as we had by this time heard of being recall'd home in such haste. However our Ship was under Sail and left the bay; on passing Corona light house we saluted the Squadron and stood to the Northward with a fresh breeze from the S. E. all in good Spirits. In a short time were round Cape Prior and the wind being off the land, we kept the shore close on board, we fell in with some Spanish fishing boats and got some fish and fruit in exchange for bread tobacco Vc. On the 7th in the evening past Cape Ortegal chased a Schooner under the land. She appear'd to be spanish by her Colours Vc. We left her and proceeded our course, took our departure from the Cape at 12 Midnight with a pleasant gale from the Southward all well.

When the Cat goes to sleep the Mice can play

On the 8th in the morning spoke the Philomel Brig on her passage to the Coast with dispatches exchanged Sigs and proceeded. Nothing particular only Wilkinson would not suffer any Merriment amongst us while he was on deck. He used to say it hurt his feelings to see a set of damnd Mutinous rascalls take the least sport or enjoyment, therefore after he took his wine and went to sleep it was our time, as the officers used to say, 'Come Boys now is your time. The Cat is away so now the Mice can fearless play,' and generally a bottle of rum from the Gun room would open the ball with this precaution, 'Be Moderate Prudent Watchfull and Wise,' then the Officers would rank themselves on the gangway to see our curious diversions and hear our funny tales and droll jests and Songs, in this Style, playing at taylors, passing thro' fire and water, hunting the Slipper, abel whackets, rule of contrary and all such diversion, then the second part Singing all sorts of Patriotic Songs duetts glees Vc. but at the same time every man was attentive to his duty such as the look out, helm, top's, on the quarters, gang ways, bows, and particularly a bright eye on the cabin door (as we like wild geese took each man his turn).

January 9. In the manner already observed, we generally passed the first Watch in Moderate weather, unless the Young Jew should remain on deck, which he sometimes did on the first watch . . . When this was the case, everything was quite the reverse . . . You might walk the deck the whole four hours and not hear a word spoke, by either Officers or Crew—except as regards the Ships duty, such as relieving the helm Vc. and now and then orders to keep a good look out foreward, or aft., but that instant the cursed fiend took his flight into the lower infernal regions, to consult his evil Genious Lucifer, then all was alive as if some evil Spell had been laid on all hands, and on the departure of the Necromancer ev'ry soul was reanimated to their former state. We must leave them to their tormented conscience and frightfull dreams, and proceed towards that fatal bed of danger; which the Prince of Tyranny had chosen, for the execution of his Cruel revenge on himself, his Country and Crew.

Sir Phillip threat'ning his crew

January 10. This morning Muster bags and cloaths, exercise guns, serve out a few dozen at seven bells, with an oath of threatening danger to all. That was 'Damn' you all, this is nothing. Before any of you reach England you Shall curse the day you first contrived your plot to bring me to disgrace, by your letters and petitions to Admiral Cornwallis, treating of the decipline on board and ev'ry trifling chastisement I think propper to inflict on you. But now you shall find the events of your conspiracy. I am your Admiral now and shall not forget to let you know it. Boatswain's Mates, do your duty or by G^d I will do mine. If you dont love me I will make you fear me.' In this manner we past the fore part of the day, and in the Afternoon haveing a brisk gale from the S.W. Made all Sail we possibly could crowd on the Ship from 12 Mer to 4 P.M. Steering N.N.E. from 8 to 10 knots pr hour. At 4 P.M. Wilkinson gave orders to steer N E untill 12 at night. and then he should give further orders.

The wilfull Shipwreck of the Hussar

Mr. Weymouth the Sailing Master says to Capt. Wilkinson (as the boy Dick said afterwards), 'Pray Sir dont you think we shall be too far to the Eastwd?' 'That, Sir, is left for me to decide. Go, Sir, and let my orders be obey'd.' Mr. Weymouth went on the quarter deck to the first Lieut. Mr. Pridham and related over what had been said in the Cabin. 'Why, Weymouth,' says Pridham, 'if ever this Ship reach Ushant Steering N.E. I will eat her,' 'No,' says Mr. Weymouth, 'according to my calculations she can not pass the Isle of Glenan, and we must be verry near run the the distance from 12 at noon by Observation we were in Latt*d* 46.17.N. and Long*d* 5. .22 West[1] —and not going less than 8 or 9 knots will nearly bring her

---

[1] If this were the ship's true position a northeasterly course would undoubtedly put her ashore on the Glenan Islands (the Saints' Islands as Weymouth calls them, using an alternative name current in the fleet that had for so long blockaded Brest as to have its own name for every geographical feature). But it is hard to believe that Wetherell heard this conversation or that it was reported to him so literally or that he would have any knowledge of the ship's exact position. My own guess is that, in his anxiety to discredit Wilkinson as much as possible, he much later worked out this position for himself, having regard to the fact that Wilkinson, before the ship went aground, had ordered a northeasterly course. But to give such an order, knowing the position of the ship to be what Wetherell says it was, would not have been so much bad seamanship as sheer lunacy, and the story is incredible. It is a pity; the rest of Wetherell's manuscript of the loss of the *Hussar* has every appearance of truth.

the length of the Saints by 9 or 10 ten O clock this evening.'
'She cannot run till 12,' says Pridham, 'and going at this rate
she will go to ribbonds in one Minute if she strike and all
this sail on her.' 'I Shall not turn in,' says Pridham. 'Nor I,'
says Weymouth. Barker heard all that. He rises off the slide
of a Cannonade [Carronade] blustering out, 'Why damn' me
Gentlemen, what are you affraid of? You wont go to hell
before your time, and my life is as precious as yours is.' 'That
is all right Mr. Barker, but we have our ideas. You Sir perhaps
have verry little regard for yourself and much less for others.
With us the case is quite on the reverse. We are studying the
benefit and safety of ourselves and the whole crew. At this
moment I feel greatly allarmed and cannot rest below.'

The first Lieut and Master are correct

At that instant Mr. Pridham goes forward and looks verry
carefully ahead of the Ship; at the same time she was flying
thro' the water at a great rate. He would then walk aft then
to the fife rail and every few minuites would repeat the same
words, 'Keep a good look out foreward there,' and every
few minuites him or the Master went foreward and took a
strict look a head; at last the quarter Master reported ten
oclock, four bells, my look out of the larboard gangway, the
helm, and looks out were all relieved. Took in the topgalt.
Studdingsails running 9 knots pr log. 'Keep a good look out
foreward' was all the cry, the night was verry dark and a
little squally. Took in the royals, and were in the act of furling
them when Something sounded like the distant roll of a drum.

Hussar Strikes on the Saint rocks

All hands stood in a state of Surprise for a moment and
anxiously listned to hear from whence the noise proceeded,
when a most dreadful crash ensued which nearly sent the
Masts over her bows. That was followed by another when she
stuck fast. Up comes Wilkinson in pretence to know where
they were going with the ship as she had just hove him from
his cot and nearly broke his arm. 'Why, Sir,' says Pridham,
'she is just where I expected, on the Saints.' 'That be damn'd

Sir, take in sail and heave your Ship clear of whereever she may be. Carpenter sound the pumps.' All hands in a state of confusion; some let go halyards others let go Sheets and braces, in fact all was terror and confusion. By this time the Ship was half full of water, the Pumps were ratling, Boats*n* Mates roaring, Ship Strikeing, Sails flapping. and Officers bawling, which formed a most dismal uproar. At last some person on the forecastle saw a large rock under the bows quite above the water. Got sails furld, Sounded, and found nearly as much water in the Ships hold as there was along side. Out boats to sound for a channel; all this time the tide was falling. The Ship fell over on her Starboard beam ends. Then knock off pumping and get topmasts over the side to prevent her falling any farther over, This was a scene of confusion; some were crying out for the lord to help them, others contriving how to raise some grog, some packing up their cloaths, others hopeing she Never would float again; some were desirous to know where the devil she was, others makeing their calculations how many could get in the boats, Vc Vc. We fired Minuite guns, hove up rockets for help, but all to no purpose, sounded with the boats, and could find one cast of the lead four feet, at the next ten, and sometimes sixteen and twenty feet water. In midst of our confusion a light was seen over the Starboard bow and was soon made out to be a man on the shore holding up a lanthorn; this gave us fresh hopes as we saw there was some place of refuge not far distant; however we fired Minuite guns and rockets untill daylight made its welcome appearance and then Oh,—horrid! All round as far as we could See from the deck was sharp ragged black rocks and on our Starboard bow was one of those destructive Masses of rock, which without either leave or licence verry abruptly had made his way thro' the bows of the Ship and was verry contentedly placed with part of his black huge body in the fore hold, and was there determined to keep possession and not to give up his hold as long as the Ship hung together. Finding such hard hearted feelings from this Sea Monster our looks were directed towards the Shore and there as the daylight approached we beheld a number of Men, and one with a flag makeing signals for us to come on

Shore. Then arose a story that the island was full of troops and they would either kill or take us all prisoners immediately after landing. Some said one thing and some another.

Landed on the Island

At last the word was passed for the third division of small arm men and Marines to get their arms amunition and every thing in readiness to land immediately; little doctor Newman to prepare his necessary articles to attend the men on Shore under the Command of Lieut Leftwidge the Lieut of Marines and my friend Smithson. They were all landed, and the men we had seen on the beach ran away and hid themselves. On the other part of the island was the town and harbour of Glenan inhabited entirely by fishermen. Their Governor was himself a fisherman and their only traffic was in carrying fish to Quimpier and Le Orient, as we afterwards learned from them.

The heroic Conquest of the town

Our little Army marched up to the town in great pomp, the drum and fife leading those daring invaders. Our gallant leaders conducted their forces up to near the town without seeing any living Soul and on the entrance of the town was two large rocks where the head Gentry had boldly ventured with their Governor in their front to know what might be the wish or request of us, also what was the cause of our fireing guns at them all night, but when they saw us advancing in such a hostile manner, they knew not what to make of our Manovres, therefore they took shelter behind those two rocks lest we might fire on them before we came to a parley. However by some means doctor Newman saw the heads of some men, as he said, peeping from behind the rocks and he was sure they were waiting a favourable oportunity to let fly amongst us, and there appear'd to be a great number of them all armed, and in the possition they were posted, they would kill one half our Men before they could see them, that he would advise the Lieutenants to return back to the Ship and get a couple of 18 pounders on Shore and more men to work them.

Then they would be forsed to lay down their Arms and Surrender the town Vc. Leftwidge burst out on him in great fury. 'Why you are a damn'd cowardly fellow, Newman. If your country had all such valliant leaders as you what would become of her Fleets and Armies? I advise you Doctor give your box to Anderson the loblolly boy, and you return to the ship, as it is my determination you shall not proceed one yard farther with us. Why Sir, you would dishearten a whole Army with your infernal imaginations. Return, Sir, immediately back.' About Ship goes Newman. Our invading army advanced a little closer to their supposed enemy when Leftwidge advanceing in front Sword in hand Saw some of the enemy peep from their Ambush. He had the forces drawn up and load their Muskets ready for an attact; the old Governor seeing our Men makeing ready for action took to his heels and ran to the town with his terrified citizens at his heels.

Adventures in Glenan

Such an army as Newman had discover'd was a great curiosity, to see them retreat from their redout, and fly for shelter to their own habitations. A few poor inofencive innocent half naked ignorant unarmed scared to death Brittouns fishermen, wanted to speak but durst not make bold enough to approach our officers. We stood like a set of Statutes stareing at them, some in frocks, some without shoes or stockings and others without hats, to see them flying from the rocks to seek refuge in their own houses, rare fun for our Men, some laughing, some roaring for them to stop, but this was all folly, home was home, with the fishermen. We advanced to the town, and took every particular description of the Situation both of town and harbour. There was a quantity of fishing boats in the port but not a Single Soldier, except the Governor was on the island, nor yet either arms or any Amunition; as Mr. Leftwidge was informed by the Governor. He spoke a little broken English and on our people entering the town our Officers were directed to where he dwelt by an old French woman.

The Capture of the Governor

Mr. Smithson was the first man to enter the Governor's Mansion. He being master of the French language demanded of a young boy where the gentleman was. The boy burst out crying and said, 'You will kill my father and my Mother and then take me away to England.' 'No, my good boy,' says Smithson; 'Your Father nor yet any Soul in the town shall suffer the least harm from any of our Shipwreck'd Officers or men. All we want is to see your Father, so that he may instruct us how to act in regard to lodging our Men on Shore Vc.'

At last the Boy took Smithson as interpreter and lieut left-widge into the next appartment where sat an elderly lady weeping. 'Where is the Governor?' says Smit*n*. 'Under the bed,' says the woman, 'but pray spare his life.' 'My good woman,' says our interpret*r*, 'we are come here as friends, and crave the advice of your good husband; it is for that we want to see him,' 'Come out my dear,' says Madam, 'those English are friends and wish your advice how to prepare for their Men.' The bold Commander crept from his concealment by degrees, looking at the officers then at his Wife; at last he got untangled from the Boats Sails where he lay and talked some time. He enquired what brought us there with the Ship Vc. We informed him of all our Misfortunes . . . He told us they had thirty boats large and small belonging the Island that three of them had gone to Quimpier [Quimper] with fish and that was all the particular satisfaction he could give, and as for lodging the People, there was no place but the Church and he would consult the Father on that point. Therefore if we could save provisions they had plenty of potatoes and might do verry well untill we had an oportunity to embark for our own country. He also informed us his orders were from his government to report any Enemies Ships Vessels or boats that might land or attempt to land on the Island by dispatching a boat over to le Orient [Lorient], but he had not as yet performed that part, therefore to clear the Governor from any neglect of his duty, it was most expedient for Capt. Wilkinson to take possession of all the boats in the harbour,

for the safety of himself and crew; this would put an end to all further altercations. Our Officers made the promise to repair directly on board, acquaint their Commander with the proposals made, and let him have an answer in two hours. In the mean time to prevent any Mistake regarding boats leaving the port to give any allarm, a guard of Marines was left in charge of the Serjeant with strict orders not to let any boat whatsoever leave the Island. In the course of all those preparations being settled Newman reached the Ship with a dreadful account of the town being full of armed Men and it was necessary to send a reinforcement of Men and Amunition also some cannon with the utmost dispatch as the enemy were in a verry strong redout when he left the Party with the tidings.

Doctor Newman relateing his adventures

Our Officers and Men left the governor and returned to the Ship at the verry time the Doctor had told his dreadful story, which for a moment made all hands on board look round themselves. The moment before every Man was prepareing to save what few things they possibly could in their bags Vc. but at the tidings of Doctor Newman it was consider'd in vain to save any thing to be taken from us directly we reach'd the Shore. However this story was quickly on the contrary side of the question, Mr. Leftwidge and the rest of his men return'd on board, gave Capt. Wilkinson every particular, and in less than half an hour the orders were all hands prepare to land immediately, and put all the provisions that can be got into the launch and Cutters with all the Amunition that has been saved from being wet.

Captain Wilkinson lands to visit the island

'Mr. Pridham, Sir, you will please to see those things all landed safe. Also all the Crew must land immediately, armed with their Cutlash and pistols, full cartouch boxes, and ev'ry Man prepared to defend himself should we be surprised by the troops from the Main. Let not any person fetch any bags or bundles with them, only what they can put on their backs,

to be ready at all calls without any incumberance. Those are
my orders, Pridham, and as it requisite for me to go immediately on Shore to consult the Commandant you make all
haste with your landing. Should I wish to let you know any
thing particular I shall write you by Mr. Mathias. Barge Men
Away.' . 'All ready Sir,' says the Coxswain. Down comes Sir
Phil. We landed him, the Purser Mr. Irwin, the Doctor, Mr.
Lawmount and Mr. Weymouth. The Master, Lord Geo.
Gordon Mid and several others landed and went to town with
Wilkinson. We returned to the Ship with the barge and assisted
in the landing our ShipMates.

The death of Jack and Nancy by slaughter

January 11. By 4 PM. all hands were safe on shore and
every Man used his utmost endeavours transporting our Stores
and provisions on shore; when we left the Ship her main deck
was in the water as She lay on her starboard beam ends in
spite of all the Shores we could invent or put over the side.
We then took each a load of the stores up to the Church, bags
of Bread beef pork Cheese butter candles Grog tea Sugar, in
short every thing that was not damaged. A favourite Goat
and the pig Jack were the first that fell victims to satisfy our
craving appetites; they were cooked on the beach and each
Man had his allowance, with bread Vc. Grog was also served
us, and after Sunset the watch was set, and the Church our
tent to sleep in by night. However be as it will there was
always something to disturb our peace. Being a fine Still
evening we were all over the place walking round, when our
Drum beat to Arms. 'What can all this mean?' says one to
another. 'Why,' says Waddell, 'it is Barkers Watch and likely
he is drunk as usual and therefore in his crazy moments has
set the drummer to beat to arms on purpose to let the old
French Governor see us fly to our post.'

Must all appear before the great tribunal

We all met at the Seat of Corrupt and absolute administration. When we enter'd candles stood lighted on the Altar and
the distributor of all good things was sat in great Pomp, with

his Officers in order on each side of him. 'Silence!' was the first salute, then the orders were given to fetch forward Joshua Porter and William Wilson.

Wilkinson disregarded in the house of God

Porter advanced up to the Bar of Pollution (altho fixed in the house of the Lord). 'Did you call me, sir?' says he. 'Yes sir, you are amongst the number of Mutinous rascals. You have struck my Clerk and I mean you to feel the effects of it directly. Where is that rascal Wilson?' 'That's me, sir,' says Wilson. 'I understand, Sir, before you left the Ship you stove in the bulkhead of my Cabin with your feet and this was contempt to me.' 'What do you want with the bulkhead after deserting it, and landing us all in this barren island and an enemy's country where you are in constant expectation to see the French come over from the main and take us all prisoners? So, Sir, you have a notion to have a little of your cruel diversion put in practice in this house of God, but I hope Sir, as we are on French ground God will shew himself above the Devil and put a stop to your tyranical proceedings in this house.' 'Gag the rascal,' says Sir Phillip, 'I say gag him, Hill.' 'Touch not a hair of his head,' says a number of voices; 'Postpone your Sham court Martial, untill a more Seasonable oportunity. This wont answer any longer. We are all determin'd not to suffer any more of your cruelties, neither in this place nor any other, so we think propper to dismiss, and go to rest and not consider any prisoners Amongst us.'[1] So good night, and out we all went, left Wilkinson to his private devotions at the Altar . . . it was a laughable scene to see the officers grin and wink at each other, some hiding their

[1] It was a legal point, frequently debated, that the loss of a ship terminated any contract existing between the ship's company and their employer—in this case the government—and put an end to the subordinates' need for obedience. In many shipwrecks—a typical example is the loss of the *Wager* during Anson's voyage—there was much avoidable loss of life as a result of the complete disappearance of discipline arising out of this theory. But Wilkinson seems to have retained command of his men reasonably well; the haste which accompanied the departure from the island, and which, in the prevailing weather conditions, resulted in such severe loss, was made necessary by the danger of the arrival of troops from the mainland.

faces a laughing, and Wilkinson, poor man, drove into a State of Petrifaction for some time and had not a word to Say to any one of his Officers present. At last when he saw us all leaving his hedious presence he rose up and vomited forth a volley of dreadful oaths on such an infernal set of Mutinous rascalls. We left him to sleep by the horns of the altar nearly all alone, only his Jew Brother Mathias was with him. We slept that night some in one place, some in another, but kept our regular watch until daylight appear'd. We then got what little we had for breakfast and at 8 AM. the word was past for the Barges crew to go on board and set fire to the Ship, which was done in a short time; then the Barge was order'd round to the cove or harbour to join the fishing Boats. Wilkinson swore he would not stay on the Island another night with such a gang of villians, so that he was going to leave that place if he went to hell in the attempt, but should he live to arrive in the British dominions he would have full satisfaction for the insults he had bore both from his officers and Ships Crew.

We Plunder the town and take their Boats

Therefor it was his immediate òrders to overhaul the houses and get Sails for all the boats, also vessels to carry water. According to orders, we ransack'd the town, took all the Sails we could find, which they mostly used for their beds, and tubs cogs bottles pitchers, or any vessel we thought any use to carry water, and at 4 P.M. went on board the Ship renewed the fires as the tide of flood had destroyed those we made in the morning. We cut away her Masts, cut the Anchors away, in Short we destroyed every thing we thought of any use to the enemy. As for her magazines they were full of water. All the Guns were loaded and double shotted on our first leaving Ferrol. We hove all the arms over the side, and finding the fires burning furiously—as a warning to us one of the Guns in the Cabin went off, the fire began to rage so fast—therefore we all Started on Shore and went up to the town. On our way we were Saluted with a gun from the old Ship and the Shot Made the rocks fly like an old pitcher.

Great preparations to leave the Island

The Ship being all in flames, her guns on the side next the town became a little troublesome to the poor fishermen. Being nearly high water the Ship was upright and now and then sent an unruly visitor into the town which gave more allarm amongst them than our first visiting them with the forces. Says Wilkinson to the first Lieut, Pridham, 'You will please, Sir, to see what Bread salt pork and water we have equally distributed among the Boats, and let each man have a little of the grog we saved. It will not harm them at present. Then let all the Sails you have collected be fitted to the different yards and sparrs you can find and placed in the Boats. As for oars or sweeps they are all supplied already, and be sure you have all the water that you can find vessels to put it in equally divided, and then let me know directly.'

The crews appointed for each of the Boats

We bent all the sails and fitted our little fleet up as well as sails and rigging would afford, and got our tubs and vessles all filled with water, which was unfortunately all render'd unfit to use shortly after we left the island; it not being cover'd the salt water breaking over the boats entirely destroyed both our bread and water, as will be seen in the following pages. Wilkinson being informed the Boats were all as well prepared as time and materials would permit his orders then were for all hands officers and crew to assemble on the Square fronting the Church, and there we were station'd to the different Boats, according to their size or burthen and formed in two divisions, the first division under Mr. Pridham to hoist a blue flag and the second under Barker a Yellow flag and Wilkinson to lead the Van with the barge.

CHAPTER

6

We Embark and Sail from the island of despair

JANUARY *11, 1804.* At 6 P.M. we all embarked and made sail with a fine breeze from the S.S.W. Our orders were to follow the barge and use ev'ry effort to reach Ushant or some of the British Ship's cruiseing off Brest. During the night the Barge was to shew a light and blue lights at intervals. We were all clear of the Island by dark; then we formed our two lines and made all ready for the nights sail. I must not forget one remark we made on our Sailing round the point which forms the harbour or rather a Cove. We all made a wonder to see More people gathered together on the shore than we had seen before on the island. Some of our Men observed they had been hid in some cave or Subteraneous vault, being struck with terror on our first approaching their seldom visited barren rock, and those few we had seen before were their chiefest Men of Valour.

The Ship shews us light and salutes us

Our small fleet haveing all passed Point look out (as we named it being the point nearest the coast of France) and night fast advanceing the orders were to Sail in two lines thro' the night and follow Sir Phillip in the Barge by his light, which was soon performed, as the Hussar thro' her great affection towards us verry friendly afforded us a most Brilliant light to arrange our grand Armada. She made a dreadful lamentation when she found us all deserting her and leaving her to the mercy of those uncultivated islanders, which was clearly prov'd because every Minute or two she set up a most thun'dring roar, as much as to say, 'Stop this night and See the last of me; then you can declare to the World you saw the total destruction of the fatal Hussar.' But Wilkinson regardless of forerunners to approaching danger rushed forward and regularly hove up rockets for us to Make all speed after him. By this time the Sky became quite cloudy and dark.

We have various signs of an approaching tempest

At 10 P.M. the wind blew a smart breeze at South; we still carried all sail in order to clear Point l' Abbe steering west dist. 15 or 18 miles. At this time we were apprehensive the wind was drawing round to the westward it being verry verry black and dismal to the S.W. with quick vivid flashes of light'ning. At 11 P.M. we consider'd ourselves to the northward of Point le Abbe, and kept away N.W. for the isle of Sein [Seins] or Point Croise, dist 27 miles, wind still from the South and westward with squalls of rain and distant thunder continually threatn'ing the approach of boisterous weather. Our Commodore still kept in his station. At 4 A.M. being by our account round the Isle of Sein we kept away N.N.W. for Ouessant [Ushant] or St. Michel's dist 24 Miles. At 6 AM the wind shifted round to the N.W. followed by a heavy squall of hail and constant lightning followed by dreadful crashes of thunder. The gale kept still increaseing, the Sea rose in entire confusion thro' the sudden change of wind, and our Sails all blew away.

Our Boats are drove before the Storm

Our oars or rather sweeps were so large and heavy that we could not make the least use of them in such a heavy sea. As quick as we got one of them over the side the sea either broke it or hove it out of our hands over board, so that all our exertions to use oars were in vain, and another unfortunate affair we had to encounter was all our water and bread entirely destroy'd by the Sea breaking continually over the Boats, sometimes nearly overwhelming them never to rise again. We bailed out the water by turns with our hats Vc and some of our Men were in constant exercise keeping the boats free and their blood in circulation, while others laid in the water perishing with cold and thirst for want of exercise and courage. About 12 Mer the Squalls of hail and rain were so quick in succession that it appear'd we must all perish. We were one minuite in total gloomy fogg so thick we could not see one of our dispersed fleet, and the next Minuite wrapt in flames, as it were, by the continual light'ning.

In the midst of danger there still is hopes

We could not hear any thing except the howling tempest and rending cracks of thunder with frequent Surges of Water rolling over us. In the midst of this disasterous situation being seperated from the rest of our unfortunate shipmates and driving before this dreadfull hurricane at the mercy of Winds and waves I somehow had hopes we should reach or drive into some place of refuge knowing the land was not far off, according to the distance we must have drifted from 12 Mer to 4 PM. Therefore I stuck close to the pump and took turns at pumping with two or three others all the time, and by this little exercise we kept in good spirits and hopes. The Boat it was my fortune to be placed in was a verry large boat and had a small pump fixed in her. This was of infinite service to us in freeing the boat, and also keeping us in motion. We were 28 Souls on board; Lieutenant Barker was our officer, and was invested with charge of the Second division of our flying Squadron.

In constant expectations to strike on the rocks

Our foresail, the only Sail we had left, was of verry much service to us in keeping the boat before the Sea and also preventing her from shipping the water she would have shipped by laying in the trough in the Sea. We suffer'd a great deal from the severity of cold more particularly in the Snow Squalls which followed each other successively. Sometimes we had a glimpse of bright sky for a moment and enjoy'd some hopes of seeing some of our dispersed brethren, or land which must be

verry near us to leeward. This small hope was suddenly o'er-
thrown by a repetition of either rain hail snow thunder lightning and wind, and within the confines of the bay with a most
frightful rageing confused Sea. However we drifted on between hope and despair before the howling Tempest. Sometimes one thought he saw a boat, another would imagine they
saw land Vc. which is a verry common case at Sea when
approaching land. Immagination can see any expected thing at
one hundred miles distance, when the real object is not visible
more than ten or twelve in clear daylight. We had a great many
false boats Ships lands Vc. reported. They all proved delusions
and dark night spread her blackest Mantle round us. In this
situation our strongest hopes had nearly fled; the only Man in
our boat who neither had hope nor dread as long as his brandy
enliven'd his Spirits would frequently hollow out, 'Pull away
you bug--s, and let us get on board the Ship. My guts are burnt
out for want of water with my brandy.' At another time he
hollowed out, 'Loose the topgalt sails and let us make sail to
clear this damn'd rocking and jolting; it is impossible to take
a drop of brandy without looseing most of it with her damn'd
kicking.' He would snatch the helm from the steersman and
say, 'Why dont you steer her Steady as I do?' At the same
Moment he would heave her broadside to the Sea and run a
great hazzard of both his own, and all our lives. Thus he
realized the old story when liquor's in wit's out. Barker would
then perhaps have a sea or a spray strike him in the face or
break over the boat and half fill her with water, then he would
power out a volley of curses on the boat sea wind and weather
and verry frequently on himself and all on board. Thus we
drove at random untill about ten at night, when to our great
supprise a gun was fired close to us, and looking round we were
saluted by a second. The water was smooth all in the same
time. We soon percieved a large ship close to us and the
weather became clear at the same instant, and we saw the land
on each side. By this time we were drove close to the Ship.
They hail'd us in French and French Taylor being in the boat
informed Barker they order'd us along side. 'Let them go to
hell,' says he; 'I shall go on shore and when the weather abates
we can run out to sea again, and not be made cowardly pris-

oners by them lousey Frenchmen. Let her run my boys out of his sight then we will all land in some cove or bay where we can get some refreshment and a fire to warm us and dry our cloaths then we are able to clear our way thro' all the ships in Brest.'

By trusting to Providence we ran into Brest

He had only made a finish of his fantastical proposition when a Boat from the Guard Ship made her appearance rowing towards us full of armed men. They came up along side and order'd us to heave to immediately; if not they would fire on us. 'Prisoners, by God!' says our brandy proof Champion. 'Heave our Arms all over board so that they may not find us armed. By this means we may fare the better.' We hove all our Muskets pistols Cutlashes and amunition over the side and hove the boat round, lower'd down our foresail and lay till the Guard boat boarded us. They enquired what we were and what was our intentions, where we were from and where bound to, in short every particular was explain'd to the Officer thro' our interpreter, Taylor. They then took our boat in tow. By this time we had drifted into Brest habour and were taken first along side the Le Indian Frigate but could not hold on.

Our foes were our most humane benefactors

Ev'ry person was so wet and benumbed with cold. They hove us a rope from the frigate but the wind Sea current and the weight of the boat caused our half frozen hands to refuse their former grasp. We drove clear of her and were again taken in tow by the Indian's Boats towards the Admirals Ship the Le Alexander 80 gun Ship. They took us on board and shew'd us the most tender humane usage could possibly be expected from enemies in a foreign land. We had brandy bread and herrings on first entering the Ship, then were placed in the Galley over a good fire, and after warming and drying our selves we had a sail prepared for us to lay down. By this time it was twelve at night. The Officers got Barker into the Gun room and with their Cogniac soon sent him to sleep. We all laid down and slept untill morning, then were roused out to have breakfast, and Make up the Sail we had to sleep on. Also to make ready for us to be questioned by the Admiral.

Not hearing of any of our boats we gave them up

About ten A.M. Barker made his appearance on the break of the quarter deck, and as some of the French officers spoke English they gave him to understand that we were going on Shore to the hospital where we would be better taken care of than we should be on board, it being the most comfortable assylum for half perish'd creatures like us. We soon heard Barker on the gangway in his stupified state of insencibility hollowing out for Graham the Boatswains Mate, ordering him to call the Hussar's to muster. The French Officer of the deck smileing at his ignorance observed to him that he must consider the Prisoners were no longer at his command, and when they were required to go on Shore they had Officers attached to the Ship able to give orders when required by the Admiral.

The first Lieut. of the Alexander's good advice

At 11 AM the first Lieut. of the Alexander came down amongst us. He was a fine old gentleman and spoke good English. He took every particular means to make our situation comfortable. He told us the steward was drawing off some wine and we should have bread and cheese with it as he expected the Admiral on board verry shortly, to send us on Shore as soon as he arrived on board. He also told us to be obedient to the Officers into whose charge we might be entrusted and then he knew by long experience a Prisoner of War was not the Most wretched mortal in existance. He also informed us newse had arrived intown from different parts of the coast with information of boats landing full of British Mariners. On the shore of St. Mathews two boats landed and their crews were Made Prisoners untill further orders Vc. The wine bread and cheese came for us and he returned on deck. The Steward gave each Man a good cup of wine also some soft bread and cheese, enough and to spare. We all eat what was required and then were called up on the quarter deck; we were placed in a line and the Admiral a fine bold looking Gentleman stood a little while in front of us then turning round to Lieut. Barker who stood on the right of us addresses him thus in English. 'Pray Sir,' says the Adml to Barker, 'were all your Ships crew such men as those are?' 'Yes, your honour,' says Barker, 'our crew were all young men.' 'Well then, Sir, I am not asham'd to tell you that such men as those are prizeable and rare to be had, therefore you ought to have taken more care of both your Ship and Men. However I know the Men were not the cause of their present situation therefore I will use my interest to make them as comfortable as their present Situation will allow. I am going to send them on Shore to the Hospital and there they will be nourished and taken good care of By some of their own Country Ladies Sisters and Nuns.'

Our kind treatment in Brest hospital

The Boats were ready and we all embarked, being 28 in number. The Admiral looked over the side as we left the Ship in the two cutters. 'Be of good courage, my men. Your confinement in France will not be long, and as it is the laws of our two nations to hold fast all prisoners at this present time My duty to my Nation compels me to transfer you to some place of confinement as prisoners of war. However your treatment shall be as good as we give our own men, and reason will not desire any more. I have sent my recommendations to the hospital with the Officer that superintends you at present, so go on Shore like Men, and you shall fare like men and Brothers.' We parted from the Alexander and made the best of our way on shore; we landed close to the back gates of the Hospital and were muster'd by the Matron of the Hospital, 28 Men; she took us up Stairs and placed each man to his cradle or bed. Then she had a number of convicts to attend the hospital and she in one word made them fly in all directions, some of them after Sheets Shirts and caps others after water to wash.

We are joined by some of our Shipmates

January 14, 1804. She also spoke to us in English telling us to be steady and not make any disturbance in the hospital. Only let her know and those poor unfortunate creatures she said (meaning the convicts in red caps frocks and a ball to their leg) what ever you want and they shall fetch you as far as our rules will allow. 'You can have wine or Beer but no spirits are allowed within those sacred walls. Another favour my dear young country men I beg you all to be verry careful not to Swear nor make use of any loose mean or unbecoming language, because that is contrary to our wish, and as we are all Christian Sisters under whose care you have had the fortune to be placed, abide by our rules and you will find yourselves comfortable clean and happy. You must take care of those Men that have to attend you. They will take any thing from you they can get hold of. Now, men, I have given you our rules therefore you have not the least excuse for breaking them, which I hope you will not. Rest yourselves a little while and you shall have some soup to nourish you and what ever will be of any good to you shall be had. . . .' We all thanked the Lady and prayed God to bless her.

Mrs. Burke relates her history

In a short time we were served soup boild beef mutton veal cutlets potatoes Bread Vc., also every man a pint of beer and before we had one mouthful our good Lady gave a blessing in the midst of us, also after eating the Same. She told to us all not to think strange of those blessed ceremonies she made use of as it was the duty of every soul in existence to return thanks to the blessed father who is the giver of all good things, and without his blessed goodness we could receive nothing at his hands. We thanked her and all sat down on the wooden benches. She then informed us that She was born in Ireland and at the time of the rebellion her Father and Mother owing to religious principles left Ireland and went to Nantes in Britany. In a short time her parents were called to mingle with the dead; she was the only child left and was by some christian friends sent to a Convent and thro' the help of her blessed Saviour was translated to the charitable office we saw her in. Her Name Was EMMA BURKE born in the CITY OF LIMERICK COUNTY OF LIMERICK IRELAND.

We find the difference between two days

January 14, 1804. By this time it was near Sunset, our Lady
bid us all a verry good night, and left the ward; we all repaired
to the beds allotted to us, and all our discours was on the
humane and heavenly treatment we found in the midst of our
most inveterate enemies; although prisoners of war, our foes
were our benefactors, and treated us with so much more
humanity than we found in the Service of our own Nation that
we could not but observe to each other what a blessed change
we had made. No boatswains mate masters mate nor yet
Wilkinson to curse and abuse us both day and night; no, the
Lord saw our sufferings were not much longer to be bore, and
thro his great Mercy towards us contrived this, as the means
to snatch us from the inhumane bonds of oppression, and to
deliver us out of the hands of tyranny. Thus we lay in our beds
discourseing untill one after the other we all fell fast asleep,
and slept till daylight next morning, when we arose quite
refresh'd and rested. Our red birds, as we termed them, were
all ready to make up our beds and sweep the room shew us
the washouse Vc.

We are informed of our Shipmates arriving

January 15, 1804. About eight o'clock this morning our
governess Miss Burke came to visit us; she enquired how we all
were, and how we had rested thro' the night, 'Well, men,' she
says, 'I have good tidings to relate to you this morning . . .
After I left you last evening we were informed that a number
of Boats had landed on various parts of the coast and all their
people were on their way towards Brest.' Those must be the
remainder of our shipmates were were all the time enquireing
after; therefore we might be contented for they would be in
Brest in a day or two . . . We thanked her for her good newse
and then were served boild milk and bread for breakfast Vc.
In the afternoon one of the red birds came running up into our
ward saying, 'Come, come, comrade, come'; and soon we
found the crew of one of our boats had arrived. They, poor
fellows, were almost exausted and wore out. When they saw us

and heard how we fared they were twice glad, first to find us alive, as they like us concluded all the other Boats were lost, and secondly to find by us they were in the hands of good Christians. They were put in a ward down Stairs and had the same tender nourishment we had already experienced. After they had some refreshment, and dry aparrel put on we sat down and heard them relate their late sufferings Vc. That evening one of our boats crew named William Jones that was in a poor state of health when we left the Ship and suffering so much thro' cold and wet in the Boat and was on our landing was put in the sick ward and medical aid was given to him but in vain; the frame was too far exausted and the Lord took him out of all his troubles to another and a better life. He died on the 15th of January 1804. We all went to our rest again for the night and on the 16th we had a number more of our unfortunate shipmates arrived. They all had the same Melancholy tale to relate in regard to sufferings Vc. We enquired after the Barge but no one heard nor saw any thing after the gale arose.

We heard of our Carpenter being lost

January 17, 1804. THUS we kept mustering our dispersed crew from all parts of the coast round Brest, and by the crew of the boat in which the Carpenter (Mr. Thomas, a fine man) was lost we understood by the men that when the boat struck on the rocks he leapt in the dark, thinking to reach the shore, and was burried beneath the boat; he was the only person lost in all that dreadful disaster. The fact is this: We kept mustering; every hour fresh parties from St. Mathews and distant parts of the coast arrived; and thus we continued untill we were all present except the Barge's crew, with Captain Wilkinson the Purser and Master, they were all in the Barge and we did not feel in much trouble of mind for the Captain and Purser, not one of us lost our dinner thro grieving for them. But as for the Master, Mr. Weymouth, he was lamented by all the Ships company. He was a sailor and a Sailor's friend. Our lost shipmates being nearly all found we began to think how good the Lord must be to spare so many Sinners.

January 25, 1804. Miss Burke gave us a recommendation

and a letter to present to any of the Sister's we might fall in with, and on the 25th day of January 1804 we were Muster'd, served Shoes Vc., to those who stood need, and in the evening we were served four days bread and seven Sols pr day beef money for four days with orders to be ready to march in the morning. Every thing went well with us in this mansion of happiness, but we had to leave it and travail in search of new adventures. Therefore we shall pursue our Journey thro' France . . . And as nearly as possible give a hint of our various over-turns scenes and curious circumstances that we went thro' before we reached our destined Prison.

7

We marched from Brest to Landernau. 15 Miles

JANUARY *26, 1804.* On the 26th of January we left Brest under a guard of Steel jacket horse soldiers and the good wishes of all round Brest hospital. We had a cart allowed for our baggage Vc. It rained all day but we got thro the days march verry well and at Landernau [Landerneau] were put in an old Castle and had straw Vc. The towns people flocked round us with Soup, fried liver Vc. to sell, and several with a drop of what most Sailors are fond of to warm the cockles of their hearts. The 27th we Marched to Landivisian [Landivisiau], 12 miles, lodged in a jail, and on the 28th went to Morlaix, 14 Miles. There we were put in the City Prison, had soup beef and potatoes served to us, and could buy a red herring for two Sols. The prison was the first place we saw the miseries of a French Conscript in Prison, and there was a great number of poor unfortunate souls, lousy, dirty, hungry, and naked, all confined in cells under ground, some singing, others cursing, some begging at the grates, some fidling, some dancing, others louseing themselves and on the other side card playing, dice Vc., dram smugling from the Gaoler.

From Morlaix to Belle Isle 22 Miles

January 29, 1804. This was the first introduction we had into a city prison or cashot [cachot]. We were verry glad when morning came for us to start from this scene of Misery and woe; Jan. 30th we left Morlaix for Belle Isle [Belle-Isle-en-

Terre], 22 Miles. There we found humanity had for some time left that place. We were wet and cold and drove into an old ruinous Church with a guard of Gendarmes round us. They treated us very uncivil. The least thing they did not like the flat of their Sword was used verry readily. An old lady of humane feelings sent her servant with Some bread and Cheese for us; the Gendearmes beat the man and hove his basket with its contents over the bridge and would not suffer any person to give or sell us any thing, but we got along with all those little things pretty well when we consider the different dispositions there always exists amongst 307 men in our situation; we had some that made two or three attempts to persuade others to join them and do great things by force, but we had good informed Men amongst us that used by fair reason always to perswade them to consider the place of a prisoner of War, even in England and they would have but little to say, and in this manner we passed over numbers of little obstacles that befell us on our march.

From Belle Isle to Guimgamp 15 Miles

January 31. We left 4 of our men in the hospital sick in Belle Isle and of the rest of us started for Guimgamp, 15 miles. Snow fell all the day and our guard could not bear the severity of the cold and heavy roads any better than us; they were the guard of the town we left and had to conduct us to the next town to deliver us up to the Mayor Vc. They are the same as Militia in our country, a composition of all sorts. In this place we had another Misfortune befell us that was nearly costing numbers of lives, entirely thro neglect and carelessness; when we arrived in this Village of Guimgamp we left many of our Guard on the way and what we had with us were glad to deliver us up to the Mayor so that the towns guard might take charge of us and they take Shelter from the severity of the weather. They put us in a large shed, their Market house, and the people and children brought us fire wood in abundance. We made a large fire in the place to warm and dry us and our cloathing, we being all wet entirely thro'.

Sir Charles White's generosity

So far all was well; our next dificulty was we wanted some victuals and saw no signs of any preparation for any. However this was soon found accomplished. In the vicinity of the Village lived a rich old English Gentleman; he had been many years resideing in the Castle and was a father and friend to all the neighbouring poor people. He kept a number of them constantly in employ on his vast domains and in short he was beloved by all around him. This gentleman heard there was prisoners of war arrived in the village and sent his vallet to know what we were and how we came into France. We told him all particulars; he told us we should soon have some nourishment from the Castle, and accordingly in a little time a cart came with raw Mutton Beef and pork, Bread potatoes cabbage beer and a pail of milk, and wood to make fire to cook with; this was a heavenly gift to us which was on the point to cost a great many lives, as will appear in the sequel. Some of the people in the village furnish'd us with large cooking pots and in quick time we shew'd every prospect of killing that that would kill us . . . hunger.

We are surrounded by Fire and Sword

I cannot refrain mentioning this dreadful accident that was makeing its ravages round us, when fortunately we discovered the rafters of the Market house, our prison, all on fire; an outcry was made, and in a few minuites all the whole village was in an uproar; the Mayor gave strict orders to the guard that surrounded us to run every man through that offer'd to rush from the prison, as they had set it on fire Says the Commandant ev'ry prisoner shall perish in the ruins or in their attempt to fly from the flames; this was told us by the Interpreter. This was the time to see us poor, unfortunate creatures run round the place, in horror and confusion, nearly suffocated with smoke, and chill'd with the barbarous consequences of our Commandants orders. We saw nothing but Death before us, the fire on one side and the sword on the other; however we were roused from our dreadful apprehensions by a lucky turn

of providence. Some of the rafters after the fire took hold of
them fell, and the roof being an old rotten concern that part
most on fire fell on the floor, which we quickly smother'd, and
put out all the fire, and the roof being wet assisted us greatly,
and thro' the exertions and activity of some of our men climb-
ing up inside the roof and knocking down the parts on fire, and
with the humane Manly aid of Sir Charles and his followers on
the outside we entirely extinguished the fire. Then you could
each face resume a contrary appearance.

Sir Charles makes intercession for us

We were as we consider'd ourselves like brands that were
snatch'd from the fire; when all the confusion was over and all
things in their usual order we had a visit made us by the Commandant and Sir Charles White. We told them every particular, how the fire made its way to the rafters Vc. Sir Charles
observed to the Commandant that it was no wonder, as there
was no fireplace, chimney, nor any place for us to cook our
victuals, only on the middle of the floor; and poor unfortunate
creatures like us almost perished with cold and wet hungry and
fatigued were much to be pitied and not to be blamed for what
had already happened. He made intercession with the Commandant to let us cook outside the house and he himself would
be answerable for any thing that might take place time we lay
in the place; and he was ready to answer for any one of us
that might desert whilst we lay under the charge of the Commandant. . . .

He describes the present state of France

At those words the guard was dismissed, and we had our
orders to behave like men and shew by our actions what we
were and to what Nation we belonged. Sir Charles smileing
says to us in English, 'My brave countrymen, I have done all
for you that delicacy according to my present Situation will
permit, I have humbled myself to the laws of France, and at
this Moment the state of things are verry tickelsome, and we
know not our friend from our foe. As we say to ourselves we
want no body Guard for one neighbour is a strict watch over

the other; this is the present system of affairs in this country; however I have reason to believe there is not an individual in this Quarter that would hurt a dog of mine, from the Commandant down to the Meanest peasant, and this comfort is all my pride. I have no apprehensions of thieves, Murd'rers, nor that of a bad name; therefore as my word is taken as security for you take care and give no cause of complaint. Let those people see that you are men of principle and scorn the idea of any thing unbecomeing the character of Brittons and Men.' At those last words we gave him three cheers and also our words that we would rather suffer death than bring any trouble on him or his connections. We thanked him gratefully for his good will shewn to us, and thus he took his leave and left us all cooking.

We eat drank and were merry yes we were merry

Some of the women in the Village assisted in cooking, furnished us with dishes, spoons Vc., and thank heaven we sat down to a good plentiful meal such as we were much in need of after our evil and good fortune in that place. We had a plentiful Supper and plenty left for next day, and after Supper we had each man a pint of Beer. Mr. White also sent us a waggon load of Straw to make us a comfortable bed to rest our wearied limbs.

Arise prisoner's and take your petit goot

February 1, 1804. We went to rest early that evening and in the morning were rose by the villagers, some with coffee, others with Milk, and some with a little drop of what Sailors mostly enquire after when on Shore. We had good and hearty food for breakfast and made ready to leave this place that made us twice glad and twice Sorry . . . We were glad on our arrival hearing of Sir Charles's generosity, and glad When the fire was extinguished and Sir Charles was our Security:: we were Sorry when the sentence was pronounced that we should perish either by fire or Sword; and Sorry when we left this assylum of Charity humanity and love. Sir Charles visited us in the morning when we started and gave 25 pair of Shoes to those most in want; he then took his leave, recommended us to the Officer of the guard, and left us. February 1st 1804 we left Guimgamp for Chatelaudren 15 Miles. There we were lodged in a Church, had soup and bread served us, with each man a dram of Brandy, and plenty of straw at night to sleep in; thus we past the first of February; on the morning we arrose early.

February 2. Muster'd and marched away for St. Brieuse [St. Brieuc], 19 Miles. There we were lodged in the city prison, there we had salt beef and bread served us with two large buckets of Salt beef Soup, pretty good. When hunger hovers round he often makes salt, fresh, and bitter or sour, sweet. We left 7 of our people sick in the Hospital and in the morning we had to encounter a severe Snow Storm. We also had a fresh guard of foot Soldiers and two carts for our baggage. They Served us three days bread and Seven Sols pr day for beef Vc. Then we started again for Lambale [Lamballe], 25 miles. There we lodged in the towns hall or the Minsipalitie as they term it. The Mayor order'd the inhabitants of the town to prepare us soup and bread, also to prepare for each Man a sheaf of straw Vc., with wood to make fire and dry our cloaths. This was the good will of the Mayor and citizens, for which no doubt but they will have their reward, as not a single charitable deed is left unrewarded by the giver of all good things.

Marched to Jugon, 27 Miles, up to the knees

February 4. The next day the 4th we again began our journey and to our disadvantage had to travail 27 Miles in rain and a verry heavy road, and our guard was not composed of the most humane men in France. They took a dislike to us thro' some of our men being unable to walk fast enough thro the middle of the heavy road; indeed the Serjeant of the guard (a Dutch man) said if we did not go faster along he would break his Sword cross some of our backs. He also made us keep the Middle of the road, and when occasions required any of us to step towards one side without leave he was sure to have a blow from one of their Muskets or a Sabre across his back. Our Officers were with us this day: before this they were always two or three days March before us. However we came up with them this day at the half way house, a village where travelers stop to take refreshment, and the Gendarmes exchange their prisoners Vc.

We joined our Officers on the road

February 4. Mr. Pridham our first Lieut, seeing a man named Robt. Devine verry foot sore and barefoot, Pridham being on horse back dismounted and made Devine mount and ride the rest of the days journey; he himself took willingly to his legs on the rough and heavy road. He said to Lieut. Left-widge publickly that he took more pleasure in walking and seeing that poor lame man ride, than he would to ride in a carriage and if it was in his power, there were more men that he saw on the road stood need of a lift. In the whole Pridham gave the Officers all a verry great hint to follow his example (they being all mounted) but they could not take an English hint (they were in France). However thank the Lord we got thro' this days trouble as well as many others, and reached Jugon, where we were put in Cells under the city prison. . . . Oh this was a horrid place; the roof and sides of those cells, or caverns, was all dropping from white parts of the rock like salt, and we being all wet and much fatigued, laid down on the few rotten blades of straw that was strew'd in the corner. In a little time the Gaoler brought us down two vessels full of Soup and some black bread but this went down verry good. It was warm and we were quite the contrary. We saw no more of any living mortal that night, our iron doors were bolted on us and we were there to fare the best we could. We laid us down like a flock of sheep to keep each other warm and first thing that we heard in the morning was the creaking of the bolts and the rusty hinges that secured our dismal bed room. We had not one glimpse of light could approach us only what was brought by the Gaoler; when he came we got a candle and eat our remaining morsel and then a Brigadier of the Gendarmes came and order'd us all up to muster. We obey'd; if we were wet and cold on entering this place of horror it was the reverse on leaving it for then we were wet and Smoaking hot, and so weak that we scarsely could walk up the Stairs of the prison. However we partly got over this when we had been a little while in the air. We left three men in the hospital, had our rations of Bread, and began another days journey towards Broons, 21 Miles. We got thro' this days work quite charmingly. The ground being froze and dry made the roads quite good. Our guards were the corresponding gendarmes. They treated us verry well and gave us plenty of rest on the road. We saw nothing of our Officers this day. They took a different rout and went two stages in one day; thus we for the present lost them. We got to Broons and there were put in a large old Castle with plenty of clean Straw, wood to make fire, and the inhabitants brought us plenty of victuals; God bless them. We were as happy as kings and laid us down quite warm and comfortable. In the Morning we had warm Soup and bred for breakfast, were counted over by the Mayor, had our orders and off we went, fine hard weather best for us to Becherel 32 Miles. We made this days journey in as good spirits as if it had been only ten miles; we had fine weather, and a good Officer and men had the charge of us. They had three Waggons that they made keep all the day up with us, and if the Captain of the guard saw any man that was any way fatigued he made him mount one of the waggons and ride. Thus we past this days journey, and at night slept in a large Barn, with plenty of straw Vc. The place being only a village the villagers brought us boild milk, Soup, Bread, Bacon, and plenty of potatoes for supper; so much for a good Officer.

February 6. . In the morning we had a plentifull breakfast of boild milk and bread, with a good share of cold Bacon and bread to carry with us and the same good Officer and guard had to conduct us to Rennes. We Started in good spirits and with 4 carts we commenced our days work from Becherel towards Montflort [Montfort-sur-Meu], 28 Miles. The weather being fine we past thro' our days journey with pleasure. We halted at the half way village during the celebration of Mass and stop in Church untill divine service was over. Eat a bite had a drink of cider and away we trudged. We reached the town in good time and for the first time were billeted on the inhabitants like Soldiers with orders from the Mayor to be nourished and lodged, which we realy were.

Our adventures in the City of Rennes

February 7. We rose in the Morning like young farmers and with our Same guard started for the City of Rennes in Britany; the weather was a little severe on our first starting but as the sun rose we had more moderate times. This day we had our baggage waggons and ev'ry thing in its former order. We past a regiment of horse soldiers on their March towards Brest Vc . . . When we got into the city we had orders to March up to the grand place, or the towns hall. There we were ranked up nearly an hour to be review'd by the General and Commandant, In the interval great numbers of the inhabitants flocked round to see us wild English Sailors, and as we stood we took particular notice of two young ladies passing up and down the front of our ranks, looking at us and laughing every few paces they went . . . Tho. Steward was in front of Me and when those ladies stood looking at us, he says to me, 'Wetherell, if I had that Girl in the red dress for what I am Suffering as a prisoner I would bear it all and ten times as much for her Sake . . . I think she is the greatest beauty I ever saw.' He speaking in English had no idea she could understand him; but to both our astonishment she turned round to Steward and smileing says in English, 'Young Man, you may wish a good while before you wish to yourself any harm; however I thank you, Sir, for the honour you have done me, and were I left to my own choice you would not be the last of my choice, but my situation is so that I am sent to this place to pass my days in a doleful Convent.' At those words the Commandant made his appearance. She bow'd her head and mixed in with the crowd; We were left in entire darkness and could not conjecture what she meant nor what nation she was from; Steward said he thought she was Irish and my opinion was that she was the daughter of some English family sent over to France to be confined in a Nunnery Vc. Thus we formed different ideas of this Mysterious Stranger. Our former Officer and guard left us, and we were put into the City prison Amongst every class of people to be found, Murd'rers thieves pickpockets forgers traitors deserters spys incendiaries lawyers and taylors composed this lousy hurd.

The Rules and laws of a prison

February 8. In this prison we were attacted by their Com-
mittee in order to make us pay the prison fee, as their custom
is to make all prisoners when they first enter pay their entrance
to the Captain of the prison as they term the chief of their
gang. He is generally the oldest prisoner, if not he is ellected by
the Majority, and all the prisoners are under his controul. He
makes certain laws and rules which all have to obey. He is
verry often an eye servant for the Gaoler, and it has been
common for those sort of characters to remain in large City
prisons on their own choice for many years and accumulate
large sums of money in this Miserable manner. However they
demanded our fee and some of our rusty lads told them they
would give them their fee over the face and eyes. This being
interpreted to their Captain he order'd them to retire and not
interfere with prisoners of War. We had our soup beef and
bread served out and a bundle of straw for four men. Thus we
finished this days adventures. In the Morning we had a Guard
of Curiaseers to take charge of us and started with fine weather
for the grand place of City hall ,and there we stood nearly 4
hours with our guard arround us waiting for the Comissary of
war and the General of Marine, to review us. About 11 O clock
they muster'd us, gave orders for our men that were sick or
lame to be left in the Hospital of Rennes, and to give Shoes
to those that wanted them. The Comissary spoke midling good
English; he asked us how we fared on the road and we told
him only verry indifferently most of the time, and at present
we had been standing in the Square all the morning and never
broke our fast; he said as for the time past there had been no
arrangements made for Prisoners of War; but this was his
present business to see regular allowance and good usuage
given to all such people; therefore for the future we would be
better taken care of; he also said he would give orders for us
to halt 5 days in Rennes untill his affairs were settled in regard
to our daily routs Vc. We also were to have 7 Sols pr day paid
ev'ry Morning, a pound and half of bread and soup beef Vc
after our days stage was completed. We also should have a
halting day every fifth day and he had given orders for us to

be lodged in the Citadella in barracks so that we might be rested and gain a little strength; for in our situation he thought we wanted some care and nourishment which was already provided for us; therefore we were going now to the barracks where arrangements were made for us. He then left us and we went down to the Cittadella; were put in good warm rooms, 12 in each room; there was a stove, bed steads, table and benches, with wooden dishes, a cooking pot and water pail for each room served us by the barrack Master; we were also served wood beef potatoes and salt for Soup, ½ pound of white bread and a pound of brown each man. We went to work first thing to cooking and some to cleaning the room utensals Vc. One Man from each room was called for Blankets and Straw. Thus we passed the 9th of Feby. On the 10th we arose quite like other men, past this day in the greatest comfort could be. We took 5 of our Shipmates to the hospital sick thro' fatigue. One of them, Charles Jones, died the third day in the hospital. On the 12th the General visited us in our rooms and said we looked quite comfortable to what we looked the other day . . .

Continue our March

February 13.   On the 13th in the Morning we all assembled in the square and had our rations of Bread, Marching money Vc., served us out and an Officer of Horse took the command of us; we marched that days journey 23 miles to Vitre with the greatest ease, and there we were lodged in Soldiers barracks, treated well, and went to rest quite happy; full bellies and warm beds. On the 14th we made sail for Laval, 25 Miles; halted at the half way house, went to Church, took a relish of Bread and cheese with the peasants, wash'd it down with a good drink of cider, and then completed our days work. In the town of Laval we were lodged in the Gaol but had the liberty to go out for any thing we wanted; our regular rations were given us, and straw to sleep on; we all went to our nests and forgot all care, untill roused in the Morning to pursue our Journey, which we did with great spirits. February 15th we tripped away for the Village of Mayenne, 19 miles. It being a cross country road made it worse to get along; however with the help of a light frost and two waggons, we made our way thro' like brave old Soldiers.

February 16. Arrived at Mayenne, the Mayor lodged us in an old Church. We had our rations and clean Straw, all things were good. Made sail in the morning of the 16th towards the village of Preenpail [Pré-en-Pail], 23 Miles. The roads were soft and heavy but our kind Officer gave us our choice of the best of it and we drove thro like lions. Our baggage waggons did not get in till late, being drawn by Oxen they travailed slow. In this place we had a larger farmers barn for our dwelling. He being the Mayor we lived like little kings on the fat of the land. The large farm kitchen was our sitting and eating room and the barn our sleeping room. We had plenty to eat and drink of the best any Man need, with a good fire to sit by and take comfort. In the morning milk and bread for breakfast and away we tramped across the fields to fall into the main road. February 17th we arrived at Alencon (Alençon], dist 16 miles, about noon, there we were put in the Skeleton of an antient Monastrie greatly reduced by time and age. However we like Monks and Friars took possession.

We all turned Monks or Friars in Alencon

February 17. Nothing but naked walls with some few traces of former grandeur and Magnificence. We traversed its vast winding passages, and galleries and down into the lower cells and caves of this large former bastile, as it appear'd More like a prison than a dwelling for Saints, after all our observations regarding the Manners of Monks and Friars with the innocent charge that was placed under their jurisdiction, and such tales as we had heard concerning this class of Christians . . . Our drum beat to Muster and away we all scampered to the gate, were Muster'd by the Mayor Comissarie de Marine General du depot and Commandant de Gendarmes, au la ville de Alencon . . . We had shoes order'd for those in need of them and a good many got shirts and some Jackets and pantaloons. Thus we fared. Here we had our orders to dismiss and go to our dinner. They left us and we took our dinner in comfort, good Soup beef and potatoes, looked round a little while then went to rest in a large room half full of clean Straw. Thus we past our day and Night in the Convent of Alencon.

Performing our Pilgrimage

February 18. Next day the 18th we had a great field day or washing day Vc., some of us looking at the curiosities of our dwelling and the extensive gardens that Surrounded it with a Wall twelve or fifteen feet heigh and a deep Mote that enclosed the Whole Structure. The only entrance was by a large gate and draw bridge; however we were made verry comfortable. Those of our party inclined to visit the town had liberty to take one of the National Guard and go take a walk where curiosity led them; our rations were verry good and plenty of them, Brandy Sneek and beer were to be had for a trifle, but that trifle was verry thinly spread; we had to send 3 of our brave comerades to the hospital. The Stoutest and most robust of our men were the first that felt the effects of fatigue and hardships by travailing. We got our things all dry and made ready to start again. Went to our roost at night and rose all ready for action; February 19th we started, with two Waggons to carry our lame and baggage. The morning was verry severe. Snow fell verry heavy and the wind blew keen and strong; however the Storm was partly on our backs.

February 19. This day our Officer and his Men appear'd to suffer more from the severity of the Storm than we did, as they stopped at every little place of shelter house or barn and took a moments comfort. We overcame this trial and in Sees [Sées] were put in the School house and had our days provisions served us with clean straw and a warm room to rest in; we had the liberty of the village but preferred a warm fire to that pleasure of wandering round a Village in the Snow. On the following Morning we were happy to see fine clear weather; our Officer Said we had best rest untill ten oclock and by that time the paths would be better for travailing and lighter for us and them: at 10 we started, February 20th from Sees for Verneuse 27 Miles, and this days journey was nothing in our way; the paths were hard and made us trip along like young hunters. We got to Verneuse in good time and lodged in the Gaol being the only place in the Village convenient to contain us and Make us comfortable; we had good hot soup beef and bread and each man a gill of Sneak (liquor like whiskey) a good fire and good lodgings all night. We could hire a good bed of the Gaoler for 3 Sols pr night each man. Some of us did and some had not the possibles, nevertheless they had plenty of Straw.

We were billeted on the peasants of Bernay

February 21. On the 21st in the morn. clear and cold; we left Verneuse and took our rout for Bernay, only 17 Miles; this we completed quite early in the day and got to our destination by 11 A.M. We had billets served by the Mayor, a kind old Gentleman, and were two or three in each house. The peasants gave us good entertainment and on the following morn. we had good warm Milk soup or whatever was in the house. Waddell Blacklock and me were at the house of the Mayor and we lived like horses and drank like Mayors. All the disadvantages attended us was that we could not converse with the old Mayor, but we made out to get along. Waddell wanted the old man to give him his daughter which Made the whole house echoe with the roars of the old Man his lady and daughter, and we all laughed Seconds. This overteure brought another large brown Pitcher of the Mayor's Rouen beer and with the help of some bread and cheese we saw the bottom of the pitcher and all went to bed pretty well satisfied. We wanted no rocking to sleep . . . In the morning we arose, took a good breakfast with our host, shook hands with all the family, and met the rest of our comerades in the Square.

In Brionne I fell into the hands of humanity

February 22. On the 22nd we left Bernay for the town Brionne, only 12 Miles, but the weather was unpleasant; small rain and sleet fell all the day and made the roads verry heavy. We got in by 12 Mer. but our Baggage never got up untill after dark. We were again billeted on the inhabitants and well used. My lot fell in a tavern where our Officer of the Guard put up, and there my treatment was verry kind. I had plenty to eat of the best and as much as I wanted and more to drink; had a good shirt, waistcoat pantaloons, shoes and stockings given me and a good bed to sleep on. They took away my wet dirty cloaths as I supposed to dry them for me in the morning, but to my astonishment in the morning the servant brought all the old things dry and tied up in a handkerchief and made me understand that I must keep them for a change when I got wet again; that the Gentleman of the house gave me the cloaths I put on to change with yesterday and as he had not yet rose he left the servant to tell me, and to give me my Breakfast and something good to drink before I started from the house, which She really did and gave Me a large slice of ham and bread to eat on the journey.

We reached the great City of Rouen

February 23. We all muster'd and after fixing our two baggage carts and some of our Men comfortable in them that were unable to march we started them off and then we took our leave of this little hospitable place where charity and humanity were their chief rulers and directors; bid them all farewell and left them and on the 23 we reached another village called Elbeu [Elbeuf], 15 Miles; there we lodged in an old church verry comfortable and warm. The peasants soon had plenty for us to eat and drink Vc. In the morning they gave us our breakfast and we all started again, this day being the 24th of Feb., and we reached the famous city of Rouen, 14 Miles. Here we crossed the great floating bridge of Rouen, and passed thro' the gates and entrenchments that surround this large City. We saw several small sea going vessels laying at the quays on the outside of the walls Vc. We were Muster'd in the grand place and then conducted to the city prison. We were placed in a part of the prison free from any of their own prisoners; and had verry good rations served us, considering that a prison is not like being billeted in a small village. We always found large Citys the worst for us.

February 24, 25, and 26. On the following day, the 25th, we halted and had a general review by the Officers of the War department, also the comissary of Marine. They gave shoes and shirts to some of our men, and the Military Physician gave orders for each man to have a pint of wine allowed pr day to strengthen them and give them courage to proceed on their wearisome Journey; this was all quite acceptable to us. We were sent to our room again and in a short time had our wine and some good veal soup Vc., plenty of good meat and vegetables, white bread Vc., served us. We sent three men to the hospital; and during our stay here Several Gentlemen came to visit us, all people that had correspondence in England or had lived there. They all Spoke English and some of them most likely were English. They gave us two louis dors to drink their healths and also informed us that our Officers had left Rouen that Morning we arrived. Their orders were for Virdun [Verdun] and ours were for Givet. They told us to be of good courage and Maintain the character we already bore and we would be well used in France, and our confinement would not be long for they expected daily to hear of the two Nations comeing to an agreement and settle all their disputes. Then blessed peace will restore you all to your homes and Commerce flourish between the two contending powers. Then all the powers of Europe may sheath their swords and rest in peace free from the allarms of War.

Our cruel treatment by the Dutch guard

They took leave of us and bid us all good night. We all gave them our sincere thanks, made our obedience, and parted. At the close of the evening we were muster'd by a fresh Officer of the guard; they were foot Soldiers the 50th regiment, mostly Dutch, and ugly temper'd Serpents they proved to us before we got clear of them in Amiens.

We left on the 26th and took our rout from Rouen to Cailly, 15 miles, fine hard frosty weather. Our Dutch guard was no ways bashful to make use of their Sabre or the butt of their Musket when any of us gave them the least cause of offence, and the first day we could not leave the middle of the road without leave from the Serjeant Vc. Lucky for us we had several of our crew that spoke Dutch, and some few spoke French and when we arrived in Cailly we told our Officer that the Comissarie de Marine in Rouen informed us that we should be treated well during our March; and not be beat and kicked about in the Manner his men had used us that day, beating us with the swords and muskets for the least offence and that we had orders from his Excellence the Commissary that if we had any cause of complaint we were instantly to let him know and he would see us justified and treated like Men; he also gave us his address how to write to him in Rouen Vc. This was all past in the presence of the Mayor of Cailly. We were then put in the Gaol, had our days provisions served and a good fire to sit by; in the Evening our Officer and the Mayor paid us a visit; they looked at our bread and then at the place we had to sleep in. They order'd us some more clean straw and plenty of wood to keep a good fire Vc. The Mayor asked for some one that spoke French, and Robt. Taylor a Guernsey man came to him. The two Officers told Taylor that they had given strict orders to the guard not to ill use any of us again; if they did by complaining to the commanding Officer we should have redress. We thanked them and told them (by our interpreter) we only wanted to be used as Men and prisoners of War by distress, not by any battle or capture, but by Shipwreck. We were cast on the coast of France and sought shelter and refuge in Brest, producing Mrs. Burkes letter, 'This, gentlemen, will inform you all particulars.' They took the letter, looked it over, then stepping a little aside they spoke to each other, looked at the paper, and again had some private discourse Vc., then turning round to Taylor the Lieutenant of the guard says to him, 'Pray inform your fellow prisoners that they shall enjoy all the comfort that my authority can grant to you all. I give my word that not a Soldier under my present command shall give any of you the least cause to complain, and any other favour in my power to grant in reason shall be allowed you while under my direction. You are poor unfortunate men and ought to be treated well; therefore I make you this promise in presence of this Gentleman the Mayor of the town.' We thanked him and the Mayor and him bid us good night and departed. We all sat talking over the whole affair some time and after several old stories wash'd down with a glass of Whiskey we all retired to our rest and past the night in comfort. On the next morning we had two carts for our baggage and sick but we had no sick just then, and so the Officer Made the carts go along with us so that if any man pleased he could have a lift on the road.

Marched from Neufchatel to Aumale, 17 miles

February 27, 28. We left Cailly on the 27th and marched to Neufchatel, 18 miles. There we were billeted by the good will of our Lieutenant and the Commandant of Neufchatel. The city is a complete little place, not Much larger than the Citadel of Valenciennes, but in this days March and this usuage after our journey we felt quite elevated. The inhabitants treated us verry kindly, gave us plenty of Meat and drink and good beds at night; next morning we had good warm breakfast and then muster'd in the square; all present and on the 28th of Feby. we set out for Aumale, 17 Miles. We had heavy rain all the forenoon and quite bad roads being only a cross country road from Neufchatel to Aumale; but like other stormy days we at last got thro'; came into the village and were distributed amongst the peasants; this was our wish. We soon were placed round good fires had plenty to eat and drink and at night good comfortable lodgings; in this days march I began to be troubled with a ball that had been lodged in my hip from the time we attempted to cut out the Revenge 64 off Brest on the 10th of Nov. 1803. This ball thro' my continual marching had worked down into my thigh and was becoming daily more troublesome and more so when I got wet, but this day it was worse than before and felt as though a needle was at times running into the flesh; however as our old saying goes, I had to grin and bear it.

Marched from Aumale to Poix 15 Miles

March 1. On the following Morning, March 1st, after a good nights rest my thigh was far better. We assembled and all present, one sick. We took our waggons along with us; it being only a bad country road and our baggage drawn by Oxen they travailed too slow for us and we left them behind waddling along. We soon arrived in Poix, a large country town, and there the Court house was our Castle. The Mayor was verry good to us; he sent a drum round informing the inhabitants they must bring in victuals and drink the same as French soldiers on March, which they did and that in abundance; also the farmers brought plenty of straw and blankets. This is the old rules of this town. We had liberty to walk round the town and view the great Castles and seats all round the shrubby hills that surround this garden of Amiens as they term it, and so they may for it is a real Eden, and the abode of Christianity.

In the Citadella of Amiens

March 2 and 3. In this Garden we were used like their own people; they gave us whatever we desired both to eat and drink, and plenty of covering when we went to rest. Our Lieutenant said he was glad to see us so well treated under his command, but in Amiens he was apprehensive that we would not fare so well; however he would use his utmost efforts in our favour with the Commandant and General of the City. He also told us he would return from Amiens and another Officer take charge of us but he would speak to him in our behalf and do us all the good in his power, which he really did; he wish'd us all good night and we went to rest. On the morning of the 2nd of March we had breakfast and then fixed our two carts with baggage and 4 sick men, the weather quite hazy and cold. Away we started helter skelter thro' thick and thin on the beautiful road to Amiens, dist 18 miles. On each side of the road was country Seats, Chateaus gardens, parks and Castles so that this days March was in the midst of Magnificence luxury and Splendour; after a little while the Sun burst thro' the haze and Made our days journey a real day of recreation as we found something strange every way we turned our eyes. At last we saw the huge Steeples and lofty Spires of Amiens on the road before us like a forest of trees.

March 3. The close of the evening we found ourselves in the city and the Citadella was prepared already for us. We were put 12 men in each room and had good Barrack fare the same as their own troops, and we could desire no better. We were warm and comfortable, went to rest, and in the other end of the Barracks was a regiment of horse Artillery. They had a guard and answer'd each other thro the night. This was a new thing to us and for some time kept us awake; however we afterwards became fameliar with que vive. In the morning we arose with the sound of the Soldiers trumpets, saw them all ride their horses to water Vc. This day the 3rd we were muster'd by the Comissary of War and had some Shoes Shirts Vc. served us, and sorry I am to have to say we sent 9 of our men to the hospital, all sick through fatigue and bad usuage on the first of our march. This is 36 we have left on the road in different hospitals, but we have the hopes to have the most of them join us again on our arrival at our appointed depot; we past the remainder of the day looking at a horrible sight.

We witnessed a horrid scene of torture

In one of the large rooms of the citadella this awful torture was that day put in forse and to be continued untill death put an end to the performance. This was a young man aged 21 of a respectable family in the vicinity of Amiens . . . This unfortunate young man was deeply engaged with a young women in the city and it was his intention to make her his bride; they kept company some length of time and were remarked by many what a sweet loveing couple they were; and so it appear'd they happned to be at a ball during the Carnival and by some Means he took a disgust to her. They left the ball and he went to see her home as usual to her Father's house; he upbraided her before she parted from some of her female acquaintance, and with inconstancy she made a jest of it and smiling told him not to be jealous. They parted from their companions to go home and on the way he took a knife and ripped her bowels entirely open so that she fell that moment lifeless on the ground with a loud groan, which brought the Gendarmes on padrole to the horrid place before he made any offer to shun the police. He then started but was taken and brought to justice, where he confessed the whole horrid transaction. He was tried and Sentenced to the inhumane torture we were there the Witnesses to behold; as a warning to all young people he was exposed in this public hall.

The manner of punishing Murderers

This young man was laid spread flat on his back on a large table or scaffold with his legs and arms drawn over to the four corners and there secured. Above his breast was a machine like a fork or spear; it had three small sharp prongs and went with a spring. Near his mouth hung a loaf of bread and when hunger compell' him to snatch at the loaf this infernal engine went with springs and would dart deep into his breast; or if he fell into a slumber the watching executioner had to toutch a Spring that drove the instrument deep again into his breast; and in this Manner he suffered five days without eating drinking or sleep; and the severe wounds inflicted in his breast by the spring spear his sufferings were most dreadful. It was on the third day of his torture we saw him and his cries and lamentations were enough to melt the stoutest heart; he pray'd them to put an end to his life and not to keep him any longer in torment, but this could not be granted for he was sentenced to die in this horrid manner.

March 4. We shall leave this horrid scene and return to our narrative. We went to our rooms, eat our suppers, and went to bed; all our talk was about the poor man his sweetheart Vc., untill sleep sent us all to silence. We arose in the morning, eat our mouthful and prepared for our journey; our baggage waggons came, and our New Officer and his guard of four Men. He was an old gentelman, spoke midling English, had in his younger days been a prisoner in England; he used us verry fatherly and his men were all quite fameliar with us; they were part of the city guard, all men of families. We took our leave of Amiens, and marched towards Corbre [Corbie], 13 Miles; we soon got thro' this days journey, were billeted in the Village, used well, and on the 5th in the morning, all well, we started again for Albert, distance 12 miles. We were put in a Church and had our victuals brought by the inhabitants. We slept well and comfortable and on the 6th in the Morning we started for Baumpame [Bapaume], 14 Miles. In this town we were quarter'd on the Gaoler and he wanted to be a little extortionate; he wanted to sell us bread and herrings Vc., at his own price but we soon let him know quite the reverse.

March 7. Our Officer came in and gave him orders to let any of us into the town to purchase what they might want and also to give us our full allowance of rations and good straw to sleep on; those orders given he left us and we soon had our dinner Vc., went to rest, arose in the morning, and after all was ready off we started towards the city of Cambray [Cambrai], 20 miles. A rainy day and the roads very heavy cut us up greatly; some of our men had to stop on the way for the baggage waggon to help them along. We got into the City and were order'd to the Citadella where we were lodged in the depot of prisoners. We were put 12 men in each room; the barrack master served us provisions and Means for cooking them, plenty of fireing Vc., to dry our wet cloaths; good bedding and clean. We were quite comfortable and our Waggon came up with the sick and our baggage so that we dried all our wet things. Of the sick five of them went to the hospital; the others came along with us and we nourished them up as well as we were able, put them to bed and in the Morning they arose with the rest of us quite smart.

March 9, 10, 11, 12, and 13. We halted this day and got rested Vc., refresh'd greatly; next morning the 9th of March we had a fresh guard of the Gendarmes, a Brigadier[1] and 6 men; we were muster'd by the General, Commandant, and Comissary, of the depot, had Shoes given to those that were barefoot Vc., we had a cart and being all in readiness, the weather quite fine and dry under foot, off we started for the town of Landrecy [Landrecies], 24 Miles, which we got through in good time and this evening March the 9th we fared well and we got all safe arrived and Billeted by Sunset. In Landrecy we fared well and on the following morning Marched away for Capelle, 25 Miles. March 10th all arrived, lodged in a tavern, well used, one man Sick, and next morning March 11th we took our rout for Vervins, only 14 miles, were quarter'd on the rich farmers round the Village, well used and nursed like their own Children; we left two on the road sick to wait for the Waggon which we generally left in the rear. March the 12th we marched to Marle, 13 Miles, were lodged in a large barn belonging to the Mayor, had plenty to eat and drink

[1] 'Brigadier' in this case is used in the French sense, of a corporal.

and clean straw to sleep on. In the morning we had our waggon as usual, put 4 Men in and our little baggage, and On the 13th of March we Marched to Roxoy [Rozoy-sur-Serre] 23 Miles.

Remarks on our March

March 13. In Roxoy we were all billeted on the farmers, and had plenty of milk Bacon and country fare; we were taken good care of by the old women and as we had some rain thro' the day they dried our cloathes and made us quite comfortable. We had good lodgings and in the morning we had a good breakfast and our Officer and his men being ready we put our sick in the Waggon and all started again across the country for Rumigny, fourteen miles, fine frosty weather. We soon passed our waggon and left them to follow. On the 14th at 1 Oclock we were in the town, Muster'd by the Mayor in the town Gaol by 2 Oclock, had our prison Soup and bread not made by the peasants but made of pease Vc. Slept in one of the cells of the Gaol or as they term it cashot [*cachot*]. So much for the Mayor of Rumigny. Our sick were kept up stairs all night; in the morning we gladly left the Mayor and on the 15th of March travail'd to Maubert, 15 Miles; we had fine weather, got in early, and were quartered on the inhabitants. They gave us share of such as they had and good warm lodgings at night; they were all verry poor.

March 19. On the 16th we went to Rocroy, 12 Miles, were put in the Gaols of the city, and served gaol allowance. Our waggon came up with our Sick Vc., and we took care of them that night, and on the 17th we halted and sent 7 of our men to the hospital. We were Muster'd by the Commandant and he gave orders if any of us wanted any thing in the town we must apply to the Brigadier and he would send a Gendarm with us . . . This was something new; however this was all well; we knew they would be more strict as we drew near our respective depot. On the 18th we went to Fumay, 14 miles, lodged in Gaol and on that Evil day as I may say the 19th of March we arrived at the last halting place for the greatest part of our young and brave Ship's crew, when we came in sight of Charlemont, Mount d'Or and Givet Prison; our hearts rejoiced to think we had at last through fatigue and Many curious turns, arrived at our place of destination; our guard told us which was to be our habitation on the borders of the river.

We arrived in Givet Prison

March 19. As we drew near the gates we saw the river that passes the walls of the prison: the River Meuse; we also saw the two towns of Givet on each side of the river and the Strong Walls draw bridges Vc., that Surround this place of Captivity situated in the Valley of death. In fine we came to the gates of the prison and were placed 16 in a room and when we got inside that was like a new life to us to see so many of our countrymen flocking round us; the day had been rainy and we were wet and cold but our countrymen soon found means to change our cloaths and make us quite comfortable. Some brought us Soup, Some Beef, Some Bread, and others brought a little drop of kill grief to drown all Sorrow; and what was singular we nearly all found Some old acquaintance neighbour or relation; after we had been in the place a little while the word was past to fetch our Straw, bedsteads, and blankets, Bread, beef, and wood, in short for all that was required in each room; which the old prisoners readily brought in for us. They fixed our rooms and we all went to rest.

Givet prison near Charlemont in France

MARCH *20, 1804.* At daylight we were roused by the Gendarmes to empty our tubs, sweep the stairs, and then all hands to muster in the yard, which was done three times a day, morn, noon, and night, by a Brigadier and one Gendarme to each passage which contained eight rooms, and each room 16 men, so that each brigadier had 128 Men in his department. The sick were reported at muster in the morning so that they could be sent to the hospital directly after muster. Bread and rice or beans was served every 4th day: 3 lb. of bread for 4 days. We also had salt at the same time. Every five days we had wood and one and half sols pr day each man but we were generally under stoppages for Windows, chimney sweeping, or some repairs to the prison; we also had to pay for our bedsteads and blankets cooking pots Vc., all out of our sol and half pr day, that is about three quarters of a cent pr day, but we never received the whole, haveing always half a Sol and sometimes more stopped daily, so that of our 5 days pay which amounted to the enormerous sum of three pence halfpenny we never rec'd more than two pence halfpenny. We had beef every two days; our rations were half a pound pr day, but heads shins livers and lights were beef.

In Givet prison all safe

March 21–25. We had everything in due season. In the Spring we had what we called staggering bob, which might be sucked thro' a quill; this was served us for beef, and they called it veal. And in the fall they gave us Mutton, but it had the misfortune to die without the knife of the contractor or butcher and was taken off with the rot. Then it fell luckily to our lot to have a whole quarter of Mutton sometimes to each mess and sometimes the Sheep were like the Bullocks, for we have positively known a bullock to be killed for the prisoners that has had four heads and sixteen legs or shin's and half a dozen livers and sometimes more lights and this was all served as beef. . . . If we made any complaint to the Commandant concerning our beef he would thrash away amongst us with his cane and tell us he would make us glad to eat our own D. . . . Thus the Commandant Butcher and Baker were all in partnerships with their yearly contracts for supplying the prison with provisions. However some of us made a struggle thro all the various overturns we were compelled to endure, confined in a prison like us ten year and four months.

However as we had got something over the fatigue of our winter's march and become habituated to the rules of the prison we became lost for want of some exercise or for something that might employ part of our solitary time and keep us from repineing at our unfortunate fate. I therefore on the 26th of March 1804 got some paper pens and ink and sat down on the foot of my bed with an intention to write something on our travails thro' France and our long Captivity, our release from prison Vc.

Sufferings while Prisoners in France

January 1805. This year we live in hopes of some means being taken by our country to either Make peace or an exchange of prisoners. The past year has proved a fatal one to numbers of our brave comerades. Out of our ships crew we have burried 57 Men from the 19th of March to the last of December 1804, and other Ships have suffered in proportion, so that the number of deaths in the Prison last year altogether were eight hundred and thirteen Souls, of the prison putrid fever; this Malignant disease was consider'd to arise from cold, and wet sleeping by night, want and ill usuage then all at once arriving at the depot, their daily exercise ceasing, they remain inactive with little or no good nourishment, lay a great part of the time in bed in order to shun the severity of the cold weather and drive away hunger and Melancholy thoughts with Sleep, and so quickly after long Marches the most of our Young robust men were the first that fell victims to the prevailing disease. When first attacted they were taken with pain in their back, head and side, then a numbness all thro' their limbs; from that to chills and fever which deprived them of their intelects and hurried them off instantly. Givet Hospital being the Military hospital for the depot on the frontiers of France and the Netherlands, we had a great many French troops in the hospital amongst our people and they suffered more than our people for all those who had any wounds or sores were sure to putrify and hurry them off immediately after the Mortification set in; this was instant death. The infection was attended with a nausious smell from the wounds even while living, which in spite of all the means used by the Most able physicians in France, such as fumigation Vc., burning juniper berries and all kinds of strong ingredients, appeared entirely impossible to keep away the bad and infectious smell that was all through this extensive building. The General doctor from Paris gave orders to have an air hole cut thro the wall under each bed to try if the fresh air would be any service, but it appeared that every endeavour was fruitless untill about the 15th of January 1805, a heavy frost set in and the cold and keenness of the frost gained the upper hand of the disease and every day the cases were less, and the deaths decreased rapidly; so that in the course of about 20 days the sickness had quite abated, and we all that were spared began to have quite a different appearance. That doleful Melencholy low spirited countenance, that doleful momently expected theirs would be the next call began to leave our habitations, and hope, the prisoners only comfort, again returned and animated our drooping hearts, with healing balm. In the Month of February our prison was quite free from the disease and we began to take more exercise in the yard Vc. In fine we became habituated to the indolent life of a prisoner of war; the frost continued untill the

Month of March. We daily had fresh crews from the various parts of the coast where they had been drove thro severe gales in January last so that the depot was kept always nearly two thousand or twenty three hundred strong. So many fresh men joining us caused a great deal of Sickness but this was nothing to compare with the Putrid fever.

Remarks in Givet prison

January 1, 1806. This being the first day of the new year we had our flour and mutton served us quite early and the steward, a verry good man, Mr. Hewlet, paid us privately 24 Sols each man. This he contrived unknown to any of the French by going into each room privately and paying them, haveing strict orders not to pay any more money from England to the prisoners; nevertheless he ran the risk. We past a quite comfortable day; I dined with two of my Old acquaintance, Leonard Knags of Whitby, and Robson Crosby of Robin hood's bay. We had a pleasant day and at night we had plenty of hot beer and brandy Songs Vc.

This Month we had some few prisoners arrived from the coast who had been captured by Privateers on the Yorkshire coast. They gave all the particulars of Trafalgar, Nelsons death, Burial Vc. This kept us some time in discourse; we then Undertook learning and some of our Men that were capable commenced School. They taught navigation Arithmetic Vc., and what still diverted us on the other hand one of the Men lately arrived, James Ruffhead, or Jemmey the fidler, brought his fiddle with him and undertook to teach us this instrument at 3 Sols per week two lessons per day Vc. He was a complete hand at his work and fit for the undertaking.

As for my part I devoted part of my time in Studying Navigation in which I took great delight; and for a change bought a violin for 6 francs and undertook this part of Music with old Jemmey; this was all grand employment and made the time pass away unperceived.

By the end of this year the Prison was one continual buzzing like a Swarm of Bees; in every room through the whole prison was from 6 to 10 or 12 scrapeing cat gut. Every person was inclined to some sort of employment, some Makeing Ships for Sale; others got work from the people in town, Shoe makers, Taylors, button makers, and chair bottomers; we also had wooden shoe sole and heel makers, barbers, Jews selling old cloathes, watches, books, fiddles Vc., and numbers makeing Straw hats; in fact the prison became one entire house of industry. It was a perfect medley for a stranger to behold. You would see a man quite busy at his occupation Jump up, take his fiddle, scrape away for some time, then down with it and to work at his book half an hour, then take a walk round the yard, back again, eat a Mouthful if he has any left, and down again to his employment. Then he could hammer or stitch away and settle all the affairs of the two contending Nations.

In this Manner we diverted away the time. . . . Health strength and fresh life seemed daily attending us. There was nothing wanting but liberty . . . We had letters daily from England and sent letters home, after the interpreter reading them to the Commandant; they were then Sealed and sent to Paris and from thence to the Carteel [Cartel ship] in Morlaix and she ran between that port and Plymouth once per week Vc. In the Midst of all this learning and bustle I still continued My Journal; and devoted two hours ev'ry Morning in writing.

We have every prospect of an Exchange from
Mr. McKenzie in Morlaix

December 1806. The close of the year drew on us apace. We were all life and spirit, as the negotiations for an exchange of prisoners was in a fair way to be signed between the two countries. The Rev. R. B. Wolfe made sure that he would not be in France 6 months, nor yet one of us that were prisoners of war. This and what we heard by our letters from England, all gave us fresh hopes of a speedy release. Mr. Mackenzie, the English Minister in Morlaix, wrote to the different Prisons informing the whole of us that Morlaix was the port appointed for the Carteels, and we might hold our selves in readiness for Marching Vc. Such good newse as this made us pass a Merry Christmass and a happy New Year's day . . . We bid adieu to 1806 and greet the happy approach of the then unknown year 1807.

The Dutch soldiers thro' their selfish ignorance
destroy all our happiness

Mr. Wolfe had made contracts for Bread Beef and vegetables which was served us every two days, and the French
allowance was stopped as the two Ministers had decided that
each Nation for the future should find their own subjects; that
was for England to find us, and France to find her subjects in
England. This was a grand change to us, but proved only of
a verry short duration, as will be shortly related. Every thing
was promiseing our immediate freedom; we made knapsacks
gaters Vc., for the March. . . . Our Prison being a Barracks
built by the Spanish when in possession of the Netherlands
was a verry extensive building, and on the east end of the
building laid the 33 regiment of foot, mostly all Dutch and
best part of them Conscripts, or as we say young Gulpins, and
our provisions had to pass their barracks as it came to us. The
Dutchmen rose in a mob and said they were determined not
any longer to suffer prisoners of War to have the best provisions in the town and leave them all the refuse and that they
would not suffer any more to pass their part of the Barracks.
When the Officers of the 33 informed the general the cause of
the men's refuseing to do any duty, unless the prisoners lived
on the same sort of provisions they did, the General informed
them that the British provided for their own subjects; they
then made answer that France should find as good rations for
her Soldiers as England could find in France for her Subjects
in prison, and they were all of one mind, that they would not
mount guard any more around the prison unless they had
better provisions or we had the same as them. This newse
struck the Commandant with astonishment. The general gave
orders that our provisions must be stopped for a couple of
days untill he had advice from the Comissary of War in Paris.
This was a severe stroke to us after our contracts were all
regularily settled and we had become habited to the fresh diet
and plenty of it, from our former Miserable Morsel of the
worst that the Baker or Butcher could contrive which merely
kept the vital spark in motion. On the third day the General
had his orders from Paris to stop all the arrangements made

by the British agent and to serve the prisoners of War their rations as formerly allow'd by the French government untill further orders. Mr. Wolfe also had advice from Mr. McKenzie not to serve us any more rations in the name of the British as he had his orders from Paris to leave France in 48 hours or consider himself a prisoner of war; he also said the French would not listen to any reasonable terms; therefore he was sorry to inform his unfortunate countrymen that after trying every way in his power to make some arrangements for an exchange the French were so unreasonable that he could not make any kind of arrangements and therefore he was order'd to leave the country with all speed; his advice to us was nearly as follows.

Morlaix March 18th 1807. enclosed to the Rev. R. B. Wolfe.

My dear countrymen. It is with the utmost disappointment that I have to address you in a quite contrary style to what I fully had determined last week at this time. However this I can say, that I have made free with all the power put into my charge by our just and wise ministers to settle almost on any terms, with the Government of this country for an exchange of prisoners, but all my exertions have prove ineffectual; for instance: the articles we agree on one day, are to be quite contrary the next, so that I am convinced they are determin'd not to come on any terms of exchange whatever; therefore my advice to you is this, bear your misfortunes a little while longer and no doubt but our wise ministers will work a way for your release. My Country men, I know your sufferings, and feel for you and give you my word that on my return to the British court I will unfold at large your sufferings, and all treatment, from your tyrannical Commandant, and his blood thirsty Dutch guard . . .

I am your friend and well wisher

Alexander McKenzie Esq.
Commissary to the British prisoners
of War detain'd in France

N.B. I am to sail in the Morning for England on board the Brig Brutus from Morlaix to Plymouth

P.S. keep up your hearts and remain to act as true Britons

adieu . . .

Now, my friend, whoever you are, I shall make free to ask you to stop a moment and reflect: supposeing yourself in my place at this moment when Mr. McKenzie's letter was read and the same day our rations were stopped I want to know how you would feel. However I can tell you that for my part I was drove almost to distraction and the truth is this altho' our French allowance was both Small and mean I was several days and did not eat half of my daily pittance, and some took the disappointment to heart so much they were taken sick, went to the hospital and died, such effect had these sad misfortunes on us after all our preparations for returning to our homes. At last hunger compell'd us like the dog to return to our old vomit and in a little while we began to do as we did before on the same diet. Mr. Wolfe used his utmost efforts to make us as happy as circumstances would admit. He sent us in our pay privately, and sometimes got liberty from the Commandant to send us in flour, which we fried in pancakes, Made stirr about Vc., as bread was prohibited. We began toward the close of the year to renew our old customs of learning Music Navigation and various employment.

January 1, 1808.   In September the City of Copenhagen was taken by the British and in the fall several vessels that were captured in Copenhagen on their passage to England were drove on the Hollands coast by severity of weather; what was saved of their crews were sent up to Givet. Amongst the prisoners was the Much lamented H. Haywood Esq., which we shall give an account of in the following pages. They kept us in Motion some daily arriveing to join us, so that we daily had some fresh newse which kept us busy settleing the affairs of the Nation, and daily Makeing an Exchange. At last Christmass stept in amongst us and finish'd 1807.

We had nothing worth notice the fore part of this year. Our Agent Mr. Wolfe helped us along; he was much respected by the General and Commandant, and any thing he wanted in reason to do for us was done without being noticed by them. He employed our Shoe makers that were amongst us to mend and Make Shoes for all that were in want of them; he made interest with them to gain permission for one man from each room to go to Market in town once per week, and also for the

Gendarmes to take liberty Men out on their own risk, that was if any deserted from the Gendarmes while under his charge the Gendarmes must be responsible for them and the rest of the prisoners liberty be stop't. This was a trust of honour which amongst us was held sacred and was never once violated, as the liberty of us all depended on it. The aged and cripples had their permission to walk around the ramparts of the two towns, Mount d'Or., Vc. Those indulgencies with what little help we received weekly thro' the various stratagems of Mr. Wolfe and his Clerk William Mortleman made our time, even on the pitiful Morsel allowed by the French for our bare existance, as lightsome and as cheerful as if we had never known what it was to see better days, Thus our time slid away in our various branches of learning and employments. Harvest took its round in our neighbourhood and we being situated in the verry Midst of the dept. des Ardennes became almost Farmers.

The treacherous Murder of Henry Haywood and Richd Gale

I have mentioned before concerning our Market every morning at the gates of our prison; this market was mostly kept by the country people. We made use of a great many potatoes apples pears Vc., which they furnished us with verry low. We could purchase a panier of good potatoes containing a bushel for 15 Sols and sometimes less, that is from 7 to 8 cents per bushel; this was our staff of life. Amongst the peasantry that attended our Market were several blooming girls and they were verry free with us. They took delight in learning words in English, and in fact several became constant companions, and in the whole I may say lovers. Amongst those young women was a farmers daughter named Rose, a blooming girl, and on her Mr. H. Haywood Esqr., Masters Mate of H.B.M. Ship Alfred 74, turned his eye (he haveing the command of one of the Daneish Ships captured at Copenhagen, on his passage from thence to England in the fall of last year 1807 had the Misfortune with numbers more to be drove on the Hollands coast and there made prisoner was sent to Givet, which proved an unfortunate land fall to him and Mr. Gale). Mr. Haywood spoke the French tolerable well and was young. Mr. Gale was a Midshipman young like himself. Those two young Officers had the liberty to go out under the care of a Gendarme to take their recreation round Mount d'Or, the ramparts, towns, Vc. However in the morning previous to their going on liberty their Girls informed them that they were to have a great harvest supper and ball in their little Village of Ransend and they were desirous to have the two young men amongst them. On those words Haywood made answer to Gale that if he was alive he would visit Ransend that evening and told his Rose at parting that she might look for him that evening if he had life Vc. Accordingly after dinner the two unfortunates went to the town attended by their Gendarme, took him to a tavern where they play'd a game at billiards, then all sat down to a bottle of Wine as was customary. The two lovers told their Guard to call for what he pleased and with his leave they would take an hours cruise amongst the Girls in Petit Givet, this being a general rule to leave the Gendarmes in a tavern and take a turn around the town then return at the appointed time and join the Gendarmes and return to the Prison. The Gendarme gave them his leave to go and return in time to answer Muster. Off they went like other lovers eager to gain the desired haven. They came to the gate called Port Ransend, passed the keeper by leaving a Crown or six francs in his possession, and then bent their course for Ransend, dist. 3 small miles. I have already mentioned that the aged and Cripples had their liberty to walk out of the prison every day and take the fresh air on the ramparts Vc. It happned unfortunately for those two unfortunate Men that as they crossed the bridge that crosses the river Meuse and divides the two towns of Givet they Met with a Monster partly in humane shape and part of him made by the hands of Man like the Gods of Nebuchadnezzar of Wood and Iron: and this brute more to his disgrace was the one selected out by them as their Cook and housekeeper; his name was Wilson, a Marine formerly of the La Minerva Frigate, captured near Cherburg, where he lost his leg, and a pitty it was that it had not been his head. However thro' compassion the Officers made him their house seervant and steward; kept him well and Cloath'd him and gave him plenty of money. In the whole he was in a grand and a plentiful situation; all they required of him was to clean their boots and shoes, make up their beds, sweep the room and sometimes cook their dinner and his own. He had all the Officers' cast off cloathes Vc., sold his prison rations, and had five francs per Month from each officer, and there was eight in the room he was entrusted with . . . Haywood and young Gale meeting Wilson as they passed over the Bridge full of Mischief and wanting to have some funn with their brother Officers, Haywood says to Wilson, 'Pegleg when you return into the prison inform our messmates that we are going to Ransend to have a nights cruise with our Girls and the country people all Met in the Village to dance.' 'Yes, Sir,' Says Wilson, and off they scamper'd towards the Ransend Gate . . . Wilson stood looking after them when the Gendarme that they had left, haveing some business across the river, came past. He, knowing Wilson, says to him, 'Have you seen your Master?' 'Yes Sir,' Says Wilson, 'him and Mr. Gale have gone to the dance in the Village. They are now outside of the Gate.' 'Then,' says la Marque the Gendarme 'I will spoil their Sport or my Sword shall fail.' He immediately pursued them. He came to the Gate or Port Ransend. Old Monsieur la Clare the gate keeper told him they had gone to the Village for an hour to see the fair and then would return as they had often done before, so that he might rest contented and they would be back at the time. 'Yes,' says the bloodthirsty savage, 'I will spoil their danceing,' and after them he went. It happned that our two adventurers a little way outside the gates stopped to look at some men quarrying stone on the Side of the hill they intended to pass. La Marque saw them and he made towards them, full of envy and Murder in his heart . . . They no sooner saw him than they ran to meet him, thinking he was going to the Village also and they would go all together. Haywood was the first that approached him and in his Merry way of talking says to la Marque, 'Come and let us go together and have a little amusement in the Village.' La Marque drew his sword, Haywood made a halt and was in the act of lifting his arm in self defence when La Marque Made a desperate Stroke at his head with all his might and split his head entirely in two so that he laid dead at his feet, Gale seeing him strike Haywood was in the greatest amazent and ran to the Gen-

darme begging for mercy when the bloodthirsty rascal up Sword
and Cut Gale down the right side of his head face and breast.
He fell near his partner. The stone cutters from the quarry
saw the whole horrid transaction and ran intending to save life
if possible, but alas poor Haywood was gone and Gale had
some signs of life left yet. . . . The crowd that by this time
began to gather took la Marque, disarmed him, and took him
a prisoner before the General. They also took Gale and carried
him to the Hospital where he expired that Night, and the dead
body of Haywood was convey'd to the dead house and both
were burried in one Grave on the following morning. Thus fell
two as fine promiseing Officers as ever graced the quarter deck
of any Ship. The Murderous Villain La Marque was confined
some few days, had his sham trial, was acquitted and sent to
some other station; thus finished the tragedy of Haywood &
Gale. On the following day the newse spread round that
Pegleg informed the Gendarme they were gone to Ransend.
We made search for him immediately, all resolutely bent to
make an example of him as an informer. But perhaps it happned
all for the best. He was gone to town, where the Commandant
soon heard we wanted the informer Wilson. The Commandant
sent Wilson up to Charlemont where he was secure from our
threatning of Vengeance which he most deservedly merited;
he was sent to some distant depot where (as we were informed)
he died on the road. Thus we were released from this Snake
in the grass or in other words a Serpent that those unfortunate
men had taken and nourished in their bosoms untill he rose
and treacherously took both their lives. This horrid Murderous
affair cast a Melancholy gloom on all around. The Country
people all cried shame and the towns people made a great
Murmering and told the Gendarmes they were an inhumane
set of Brutes. The prisoners all prayed they might live to revenge
the Murder of their two countrymen then they would be
Satisfied . . . Sometime near the close of this year 1808 we were
reinforsed, as we used to say, by a party of our country men
prisoners from Arras prison. They brought us the glad tidings
that the Murdrer la Marque when he left Givet went to Arras
and by some means his reason for leaving Givet was made
known in Arras. This villian during the time of Carnival or

Masquerade was run through the heart by some one in the character of a French drummer. Thus ended this year of trouble.

Further remarks in Givet Prison

January 1, 1809. We welcome the new year in a number of different ways. The greatest part rises in the Morning and makes the new year welcome with a bumper of brandy and beer made hot, which they have been gathering perhaps two months back. Every spare Sol they had was put in the Christmass bag, and that bag could not be drawn upon even on the greatest necessity but was in the charge of the Chosen Captain or President of the room, and he was to expend it to the best advantage in Victuals and drink to be used by all the room mates at Christmass and new years. And sometimes our bag was so strong we could have two or three friends to dine and pass Christmass or new years in love and unity. Some Again took quite another Method. They spent all their spare Sols in brandy and depended on the old word or as some say the old Proverb that was to let tomorrow provide for itself, but when tomorrow came and our bag brought forth its contents I have seen Mr. Tomorrow verry glad to sit down and take a taste of the gatherings which the bag had plentifully furnished our table with. Others devoted Most part of the day to their various religious dutys. We had church twice a day and an able Minister to perform divine Service.

Our Agent was verry diligent and used every means to make us comfortable in regard to what was under his Jurisdiction, that is to say what was allowed us by our own nation . . . This Month was verry severe and we kept close to our rooms so that there was little or no politicle business transacted amongst us. Music or learning was the chief employment in cold weather.

In the Month of February we had another draught of prisoners from Arras to fill up our prison again, and those poor creatures suffer'd greatly on their March by cold and stormy weather which caused a great deal of sickness amongst us after they joined the depot; the most part of them were taken down by the fever and Ague.

At this time I had the good fortune to fall in with Andrew Smith, afterwards my Son, Brother, and companion. It was a cold rainy day and we had the newse of a draft of prisoners being down at the Gate. As was natural for us to wish to see them we flocked down to the gate. The rain was pouring down and they poor fellows were turned in amongst us to wait untill the rain was done, and then the Commandant would place them in the vacant births amongst us.

Proceedings in Prison

February 25, 1809.   On their entering the prison yard some found a neighbour or an old Shipmate; others found relations and many found townsmen Vc. In short they were soon dispersed round the Prison to take some refreshment. Some of them were left without any one to take them to their rooms, and amongst them I remarked a little boy appeared quite dejected and trembling with cold; no person took any notice of him. Poor little fellow; I felt for him and went to him, took his little bag and desired him to follow me up to my room. I made him strip and put on some of my dry cloaths untill his own were dried by the fire. We then gave him some hot soup bread meat Vc . . . After he was a little refreshed I enquired where he belonged and what was his name, what Ship Vc. He answer'd me that his name was Andrew Smith of Sunderland taken in the brig Friends from Sunderland bound to London. I then enquired his father's name and found him to be the Son of George Smith my former benefactor when I was a boy prisoner of war in Vallenciennes where he took care of me the same as his own Son, George. After the little fellow had related his tale to me my heart was overjoyed to think that I had an oportunity to return the part of a friend and benefactor to the child of him who formerly was to me a father and instructor. Andrew informed me that his father was master of the brig Friends and took him along with him with an intent to let him stop a little while with his relations in London; that William Rutherford was Married to his Sister and was mate of the brig, and on their passage to London they had the misfortune to be taken by a Privateer and carried into Bullogne and from there they were sent up to Arras prison. Three weeks after their arrival in Arras his Father was taken sick and died

and left him with his brother in law Rutherford. It happened
shortly after, there was an order for Volunteers to put down
their names for Givet. Andrew haveing heard that his brother
Robert was taken and in Givet, went immediately to the
Bureau and had his name enroll'd for Givet; this was his
motive, to meet his brother. Haveing heard the whole of his
story and he being quite comfortable my first care was to find
out his Brother. I knew we had several Smiths in the depot
and in a short time I found his Brother Robert. This Robert
Smith was an interpreter and was a writer in the Bureau. This
young man considered himself far above any of us; in fact he
was a great dandy, and when he heard of his little Brother's
arrival in Givet it gave him no small mortification. However
he came to see him and after hearing the youngster relate his
tale, the reason for his comeing thus to Givet, the death of his
father Vc., he turns round to me and asked me if I would take
charge of his Brother. I then answer'd him that it was my duty
to do all in my power for him, and related to him what his
father had done for me Vc. 'Well,' says he, 'take care of him
and I will put him in your room as you have one vacant birth.
You will see that he wants nothing and I will take care you
shall loose nothing by him. In my present situation it is not
in my power to do for him as you can, therefore I wish you a
good night.'

February 26. Employed my time in altering cloaths that I
could spare for the boy. Robert was verry good; he gave the
boy his rations along with our allowance of Bread Beef Vc.,
and our beef he took care was the best the butcher had in his
shop. This was in his power as he had to see the rations served
out to the prison and give an account every morning; the
number of sick, how many in each room, and how many in
Charlemont, in the Cashot Vc. March the 1st I put Andrew
to School. We had good Schools and able teachers in the Prison
supported by our own country, conducted under the patronage
of the Revd. R. B. Wolfe. On the 5th day of April Robt.
obtained passports for his Brother and me to go to town every
day, walk the ramparts on Mount d'or, and take the air; only
we must attend all Musters at the prison. If we did not attend
Muster we forfeited our liberty.

In the Month of May I sent home a will and power to my Mother enableing her to draw on the Navy Board for part of my wages, and for her to remit part of the money to me thro the hands of Couts and Co. bankers in London and their connexions in Paris, Peregause and Co. This was the channel at that time by which we had a regular correspondence between the two nations. We had daily draughts of Money for the prisoners thro the same channel, both kings men and merchant men. Such indulgencies as those soon made an overturn thro-out the whole prison that long lost cheerful countenance began to make its appearance on every side. Plenty and good fortune seemed combined together with full intent to overthrow that tyrant Want and reinstate Plenty in the midst of us. Mr. Wolfe rec'd a quantity of books from England which were lodged in the Schools for the use of the Prisoners, so that Givet Prison became Givet University. We had letters daily from England, sometimes 80 or 90; in short our prison was more like some exchange or place of great business than a depot of prisoners of war. Every Mail brought some fresh tidings so that we were diverted from day to day with something new.

June 4, 1809. This was a great day amongst us. Old George[1] was verry much honor'd by our loyal Sons of Bacchus calling his name in question with every glass, and that was not a few.

In July we had great rejoiceings amongst the French owing to a victory gained over the Austrians at Wagram. What cared we for that?

In Sept. The French Squadron returned from the North Sea after destroying the British Whale Ships; they sent us a fresh supply of Prisoners.

In October Robt. Smith was detected in his elopement with Madam Gammant, the Second Commandants Lady, thro' a letter she sent him from the environs of Antwerp. He was sent in irons to Charlemont and from thence to Bitche, there to lay in cells under ground on bread and water. So much for loveing another Man's Wife; a Snake in the grass. Madam Gammant had eloped from her husband in Givet and went down to Antwerp where, as they had planned the trick,

---

[1] They were celebrating the birthday of George III—Wetherell's 'old George.' For the same reason June fourth is still celebrated at Eton College.

Robert was to wait untill she had found some means of con-
veying them to England; then she was to write young R
Smith to make the best of his way to her where she lay conceal'd in the house of a Boatman in the neighbourhood of
Antwerp, all ready to Make sail. The letter she sent was
directed to a young Apothecarie which had been entrusted
with their whole contrivance and he was to assist Smith in
effecting his escape from the prison and finding him a private
conveyance down to Antwerp, where the Witch of Endor
lay concealed. Madam Gammant was missing; no one had
seen her and her husband was almost distracted. He searched
every way but all in vain. Several days passed without any
tidings of her. Gammant had nearly given her up for lost;
sometimes he thought she had drown'd herself in the river,
at others that she was murder'd. In this Manner he past ten
or twelve days, while Bob and the Doctor were laughing in
their Sleeve at him and watching the post for a letter from
Madam Gammant. During the interval I was much astonish'd
at Bob. He gave me the most of his Cloaths saying they would
alter for Andrew and he would buy himself some new.

October 25, 1809.   It happened this morning as Gammant
was turning over the letters in the Post office (as was his usual
custom sellecting out the letters for the prison), he turned
over a letter and snatching it up, says, 'This is my wifes
hand writeing, and if it was not addressed to the Doctor I
would swear to it.' 'Well,' says the Post Master, 'let me open
the letter,' which he did and found out the clue to the whole
affair. Gammant stood a little while like a Statute and then
exclaim'd, 'Was there ever such a fiend of hell as this Woman,
and such an ungrateful Monster as this Boy that I have been
lulling in my bosom untill he has stung me to the heart? Oh,
cruel young man! Now Shall my Vengeance fall on both their
heads.' He flew to the Bureau. Bob was not there and well it
was for him as Gammant was determined to lodge his sword
in his bosom. Bob was in town and Mr. Peytavin the first
Commandant sent a Guard in search of him with order to
take him directly up to Charlemount, and keep him from the
sight of Gammant. Those orders were obey'd and Gammant
was informed where the destroyer of his future happiness was

lodged. He made Bob secure and Gammant being some-what [overwrought] Mr. Peytavin dispatched a brigadeer of Gendarmes with all speed down to Antwerp to [find] my lady and bring her back to Cambray where [she could] be in confinement and clear of Gammant. [Accor]dingly she was taken brought part of the way and lodged in the citadella of Cambray, not to have any liberty from the citadell whatsoever and not to have the liberty of writeing nor receiving any letters, or haveing any correspondence by any means. Madam being secured the Doctor was sent to the Military depot at Liege to join the army, and poor Bob was condemned to Bitche; a horrid place. On the 1st of November 1809 Robert Smith was marched from Givet in irons. His brother Andrew and me went to see him before he started and as soon as he saw us he burst into a fit of laughter. 'Wetherell,' says Bob, 'you see what a load of trouble that infernal Woman has brought on me and herself, but I dont care. When I get to Bitche I will write to the Minister of War, and I know he will be my friend and restore me once more to my former station.'

November 1, 1809. Andrew and me took leave of poor Bob. He parted in good spirits; his last request was that for the sake of his poor Father I would take care of his Brother, which I promised to perform as far as lay in my power. 'Andrew,' says Bob, 'there is no fear of me; my tongue will always stand my best friend. I will write as soon as I reach Bitche. Good by. Here we go,' and off he started, poor boy. The Rev. R. B. Wolfe used every possible means to have him stop in Givet but the Commandant and General said it was not prudent as he would only hurt the feelings of Mr. Gammant and some evil consequences might arise thro it. Therefore it was right for him to leave Givet. Robt. Smith was a favourite of both the General and Commandant also of Mr. and Mrs. Wolfe. The General said it was a pitty such a smart young lad should be led astray by that wicked deluding Monster, but he hoped this would be a warning to him and all other young men never to be led astray by the flattering tongue of Woman. Mr. Peytavin the Commandant sent for Me and young Andrew. He told Andrew that he would always respect him on account of his Brother and any favour that he craved in reason should be granted. He recommended him to Mr. Wolfe and advised him to pay every attention to learning the same as Robert had done, that being the first step towards promotion. Mr. Wolfe being present said he made no doubt that Roberts Missfortune would be a caution to him and all young men in the prison never to stray beyond the limits of reason, nor like the Snake in the fable rise and sting their best friend and Benefactor in the heart. They also said to me they hoped I would take care of the young boy and instruct him in the paths of Virtue Vc. Mr. Peytavin told us we should continue our liberty the same as when Robert was with us and as for me they frequently needed my assistance in the Bureau and he would speak to Mr. Gammant so that I might attend the Bureau.

CHAPTER

9

WITH the assistance of feast days rejoiceings Carnivals and such like passtimes we found Christmass calling out for us to prepare for the approach of another year, which according to the predictions of the learned philosophers in France, is to be a Year of great overturns in Europe. And My prayers were that the greatest overturn we experience might be to turn from France over to England.

Remarks in Givet prison in the year 1810 Vc Vc

This year commences rather rather Gloomy. Our first salute was the death of General Moore and the whole account of his retreat down to Corunna. This we learnt by letters from British State prisoners in Verdun, Vc. We also learnt by the Bulletin the surrender of Seville in Spain to the arms of France. As we have past so many years in this great University and been constantly in the practice of Study, we have become great politicians and pay great attention to the Various revolutions and overturns in Europe. We are like some of the old Barbars or tavern keepers in England that can give all the particulars of two Contending Armies or Fleets with more punctuality than those who had been eye witness to the verry subject of the present discourse, which every one may readily prove while waiting his turn on a barbar's Shop. We were as most Men that have that patriotic spirit kindled in their heart would be; and as all men ought to be, sorry to hear any tidings that were contrary to our wishes, particularily any thing in favour of France; but on the reverse then we were somewhat elevated, although we had to keep our ideas confined within our own district or our own class of people that could think much and say but little.

January 12, 1810. Peter Borden or Pierre Badeau, formerly a Clerk to Pereguan, Banker in Paris, haveing by some means offended some of Clarke's[1] tools in Paris, was arrested and hurried off to the depot of Prisoners of War as a State prisoner. After laying amongst us a little while he made friends with the Minister of Police to recommend him to the Commandant and General in Givet, where he soon was made an interpreter to the Depot in the place of Robert Smith. He was then appointed to the interpreters room, which made up our former complement of four. That was William Aplen Interpret, Pierre Badeau Interp, Andrew Smith and John P. Wetherell interpreter and nurse in the Hospital as I afterwards was made,

In February I went by the request of the Commissarie General Purnier [Fournier] a Provender Pour 1. Armie du Nord. He lived in town and I only had one horse to take care of and attend the distributions of Grain hay straw Vc., to the horse Soldiers. My pay was 25 francs pr month and 25 francs for my prison rations which made me quite rich. In this Month we had the account of Rome being annexed to France.

In March that dreadful Malady the putrid fever made its appearance again in the Hospital, it being at this time full of wounded Soldiers from the Armies in Germany and Spain; made it verry allarming. Richard Baker Nurse in the Hospital broke his leg and near all the French Nurses died of the prevailing disorder.

In April the two Irish recruiteing Captains made their visit to our Depot. Capt. Devrause [Devereux] and Capt. Mackay, to enter volunteers from the prison in order to form two battallions or Brigades; the prison gates were hove open and a great number enlisted under their banners. Every one was taken that said he was an Irish man Dutch man Swede Dane

---

[1] The Clarke here is the Duke of Feltre, Napoleon's Minister of War for many years. Like Marshal Macdonald he traced his descent from an ancestor who had taken service in France as a result of the dynastic troubles of England.

Prusian or any nation, only not to say openly they were English.

In May Serjeant Hatton committed his treachrous information. This inhumane Monster was formerly a Serjeant in the 13th British light draggons and on General Moores retreat thro Spain this fellow being an out picket, deserted his post, and like a traitor to his country went over and delivered himself, Horse Arms and accoutrement up to the French advance guard. He was taken to the French General and desired to give his reason for deserting his colours. His answer was that his desire was to serve under the banners of Napoleon, and this was his plan to effect his long intended design. Hatton haveing revealed his mind to the French General was disarmed and that night kept in confinement. On the following day my brave Hatton was conducted to the Generals tent where he received 25 Crowns, the price of his horse and accoutrements, and this unexpected newse was related to him by the interpreter, that he was to consider himself a PRISONER OF WAR, oh, shocking, since he as an Officer on the British Army had betrayed the trust he was in charge of and would not stand true to one Nation. No man of any understanding would ever trust such a false traitor to be enrolled amongst his brave country men and the safest place for such Cowardly traitors was to be kept safe confined in a strong prison where he could not betray his trust again, as he had done, nor deceive any more his companions in War. He was deliver'd over to a guard of Gendarmes and Marched with other prisoners through Spain into France, and on his march he being a good Scholar gained considerable hold of the French language and when he arrived in Givet he passed for a Serjeant of the 13th that had been taken on the retreat to Corunna, and he drew the Lloyds Money and every other advantage as an honourable loyal British Subject. What a hoax.

As such he passed amongst us and by his false tongue made himself a great many friends in the prison; by this time he was Master of the French language. He made interest with the Commandant and had in a short time liberty to go out to town every morning to Mass Vc. He got liberty to keep a Canteen in the prison in Co. with the much to be lamented John Mclagan. He in fact made himself acquainted with every person both in town and the prison, and being a Clean, smart Soldier in his uniforms the Commandant was quite partial to him and granted him many favours. Thus we Nourished this Snake amongst us.

June.   Bonapart's Marriage was celebrated in Paris. On the 8th of June Mr. Peytavin the Commandant and Mr. Wolfe the British Agent sent for me and they requested me to leave the Commissary and go to the Hospital in order to assist Tho. Stevens attending on the sick. Several of the French and English nurses were dead and the sickness spread such terror thro' the town and prison that every person was afraid to undertake the unwelcome office of Nurse and interpreter. I obey'd the call went and render'd all the assistance in my power.

July.   I had a bill from England paid me in Givet of fifteen pound sent by my mother from England and in August another of 30£ by Peregause & Co.

September.   The sickness was very severe and proved fatal to nearly all the wounded men. Their sores would mortify and hurry them into eternity in 4 hours. One curious circumstance I wish to mention that took place one night on my middle watch from 12 to 4, as I sat nodding on my Seat near the Stove in the centre of the ward; my patients at the time were all quite silent, the Lamp burning quite dim and every thing was silence when to my astonishment a heavy stroke on my Shoulder made me start with a terrific supprise, and looking behind me there stood a huge tall Skeleton of a Horse Grenadier, 'Come,' says he to me, 'make no delay but carry me immediately to Paris. I am ordered to bear those private letters to the Emperor.' With that he tore me from my seat, leapt on my back, hove his long Arms round my neck, and with his heels he kicked my Shins, hollowing and driving me up to the door of the Ward (which we made a practice to lock every night and hide the key). When he got to the door My Jockey dismounted and verry Sternly demanded the key in all haste I then answered him that the key was under my pillow and he must let me go after it. He then quit his hold of my Jacket and made me promise to make all possible haste back with the door key. After being released from the pondrous weight and the rough feet and hands of my rider I made no delay in makeing my escape from his unmerciful grasp. All the while he was

bellowing out for me to make haste with the key, or he would
be too late to reach Paris that day. I kept answering the fellow
all the while that I was comeing which he soon found out. I
went to the Bed where Tho. Stevens and me laid in turns. I
shook Tom and told him to look at my jockey standing by the
door and he would shortly see some sport; I then went to the
fireplace at the upper end of the Ward and got my Broom
which had a brave long stout handle and with this weapon I
made bold to advance my horrible ghastly impatient trooper
swearing he was out of all patience waiting for the key. He was
reaching his hand for the key when I gave him a bounder across
the shoulders with my broom stick and made him set up such
a dreadful roar that he rose nearly every person in the ward. I
followed my blows with all my strength so that my trooper took
to his own legs in the place of useing mine and made his way back
to his bed, and I followed close at his heels dealing out my broom
Physic in unwelcome portions to the flying horseman roaring
out for quarter as he retreated towards his bed; the rest of the
patients all rose up in their beds and those that were able came
to the scene of action. Tho. Stevens all the while roaring out
to the horseman for him to turn round and Mount me in all
haste and he would help him to mount his horse but my
medicine had such effect on the patient that he sought shelter
beneath his blankets and hid his face from the naked group of
both his own and other nations. Some of his own regiment
laughing and shakeing him, asking if he wanted another ride
to Paris. Thus was finished this secret expedition and all hands
returned to their tents to take their repose the remainder of the
night. Nothing more was worthy of notice until 9 in the morning
when the Doctor came to pass the Morning visit; Stevens and
me went round with the Doctors as was usual; we passed round
untill we came to my bold Grenadier. 'Well my man,' says the
Doctor, 'how do you do this morning?' No answer. A number
of patients were all listening to hear the Soldiers tale, but he
said nothing. 'What is the matter?' says the Doctor, at the same
time takeing hold of the bed cloaths that cover'd his face, in
order to look at him, but the Soldier kept them fast over him.
At this Stevens and all the spectators burst into laughing. The
old doctor looked at me smileing. 'What does all this mean,

John, that he is ashamed to shew his face?' Stevens in his lively way says, 'Why, Doctor, you must know that the poor man is quite wore out with rideing; he had been to Paris last night on express and on his way his unrully horse hove him, and has kicked and bruised him most horribly, so that he was glad to seek refuge under cover in order to Save his life, and now he trembles as you see him lest his horse should again repeat his unpleasant dose of broom essence.' The Doctor smileing desired Stevens to unravel this mysterie; Stevens then related the whole farce, made the Doctors and all the spectators laugh at the joke; the Doctor then desired us to uncover him, which was no sooner done, than the doctor pronounced him cured. The fever was turned and he was quite feeble, poor fellow, and looked verry pitifull; however he recovered hourly after this, and the Doctor used to tell him, that the balsam of broom saved his life. . . . He daily gained strength and when I came to his bed side he would kiss my hand would smile at me and say, 'Oh my good nurse it is to you that I may always pay every respect as a friend and brother; you and you only were the cause of my being as I am at this moment.' In 5 or 6 weeks he recovered so fast that he was able to walk on the ramparts and in a short time he left the hospital and went to Barracks quite hearty. Whenever he chanced to meet me in Givet we must be sure to have a glass before we parted. In a little while he left Givet to join his regiment in Germany. At parting he gave me a razor and pen knife to keep in memory of him . . . Poor Young Man.

October 4, 1810. A day never to be forgot by those who had the hard fate to fall under the horid feelings we had the misfortune to suffer that day. It had been long in preparation to undermine the Prison Yard from a Stable that was constantly shut up. You must understand that the Prison was first built by the Spaniards (at the time they had possession of the Netherlands) for a horse barracks, so that the under Story of the whole building was Stables, many of which we converted into Canteens and dancing rooms. This Stable, where the Mouth of our Subteraneous passage was, laid under a room we used to call itchy bay and was always kept for the purpose of a room for those who had that filthy disorder to rub in and keep them from the rest of the Prison. It was in this room that all those concerned in the Plot used to meet; they had a private passage from the chimney down to the Stable where they took their regular turns digging in the Secret Mine and piling their earth all around the Stable; this was a laborious task and attended with great risk and Secrecy. Those who went down used to strip in the room above, put on an old Shirt to work in, and on their signal being given by one always to watch (whilst they were at work) they would instantly repair up to the room, wash and dress, then all disperse. Their work was on the point of finishing; they were thro' under the Yard and had the stones loose that formed the foundation of the wall and faced the bank of the river Meuse; every thing was ready, the night appointed for this intended escape, which was to take place the first night of the new Moon: this was also their pass word.

Serjeant Hatton all this time had been list'ning to their various proposals and intentions. His Canteen being close to the Secret Mine they used to go in there and take a glass or drink of beer and often times meet there to consult each other with their private business Vc. This Audacious Monster on that verry day that they had proposed to start at night, and at the verry Moment they were some of them in the passage moveing the last Stone, he starts to the Commandant and reveal'd the whole Mysterie. Mr. Peytavin the Commandant could not believe him but smileing shook his head at Hatton and said this was all passtime Vc. Hatton swore it was so. Peytavin went into the prison yard as he was used to do every day and look at the Boys dancing and fidling Vc. He walked round and took no notice. When at the fatal spot he stopped short, looked in the window, and there to his astonishment he saw the Stable piled nearly full of fresh earth, he walked away, took no notice, but went to the Guard house and sent all the guard to the fatal Stable. They had just got out of the mine and were putting on their cloaths when the Gendarmes burst in upon them, took 15 of them to the Cashot, and then drove every Man to his room to Muster. Afterwards locked all the doors untill the Mine was filled up and Made secure. Then the doors were op'ned and things went on as usual. Two or three days passed over when the 15 men were sent to Charlemount.

It happned a few days after this some of the men were out on liberty with their Brigadier (a fine young man had been prisoner in England and with several more escaped from Plymouth with a beer lighter). The Brigadier, Monsieur la Garde, spoke some English and being in Madam Berrie's Auberge drinking with some of his liberty men he chanced to say, when he was in English Prison, Should any of his prison mates discover his means of escape, the same as that blood thirsty Hatton had done, they would not have let them live to see the light of another day. William Shead was the man in discourse with him and answer'd him thus, 'Sir, if our people in the prison knew positively that he was the informer, no men in the Universe would be more ready to seek revenge on such a vile Monster.' 'Well,' says la Garde,' let my name never brought in question in Givet on your word and honour.' 'No Sir, May I never see God if I do,' Says Bill Shead. 'Then,' says La Garde, 'the truth is that infernal Serjeant Hatton relates every particular circumstance that takes place in the prison daily to the Commandant, so I give you timely notice to be ware of him as he is far worse than an Assassain that lurketh in the dark and stabs his adversary to the heart when he is least prepared for him. Now, William, I shall feel content since I have warned you all to be ware of that viper. I consider it my duty between God and Man to reveal his cursed designs to you, and my advice to you is to put a stop to his carreer as soon as possible. He is a pest to us as well as to you. If we chance to take a glass with any of you in the prison we are sure to hear of it from the Commandant and all thro the treach'ry of that audacious bloody villian. Mind your promise of Secrecy and punish infamy.' Thus they returned after their afternoons recreation back to the prison in time to answer evenings Muster. Shead did not reveal his secret to any of his companions that were in town with him, nor yet to any of his room mates that night, but next day was the day of retribution. This was the 4th day of October 1810. William Shead stood down by the gate with many others looking at the French girls selling their Market stuff. In came Serjeant Hatton. 'Well, Serjeant,' says Shead, 'have you had any tidings to the Commandant this Morning?' 'What is that to you?' says the villian. 'Yes, you damn'd informing rascall,' says Bill, 'Look at the poor Men on the Mount'; ' I will take care of you when I go out again,' says Hatton. At those words the fire began to kindle. 'What was that you said?' says one. 'He is going to take care of Shead when he goes out,' says another. 'He proves himself an informer,' cries out two or three more. 'Let us pin him and make an example of him' was the general cry thro' the whole prison. He went to his Canteen in haste. This infernal Canibal was no sooner in his cave than the cry of revenge flew thro' every room in the prison. This was the allarming Moment when Uproar rose its horrid head. This Monster Stood in conscious dread his looks his fears confes't. His partner Mclagan enquired what was the cause of such an uproar round the door for at this time a great multitude had assembled with full determination to have revenge. 'Drag him out' was the cry from every side. Mclagan went to the door to hear the meaning of this strange Mysterie where he soon learnt the cause of Hattons paralytic fit. 'Take him out of this quickly, the infamous bloodthirsty Savage. He shall not remain in the same room where I am.' At the same time Mclagan turned him out to the Mercy of a set of Men in full determination to have revenge and make an example of him for the first; I· must say it was something rather awful to behold. He was no sooner in the Yard than Jack shut the door and he was laid prostrate on the ground by a blow from a large Stick. Hatton roared out for the Guard but this noise was quickly put a stop to with the toe of a man's Shoe. Some danced on him, some kicked him, some beat his head with sticks, and some ran knives in him, while another party were busily engaged fixing a rope to the lobby of the passage in order to hang him up, where they dragged him to the place of the intended execution. . . . All this time the Centeniels round the prison turned their backs and smiled at the fun, he being an enemy to them as well as us. Haveing got him to the scaffold and the rope adjusting to his neck, a Dutch Brigadier chanced to come down the Yard. He saw the Mob and ran to see the cause. At that moment the rope was hauling him off his legs. The old Brigadier drew his Sword and rushed thro' the crowd, cut several that did not quickly

give him way with his Sword, and cut down the informer and
hollowed for the Guard, who had to obey his orders. They
rushed in amongst them sword in hand, rescued the Serjeant
sore against their own will, drove the Men all to their rooms,
locked up all the passage doors, and took the mangled body of
Hatton to the hospital. Stevens and me were both verry glad
that he was not put in our Ward No. 3. He was put in No. 1,
the only French ward in the hospital; all the other were French
and English intermixed. He was entirely cover'd with blood
and wounds and by his dismal groans was not expected to live
through the night (which numbers hoped might be the case).
The prisoners on liberty were all sent to the prison to wait
further orders. The Commandant gave orders for Tho. Stevens
and John P. Wetherell to remain in the Hospital as usual but
all others Must go to the Prison untill he wrote to Paris. On
the 5th in the morning we were sorry to hear first thing in the
Cook house that the informer was not hurt anything like what
he appear'd to be when first brought to the hospital. After he
was washed and changed, he certainly had several cuts and
bruises on his head and body, but none of them any ways
dangerous. He recover'd every day, and on the ninth day of his
being in the ward he was able to walk round the hospital
Yard.

All this time the prison gates were closed, no liberty nor any
priviledge to buy any thing at the prison gate. The Old General
of the town was greatly enraged at the prisoners for attempting
to chastise such a useful tool as the Serjeant had been to him.
The Commandant was quite the reverse; he was a Gentleman
of great honour and disdained the Man that was guilty of any
thing beneath honour. It was on the 20th of October 1810 in
the Morning we had orders to be in the prison to answer
Muster at ten in the forenoon. We also learnt that the 33rd
regiment had orders to Mount guard round the Prison and
that the Commissarie de Marine was to pass a review of the
prisoners. Also the Serjeant was to pass thro the ranks with a
strong guard and point out those he had seen in the fray of
the 4th. Tho. Stevens and Me went in according to our orders
at ten to Muster Vc. We stood some time in our ranks when
the whole regiment of Soldiers Marched in front of us; all the

Gendarmes, both horse and foot, were under Arms, four pieces of Cannon were planted at the prison gates, and then in came the General, the Commissarie, Commandant, and several officers of distinction, followed by the infernal Serjeant and a strong guard of horse Gendarmes, a verry grand review. The Soldiers were formed in a line fronting us, where they loaded their pieces with ball cartridge, and then the Brigadiers called all our names. This done, then began a scene made our blood run chill. That fiend of hell was sent loose and ran the gauntlets thro' our ranks as he passed up and down the ranks. Every person that he had any kind of dislike to he made a motion to the guard and they were dragged that moment to the Cashot. When he came to William Shead he had him taken away. At the same time we all knew Shead never lifted his hand to him. Another young man that he had a dispute with a month before this affair, named Ja. Boatfield, who at the time of the plot being discover'd was laid drunk in his room, was taken, and in the whole of the 27 that were dragged away there was only nine that were leaders of the advance line of Correction.

After this lottery, as we termed it, was done drawing we were all drove again into our rooms and locked up as before, and in the evening Stevens and me, Mr. Wolfes Servant and Smith the Jew, with two or three more, had our liberty to return to town and resume our former stations; the hell hound of a Serjeant was sent to the hospital on Charlemont to be out of the way of any further danger. The 27 men were sent to the Cells on the Mount and on the second day afterwards they held what they called a tribunal, but we called it a court Martial. It was a Meeting of Officers composed of Generals, Commissaries, Commandants, and officers of the 33 and 34th regiments. This court was called to pass sentence on our poor fellows in confinement—in all 42 men. They sentenced the 15 taken in the secret mine to the Bullet at Liege during the war and the 27 drawn Men to Bitche the same term. When that happy day came, out of the 15 in Slavery at the Public works at Liege ony 3 lived to see the restoration of their liberty; the other 12 all died of grief want and fatigue, and those sent to Bitche fared much the same as in Givet. Hatton was sent away privately to the South of France where he changed his name and passed for some other Nation. This we were told afterwards by the Gendarmes and many times afterwards I have heard the young Gendarmes say if ever they chanced to Meet that notorious rascall he should never make any more Mischief either for them or us. Thus we leave Hatton and give a small hint of our Noble Irish Brigades as Clarke the Ministerre de Guerre used to address them. Their depot was in Landeau [Landau] near the Rhine and being disciplined and formed into two Battallions, each 15 hundred strong, the Emperor was desirous to let them try their Courage. The first bat.[n] was sent down to Flushing where they got such kindness shewn from their countrymen then landed in the Island that they killed them with their kindness and verry few returned back to Landeau to give an account of the kind reception they met with from their countrymen at Flushing. This great disappointment put Clark to his trumps; finding the British had no mercy on his countrymen in Holland he was determined to have satisfaction and prompt them up to take satisfaction of the British in Spain for all their ill treatment in Flushing.[1] Accordingly he joined the remains of the first to the second battallion and called them the Bat*n*. of royal foreign Brigades. They were upwards of two thousand strong, a great number of them English Sailors. They were sent to Spain and joined the Army under Gen*l* Messina [Masséna] and at the Battle of Burgos they proved their gallant courage. Those Brigades were placed in the centre of the French Army and at the time the two Armies Met on the field in Battle array (those Brigades had so contrived their plan that should they have any chance at all they would fly to the British colours, arms and all their

---

[1] The fighting at Flushing, where the Irish Brigade met with this hard treatment, took place during the Walcheren expedition of 1809. As regards the subsequent transfer of the brigade to Spain, there is no doubt that Joseph Bonaparte had in his service there a foreign regiment called the Royal-Etranger, (Wetherell's 'Royal Foreign') which was notoriously leaky, its men deserting to Wellington at every opportunity. But it is to be feared that there was no dramatic mass desertion such as Wetherell describes. There was fighting round Burgos, but no 'Battle of Burgos,' nor was Masséna in command there. But some time later, during the fighting in the Pyrenees, a whole regiment of Nassau troops succeeded in escaping from the French lines and went over en masse to the British. Wetherell probably heard an echo of the incident.

whole Baggage accoutrements Vc., and give themselves up to
the Mercy of Wellington) the Battle began and was for some
time disputed by both sides. However the French General
thought he saw an oportunity to charge the centre of the
British, it appearing to be their weakest point. The orders
were given for the French centre to advance, which was composed mostly of Germans, Swiss, Italians and the Brigades.
They advanced a few paces; the orders were to halt and
engage but the Brigades in the lieu of halting quickned their
steps, left the Wings behind and made right up to the British
army. Wellington saw the Movement and caused the British
to open right and left. In this Manner the Brigades passed
thro' the centre of Wellingtons Army, laid down their Arms,
Colours, Vc. The centre closed, broke in upon the French
broken lines and in this manner gained a complete Victory
over the French near the Walls of Burgos. At the same time
the Staff of Brigades had recruited a great number more Irish
from the different depots of Prisoners of War, in Givet, Cambray, Vallenciennes, Arras, long why [Longwy], Besancon,
Briancon, Bitche, and other small places of confinement,
nearly eight hundred strong; numbers of those poor fellows
fell into this cursed Snare thro' a desire for their liberty and to
follow their Brothers, Shipmates, townsmen, or their companions that enter'd on the first enlistment with Deveraus and
Capt. Mckay, two roaring Vinegar hill Croppies. After the
Battle of Burgos the tidings soon reached Paris and the
treach'rous conduct of the Brigades made their Countryman
Clarke stamp and curse their treach'ry. Bonaparte gave
orders to break up the Brigades and never let the name be
found amongst his brave troops to lead them to death and
dishonour. Accordingly orders were sent to Landeau to dis-
arm the Brigades, take away their Uniforms, and leave them
only their furrageing cap and barrack dress and then disperse
them thro' the different depots of Prisoners of War. One
draught nearly three hundred were sent to our depot and
intermixed amongst the old prisoners which was verry near
causeing verry serious consequences. The old prisoners that
had remained true to their colours thro' all our sufferings and
hard trials could not bear the sight of Men that had taken up

arms to fight against their own country, their Fathers, brothers, and friends. To be intermixed with treach'rous rebels caused constant fighting and disturbance; the chief Commandant seeing the cause of such constant uproar Amongst the prisoners wrote to the Minister of Marine in Paris concerning them, and in a short time the whole of the Brigades from the various depots were all sent to the Citadella of Cambray and thus we once more regain'd our old rules and customs, and Givet prison was once more transferred from a place of Execution for information; and a nursery for Brigades into its old occupation, that of a University of the Fine Arts, Mathematical Arts and Sciences, Modern languages Vc. The liberty of the ramparts for the aged and infirm was again renew'd, the various sorts of Mechanics were again at their work in town. The Rev. R. B. Wolfe paid us Lloyds money and kings pay as before and we wanted nothing but our liberty to return home to complete our happiness.

On the 1st day of November 1810 as the porter was opening the Hospital gate we had the pleasure to see our old friend John Smith the Jew with an invitation for Tho. Stevens and John P Wetherell to attend his Christ'ning at 8 that morn. We gloried in the sport, went and had a jovial day at Madam Debausc's tavern; we had Smith baptized, Married, and turned from a Jew to a Catholic by ten that morning. He married a fine girl, Servant to the Mayor of Givet and a curious Christ'ning and Wedding this realy was.

The Emperor visits Givet

November 10, 1810. On the tenth of November a messenger passed through Givet and brought information that the Emperor, Maria Louisa, and all their train would sleep in Givet that night, as the Emperor was on express to Paris and left Namur that day at 12 Oclock and would reach Givet by 8 P.M. This unexpected newse made Givet all in a bustle prepareing the town hall for the unexpected visitors. The prisoners, every Soul, were sent immediately to the prison excepting Mr. Wolfe and his family. We all slept that night well guarded from robbers. The Cannon on Charlemount were all blown off, the Soldiers and Gendarmes were all under Arms, the city Guard were all drest in their best bib and tucker—all the town was in as great a bustle, as they were afterwards in 1814, when the advance guard of Cossaques entered the Gates of Petit Givet. Towards evening all was in readiness and under arms waiting to hear the Guns at Dinant which were to fire on their passing thro Dinant; all this time the rain fell in torrents and had done so several days successively which caused the river to swell verry high and run with great violence against the light Moored Bridge of Boats where the Royal Visitors were intended to pass. At 6 the guns at Namur or rather Dinant were heard and at 8 Charlemount made our Castle all tremble and thus continued till nearly nine Oclock when they ceased and we all went to our beds. Next Morning we were Muster'd in our rooms and then all locked up again so to remain untill the Emperor had passed the prison at 8 AM. The Guns on the Mount began again to roar and we kept looking thro' the Windows to see them pass but looked in vain. By and by the Packet was that Daniel Owlet the first Interpreter with two or three Gendarmes and the Second Commandant were running towards the prison. This was true; they came into the yard and called the liberty men Nurses and Mechanics. Stevens and me were the first two, then Mark Taylor and several carpenters, William Crown, Saml Clark, and a number of Active Young Men, Edward Cardiff, Walsh Vc., in all we were thirty three. 'That will be enough,' said the Commandant. We were musterd and away we went and where we were going no one of us could think. And it would be impossible to relate the different conjectures of those left in the prison; however we soon found what we were wanted for. When we got to the Bridge to our astonishment the Bridge of boats were all gone and the current ran with such force that the French people could not cross the stream with a boat by any means whatever. They had been striveing all the Morning in vain, and only one boat had been able to gain Grand Givet; the others were drove some distance down the river before the foaming current . . . In the boat that got across was one of the imperial Officers with a Message to the General and Commandant requesting them to send to the

Prison and fetch some English Seamen and they would find a way to cross the river in a short time, and that he was not in the least affraid to trust his life in the hands of British Mariners. This was related to us by the Commandant and to work we went; got two of their largest flat boats; in one we coiled nearly three hundred fathoms of Small line, and four Men to assist with rakes; in the second Boat we put eight Men with rakes and two to Steer or attend the boat. We then Made the Boat with the lines in her fast to the stern of the other Boat, towed them up the side of the river some distance, then let them Make the best of their way across. This was the time that those large wooden rakes were dragged through the water of the Meuse and over they went nearly at the landing of little Givet bridge where lay all ready a large hawser kept on the purpose of crossing the river in the time of ice. This they made fast to the small rope, the end of which was made fast to a tree in Grand Givet. They made the other end of the large cable fast to the Cabstern in Petit Givet, then took the most of the hawser or Cable in the two boats, hauled on the small line, and when nearly on the other side made the end of the Cable fast to the line and let the people on the Shore haul the end on Shore and make it fast to a tree and heave it tight with the capstern in little Givet. Thus in fifty minuites we effected the Means of a safe conveyance across a Stream 327 Yards wide running from 8 to ten Miles pr hour. When our Cable was hove tight by the Cabstern in Petit Givet and found all secure our next care was to prepare a vessel to convey the Carriages, horses, and all the Imperial train across the river. When the Bridge gave way on the night before some of the large flat bottom boats drove on the Shore on each side of the river. They were verry large and the verry vessel we wanted. We took one of those boats (they being square) and we got a large block and made fast to one corner of the boat, then placed the cable in the block and by useing a little exertion the boat crossed the Stream and gained the opposite Shore amidst the Shouts and acclamations of the numerous beholders. We then transported two heavy Carriages and 8 horses also a number of Soldiers across without any trouble, landed them in Grand Givet with another cheering Match. Our next freight was the

Emperor, Wife, and all the Nobility, which we transported across in a short time all safe. Our next voyage was the heaviest cargo that was the Imperial travailing Carriage where they slept and eat their Victuals.

After we got over to Grand Givet we had a misfortune happned. One of our men, Edward Cardiff Walsh, in landing the Emperor's Carriage, had his arm thro' the wheel lifting it on the side of the boat when the crowd on shore dragged the Carriage with such force that the Wheel broke his arm. He was sent to the hospital with all speed and orders from the Emperor not to let him want any thing. We transported the whole train across the Meuse by noon that day to the satisfaction of all beholders. We were then all called to give in our names to the Prince de Neuf Chateau [Neuchâtel) which we did. The Emperor then told us that we should all be sent home to our Native country after he arrived in Paris and could make propper arrangements; we should have cloathing and other presents to make us comfortable on the road; he also recommended us to the General and Commandant. His Carriage being ready he went to Col. Flayel's house, stood god father to his Son, and then took his leave of all the Officers and Quality, enter'd his Carriage amidst the Shouts of the Spectators and the constant roar of Cannon, Music, bells Vc., and off they scampered helter skelter for Paris. As they passed the prison the prisoners made their Obedience to him. He took his hat under his arm, bowed his head to them, wove his hand and disappear'd. I shall leave them on the road to Paris and return to our own affairs. We all stopped at Monsieur Barretts to wash down our future prospects of liberty and our return home with a drop of Cogniac brandy. I shall now take time to relate a little singular joke that took place in the boat at the time we were transporting the Emperor across the river. . . . We all had been a little free with the bottle that passed round plentifully. The Emperor and Prince of New Castle [Neuchâtel] were laughing at the droll expressions some of our Men made use of. Some wanted to know which was Boney, others said his wife was a fine lady Vc. A young Man named Tho. Thompson seeing the Emp. present his snuff box to some of the Nobles that were in discourse with him. 'Damn me,' says Thompson, 'but I should like to have a pinch out of the Emperors box.' Bonaparte Smileing said, 'Yes my Man, you shall with pleasure.' He then presented the box to Thompson. The youth seemed dashed when he found the Emp. understood what he said. 'Come my Man you need not be the least allarmed. Perhaps you may never have another oportunity to do the like again.' The Emperor then presented his box to Thompson; he took a pinch made his obedience and went towards the rest of his countrymen. 'Give me a grain,' says one. 'Let me have a snuff,' says another. 'Here,' says the Emperor. 'Take each of you a snuff.' We then each man took a dust of his mill, made our Obedience and to our duty, greatly elevated at the honour conferred on us, to take a pinch of Snuff from the hand of an Emperor. My God, this will carry us all safe to Heaven; we shall be no longer in need of any Support. Such nonsense passed amongst us afterwards when we Met over the Social bowl, or amongst any of the French people in town. After a few days carrousing in town and in the prison we began to think about the promise made us by the Emperor, that in a few days we should have an answer from Paris.

Cardiff Walsh was recovering quite fast in the Hospital.

We wrote a petition to the Emperor

November 20, 1810. Day by day passed away and brought us no tidings from Paris. Many of our Men had gone so far as to sell their cooking utensils and every thing they had to spare and bought Shoes, gaters, knapsacks, and other thing necessary for a March, being confident that they were going directly home to England. Many of our townsmen had wrote letters for us to take home to their friends. Yet no answer whatever. We consulted the Commandant what was the best means for us to take. He wished to see the General and Mr. Wolfe before he could give us any advice. We also enquired of Col. Flayel what he thought was the reason we heard nothing from Paris: he said he could allude to nothing only that some verry important business must have taken the emperors time entirely in attending his private counsellors.

On the 20th Nov. the Commandant informed us we must write a handsome petition to the Emperor, and the General, him, and Col. Flayel would sign it and forward it to his Exelency le Duc de Feltre Ministerre de guerre, and he would lay it before the Emperor and by that Means we would have an answer. We had a petition wrote in a verry submissive humble manner and it was signed as proposed and sent to Paris and time passed away in expectation of an answer. At last the day came that put an end to our expectations. The General had a letter from the Minister of War which was to this effect; he had received the Generals letter and our petition which he laid before the Emperor and had for answer that the Emperor had considered it would be a verry unwise action to send us to England as it would cause great murmering amongst our countrymen left in France. It would also cause great discontentment in the prisons in England when the Frenchmen there confined heard the newse that 30 British prisoners had been released from Prison by the Emperor. He therefore had considered that could not be done but every liberty and favour that could be given to us in France should be granted. We also were to draw a louis d'or each man and suit of cloaths of a superior quality Vc. This was our Answer; and this our long look'd passport that was to take us down to the water side to embark. 'Oh, oh. Now what must we think of the word of an Emperor?' A mere puff of wind!

I think this was the greatest disappointment I ever met. All the men in the universe could not have made me believe that an Emperor would act so mean, as run back from his word and honour, with as little concern as a tinker, or even, as they say in France, a Savoy [Savoyard], and that thinks no more of his word than the bark of a dog. But when we come to reflect, and consider what Man it was that we were placeing our confidence in, then we might have looked back a few years to the revolution where he as well as many others swore to do away all crown heads and royalty and make him Consul for life. This he grew too large for; his consul robes all grew too Small for him, he could not wear them any longer, but it happned that they found a Suit of Kings robes that just suited Nappey; they put them on him, and he felt quite comfortable, therefore

the People said he should wear that suit and still be their ruler
untill they could muster Money enough in Germany and Holland to purchase him a more costly suit for any Emperor. This
suit was made and put on him. He liked it well but poor old
Josephine could not help him on with his imperial robes;
therefore she was discharged with this fault, that she was too
far in years and not able to do up his imperial linen. He then
went to Vienna in Germany where they heard of a famous
laundry maid, named Maria Louisa. He knocked at the Emperor of Germany's door; when the porter asked his business,
he said he heard there was a girl within named Maria Louisa,
and he wanted to engage her to do up his linen. The old porter
told him to wait, and he would inform his Master what business he came about. 'Well, be quick,' says Nappy. The Porter
not returning in time, my noble fortune hunter followed him
in to the old Germans house, took the laundry Maid by forse
and hurried out of the country destroying all the toll gates that
offer'd to oppose him, makeing all the Stage coach offices
furnish him with coaches free of charge—if not he took them
at his will and pleasure. This is the Man we were placeing
confidence in.

Well we are disappointed and must do the best we can to
get over it. Numbers were worse situated than me, or even my
young messmate Andrew Smith. I had plenty of Cloathing,
books, Music, Vc. I left the Hospital and came back to the
Bureau where Andrew had been improveing his time during
my time in the hospital. We began again to live as formerly
and devote part of our time to political affairs Vc.

DECEMBER *1810*. My inclination led to drawing and music, to which I devoted the greatest part of my time all this winter, by the side of a good stove, which we supported by keeping a canteen in our room, called the inter-preters hotel; it being the room where we that were inter-preters all lived together. We were six Messmates, and a young man Named George Critchlow was bar keeper; we got our liquor at the lowest rate, had permission to have our beer from the brewer by the barrel, and we used frequently to share from four to five crowns each man, weekly clear of all our expences.

January 1811. Verry severe frost, the river all frozen over. Verry little alterations took place amongst us untill the middle of March, when Lloyds coffee house in London contrived the means of assisting the Merchant Mens crews that were in France by the Means of the tonnage money Vc., which was all sent over for the prisoners of War in France, and we that belonged to the Navy had three Sols pr day from our British wages, paid every ten days; we therefore gave our part of Lloyds money to the Merchant men; and that made them nearly equal to us; this made us all quite comfortable. On the 20th of March 1811, a great day in France, Bonaparte's son was born; Charlemount made the prison all dance with its peals of thunder from its three hundred guns. In April we had the newse that all the old men and crippled were to be returned to England by the way of Morlaix; May, the Old men and Cripples were all granted permission to walk out of the prison round the ramparts Vc. Letters and money were daily arriveing from England. We devoted great part of our time to Music. A number of us formed a Society, and bought Instruments in Order to form a band amongst our selves; we had several of the first performers on different instruments that had been captured in Spain and sent to our depot. The Commandant was so good as to give us a large Officers room to practise in. We bought Instruments for the Musicians from Spain; they took delight in giveing us every instruction in their power, so that in a short time we mustered a complete band of 24 in number; we made such progress in this delightful Amusement that in the course of a few months we could perform some Verry grand pieces. We made exchange with the French band for their different pieces, we gave them ours, and in the course of a Short time could surpass them in their own Music. This simple Amusement put away Many solitary hours throughout the whole prison. We were frequently visited by numbers of the French Officers and Musicians from diferent regiments, passing thro' Givet. Another beautiful Manner of employing our time to advantage was Sacred Music in the Church, which was brought to great perfection amongst us; we had an elegant Choir of Singers, and the Revd. R. B. Wolfe took pleasure in provideing the Works of several authors such as Rippons collection of Sacred Music, so that Givet Prison was called by the French a repository of Arts and Sciences.

In this Manner the time crept away and in rapid strides this year passed away. We began to think that it was mere folly to think of ever being released; therefore we might make ourselves as happy as our situation would allow, and thus we brought Christmass close to hand before we thought of it. However, we made timely preparations for our yearly feast of Hams, brandy, and strong beer; thus we pass our time in captivity, from year to year. We also had some Malteese, and Italians, taken in the English employ up the Medeteranean. Those men performed Operas, and plays, for amusement; we also had free Mason's lodges, Odd fellows societies, Orange Clubs, and a number of free and Easy Meetings; Methodist, and other professors of religion, also had their Meetings. The

Canteens had their days appointed, for singing and Music, where we were generally visitors with our band, which caused them to sell great quantities of the liquor. On those days we were frequently visited by the Commandant, General, gendarmes, and inhabitants of the town, on which days we performed a number of Select pieces, such as the battles of Egypt, Prague, Agencourt, a great Many Choice Marches, Rondeaus, and Waltzes Vc., both French, German, English, Prusian, Vc. Our Depot at last was entirely the chosen place of the Gentry from the town when they wanted to take a pleasant afternoon's excursion with visitors from other parts of the country, so that Givet College was no longer a prison but a repository of Arts and Sciences.

Midst all those various ways we had to kill time, as we used to say. Time was not laying idle; he found means to be killing some of us day by day; Mr. Joseph Williams, a fine young man, one of our ablest Scholars in the depot, was called to his silent tomb in the midst of health, and promiseing abilities. He being a free Mason, the Commandant and Officers in town requested him to be burried with all the honour due to Masonry. All the Masons in the prison were present. All the French Officers, and townspeople, were also there, and Our Band led the procession through the town to the burrying ground, playing the dead March in 'Saul.' This was what had not been seen before in Givet, but was frequently made use of afterwards both over the French and English Free Masons.

This being the 24th of December, we then returned to the depot and began to look forward to tomorrow (Christmass day). We past our hollidays as usual, and Welcome the New Year.

January 1812. Principal remarks in Givet depot this year promises us many flattering prospects which all proved only false delusive stories; nevertheless we drove Jack Frost as far from our presence as possible; and in our various Amusements, over a good warm Stove, past away January, February, and March.

On the 1st of April the Boys in the depot were all muster'd by Mr. Wolfe, and Jack Jones appointed as boatswain over them: to instruct them in their duty on board of Ship. They had three Masts, all rigged with yards, and rigging, complete, in the depot, where he taught the boys to strip her, rig her, send yards up and down, bend Sails and unbend them. He also taught them how to splice, heave the lead, Vc. The masts and rigging were large enough for boys 12 years of Age to pass up and down the rattlings, to send the yards up and down. It was large enough for a vessel 50 or 60 tons. This was fine Amusement for the Boys every Saturday.

On the 5th of April the Commandant had orders from Paris to give all the Americans in the depot liberty to enter for the American Brig True Blooded Yankee laying in Brest. We had a number of Americans that sent their protections to Paris and were released immediately, to Join the brig. We also heard of the invasion of Canada by Genl. Hull of Wellingtons takeing Cindad Roderigo [Ciudad Rodrigo] in Spain. On the 13th, 14th, and 15th of April the Armies of France passed our depot by forced marches on their march towards Rusia. Such a sight as we had never seen before. All the Waggons, Carts, Vc, through all the country they had to pass, were ordered to meet the Comissaries at certain appointed stations, in order to transport the troops thro' the country, without the least delay, and this was the means they took to transport the Army to the Frontiers in such a short space of time. . . . When a Soldier was fatigued, or foot sore, he was put into a Carriage and rode; provisions was ready for them at every town, when they arrived, one division in one town, and Another division eating in the next; and so they kept on continually Marching, day and night. They Slept in Carriages, takeing their regular turns to ride and Sleep, eat, and March, by day and night. Such regular order was kept thro' the whole Army.

Our depot being situated on the Grand route de Paris on the Main road from Paris thro' the Netherlands, to Mayence, where the Bridge crosses the Rhine, gave us a fair oportunity to see all the Army that passed by day, and hear those that passed by night. On the third day of their passing Mr. Peytavin the Commandant came to the prison with several of the Officers and desired us to turn out with our band, and Salute the Army as they passed, which request we willingly complied with instantly. We assembled at the gates where they passed, and Struck up Bonapartes March and Made the Yard and Charlemount echoe with the sound. The French Music ceased playing, and we played different National Airs, untill all the Main body of the Army was past, and then we gave them the Austrians retreat, and dismissed. Mr. Peytavin and the rest of the Officers were very much gratified with our conduct, and performance; and gave five Crowns to drink. One of the Colonels gave Leversage, the Bass Drummer, a Crown to buy him a set of heads for his drum, and said as he passed out of the gate that he never was more astonished in his life than at that time, to have the pleasure of hearing so many of his own country's favourite Airs performed in such grand order and so verry correct as had been done by the British Seamen that day in his presence. The Commandant laughing reply'd, 'Ah, Monsieur, those are my Children.'

We will now leave the Army to their commanders and look a while at our own affairs. I shall mention a singular circumstance that took place at our depot. It is already observed that the Aged and cripples had liberty to walk out of the Prison. One of those Cripples named Edward Bonner, a verry sober religious little fellow, and a townsman of my own, had unfortunately lost his Arm on Board HBM Frigate la Minerva at the time she was captured under the forts of Cherbourg in 1803. This Bonner was the Man, the verry little fellow, that deceived all who knew him, haveing, as was customary, taken a walk to town in the afternoon, and passed the gates that lead to Dinant with an intent (as the gate keeper thought) to take his daily country walk. But Bonner was bent on trying a longer walk than usual. He forgot to return that evening, but bent his course down to Ostend. When the evening Muster was called, Bonner was absent. At this time there had been a verry heavy spell of rain for some time, so that the river Meuse had rose to a great height, and the current ran with great fury. When Bonner was missing the Gendarmes said he was drowned in the river; otherwise he would not absent himself from the Depot, they were certain. Next day no Bonner; even his bedfellow could not form any idea what was become of him. Bonner was a good free Mason; he kept his own counsel, and even his most intimate acquaintance were all kept blind in regard to his intentions. Well, days, weeks, and Months passed over and not the least tidings of him. In fine, the Commandant, General, and Mr. Wolfe all concluded Bonner was drowned, poor little fellow. In a short time we were all the same opinion, and were sure, poor fellow, he was gone— yes, gone. 'What a pity,' says one. 'He was such a clever little fellow.' 'Yes, and such a sober steady Man,' says another. 'Ah,' says old Dick Hornsby, 'I always thought something would happen him. He was so sad and could scarcely smile at any thing he saw or heard; this was a certain forerunner of his death.' 'Well,' says Robin Gray, 'he has gone to Heaven by water, and will not be able to ferry himself across the river Styx: only haveing one arm, so that he will wait there untill some of us meet him and help him across the river.' At last Bonner was forgot: he was drowned and no more thought about. But only listen a while, and you will laugh at the jest; Bonner got into the woods first night he left the depot, and the following day laid in the wood untill night, then made the best of his way towards Ostend. He continued this Mode of travailing for Nine successive Nights, and only called at small cottages where he was verry singularily directed to the Sea coast, close to Ostend. On the tenth day he ventured into Ostend, went down to the Port, where he heard some men in a Boat Speaking English. He watched their motions, and followed them up to a Tavern which proved to be kept by a Man from Dover.

'Old fellow,' says the landlord (to Bonner), 'where the devil have you sprung from with your one flipper, eh?' 'Well Sir,' Says old Ned, 'I have sprung from Antwerp where have sold our Boat, and I am going over to Deal to buy another, to come over again after the rest of our Men, and a large quantity of lace we have bought with the price of our old boat; we sold the old boat to a French Merchant that is fitting out a large lugger as a Privateer, and wants our boat as a galley, to board vessels and if required to row away.' This discourse brought the rest of the English men round so that according to Bonner's wishes, they all sat down and joined in company. The bowl passed round and Bonner was soon convinced that he was in the Midst of a set of Deal Smuglers, and they were to Sail at ten the next evening if the coast was clear (that was clear of English Cruisers). They offered Bonner a passage over to Deal; this was just the thing his heart was wishing, only he was afraid to ask for his passage, lest they might suspect him to be a prisoner or some imposter: he verry humbly thanked them for their kind offer, and called for a bottle.

They passed that night quite jovial, and at an early hour in the morning went to rest; he got a bed in the same house, and next day kept very close quarters; the rest of the Smuglers were all employed, settling their various accounts.

Next evening the Signal was made that the coast was clear; they settled their accounts with old Walter Jones, the host, embarked, and Sailed along the Shore; the wind being light they lay under the land all day near Dunkerque; and next night with a smart breeze they all landed safe in St. Margaret's Bay, close to Deal, landed their goods, and Made all safe. They all went to Deal, where they had another day's carouse. Bonner then took his leave of them all, returned his sincere thanks for their generous treatment, and parted. Bonner made the best of his way to London, went to Somerset house; in Short, he drew his pension, Wages, and some Prize Money. With this he took his seat in the Coach for Stamford, the place of his birth, where he meant to pass the remainder of his days in comfort. But Bonner, like other Birds that have Made their escape from a cage, and being overjoyed at his good fortune, and happy release from prison, made a little free with the long wish'd for Lincolnshire Ale. He arrived in Stamford, in the Middle of the day quite happy; and as he passed my Mother's door the old Woman was looking out and saw him looking round like a stranger. She says to Julia my Sister, 'There is a poor Sailor looking for some person. Go and enquire what he wants.' She went and found he wanted his Brother John Bonner; but alas, John was dead, some years before. Mother called him to her, asked him where he came from, he said from French Prison. 'Come in,' says the old Woman; in he went, and she soon found by his discourse that he was from Givet and was particularily acquainted with me. He informed her that he left me in good health. Mother then took him to the house formerly ocupied by his brother John.

It was then a boarding house kept by a Widow Toulson, a particular acquaintance of my Mother's; with this woman Bonner took up his quarters, and lived there until I returned from France and met him in Stamford after the overthrow of Bonaparte, and the restoration of the Bourbons, Louis 18th, to the Crown of France. However, in the interval Bonner was not idle; he made love to the Widow his landlady, and so far gain'd her consent to Marry, that she would have him, if she could get a line from me, to prove his Character in France, and that he was not married in Givet, as She understood numbers were. However, this line they never got, untill I was the bearer of it. Nevertheless, they remain'd faithful to their Words, and two days after my return to Stamford, which was the 7th of June 1814, Edward Bonner and Jane Toulson were Married, in the Church of All Saints in the Parish of St John, Stamford, Lincolnshire. I gave her to Bonner for Better or worse, but she was good.

I shall now leave Bonner alive and happy in England and return back to Givet, where his unfortunate body by this time must be nearly destroyed by fish; he is drowned, gone, and almost quite forgot. In the Month of June the orders came to Colonel Flayel the chief engineer, and the General of the town and Garrison, to commence the necessary preparations for building a Bridge of stone, across the river Meuse at Givet. Those orders were immediately put into operation. The wood for Spiles to lay the foundation of the pillars on was soon conveyed by water down the river from the forest of Ardennes. Stages were made and the Machines all made ready for commencement then; the Prisoners were called to put down their Names to work at the Bridge; the rules were to have one Shilling pr day, and one Shilling pr night, to work, watch and watch, day and night; this was a real treat to the prisoners. Numbers of them had never before been out on liberty, and this to them was welcome Amuesement; they were one hundred working Men that had not before had liberty, and fifty that had passports; those were interpreters and leaders of the work. There was a number of Mechanics employed, besides the labouring men: such as carpenters, Masons, blacksmiths, Vc. this made entirely a turn over through the whole town and prison. Numbers that had suffered extreme want at different times in the prison felt the good effects of this daily employment, owing to the Commandant granting liberty for the Men to change with each other daily if they thought fit, only to keep up the complement of 150 constantly at work day and Night. The work went on with great success all the remainder of this Year. When the winter set in and ice began to make in the river, they had to leave off their works untill next Spring. In the papers we have daily Bulletins from the Grand Army; in Novem. we heard of the burning of Moscow on the 14th of Sept., and the close of the year brought daily fresh losses from the Army, their sufferings by the severity of the Winter, want of provisions, want of rest and nourishment, and worse than all the unmerciful Sword and lance of the Savage Cossaque that harassed their rear, both night and day, spareing none that fell in their way. This was the newse, at the close of the year 1812, which we, to speak the truth, were glad in our hearts to hear anything that had the smallest signs of overthrowing Bonaparte, and his numerous Army. We said nothing but thought the more. We were all fully convinced that nothing but the overthrow of Bonaparte could ever restore us to our friends and Country, once more to enjoy the blessings of Sweet Liberty, and we again began to enjoy some small hopes that that happy day was not far distant when we should burst the chains of tyranny, and trample his cruel orders under our feet, and he, seeing his bloodthirsty Eagle lay gasping, beneath the outstretched paw of the Lion, should burst his heart with panting for revenge and leave Europe to enjoy that blessed peace she has been many years longing to enjoy. Thus we passed away our Christmass and new Years, eating, drinking, and wishing the lord to strengthen the Arms of bold Alexander.

January 1813 commenced with a violent Snow Storm which continued 4 days. The mails bring the Bulletins from the Grand Army, with most dreadfull and destructive accounts of their deplorable Situation and daily losses by the Cossaques that are constantly harrassing the rear and wings of the Army. They frequently cut off some hundeds of Men and take great part of their baggage and at times both Artillery, Ammunition,

arms, Colours, and what was worse of all verry often cut off
their supplies of Provisions. Even the horse Soldiers had to
March on foot, their horses either dead or unable to proceed
any further entirely thro' want of forrage. They eat the bark
from the trees when they found any uncover'd with snow, but
this was nothing amongst Such a numerous train of Cavalry,
flying Artillery, Cannon, Ammunition Waggons, Comissary
Stores and Baggage Waggons, the greatest part of which fell a
prey to the pursueing Enemy or died through fatigue and
Want. And as for the poor Men, alas, their situation was too
dreadful to be described. They were harrassed day and night
thro' deserts, o'erwhelmed in Snow, no shelter to take a small
repose; only the Cannopy of Heaven for their covering and a
snowey rock to lay their wearied heads, even that was rare to
be found. We used to murmur at our hard fate, but how happy
and comfortable we were situated to what those unfortunate
Men were that some few months ago past Givet, in great
pomp being fully persuaded they would make an easy conquest of all the Empire of Rusia.

Those daily tidings made us often reflect and say to each
other how happy would those poor fellows be if they were in
our situation or even in the Cells of Charlemont. Those reflections caused us to make ourselves quite content and say it was
all working for our good, and was the only Means by which
Bonaparte could be subdued and we all be restored to our
Native land. We all were convinced that nothing but the
overthrow of the French Army or the destruction of Bonaparte
could release us from our threatned imprisonment for life. On
the 24th of January we had the account of Bonaparte at the
bridge of Vesselovo [Viesselovo] on the 27th of Nov. 1812.
This was another Article in our approaching treaty of release.
Everything seemed to be in our favour; the British Army were
triumphant in Spain and the Prusians under Genl. York
deserted Bonaparte and fled to the Standard of Alexander.
All in our favour. Thus we passed January and February
debating on the Politicks of Europe.

In March we had a letter from Robert Smith directed to me
and his brother Andrew in which he informed us that after he
had been in Bitche some time he gained the good will of the

Commandant, the commander of the fortress, so far that he was made the Commandant's Clerk and in a little while after that he made intercession with the Com^t. to use his interest with the Minister of War so far to as to grant him liberty to Marry Madam Gammant; she, thro' her intended elopment with Robert, haveing been divorsed from Mr. Gammant, was single and at liberty to marry at her own pleasure. The Minister of War gained him the grant to marry her and he sent to Cambray for her. She went to Bitche and they were lawfully Married. This was the subject of our letter which caused many a laugh both in town and the Depot.

On the 12th of March the Bridge commenced again with all speed. The Prisoners went to work at it the same as the last year; 150 of the prisoners and as many French were employed day and night to complete this great undertaking. William Carter and William Applen returned to Givet again after being two Serjeant Majors in the Brigades. Our depot was kept full with prisoners taken in Spain. Small parties frequently joined us from Hospitals and various prisons between the depot and the frontiers of Spain. William Carter was married to Jannet Rankey and Young Andrew continued in the Bureau and as for my part I worked by turns at the Bridge, fine exercise every two days to have a good day's exercise and the same every other night. We were laying up money for a rainy day, or for a hasty turn out of our present habitation. We daily hear of great works going on to the eastward all in our favour. Wellington causes a great deal of Whispering, wry faces, thumping tables, and stamping on poor inoffensive boards, accompanied with many a Sacred oath, or Curse, on the English. Bavaria and several other Austrian kingdoms or princedoms had rebelled against France. Indeed it is plainly seen that Enemys are on all sides of France and they are determined to work out our long treated for in vain release from prison.

August 27, 1813. We got the inteligence by some men that had the Misfortune to be taken in the same affair regarding the great Battle of Pampelona [Pamplona] in the Pyrennees. It is in this manner we have to keep up our doubting hearts, being fully convinced that nothing but the fall of Ambition was of the least benefit to us, and by what we can learn that day is not far distant. Therefore we content ourselves with hearing, seeing, and saying nothing.

In the Middle of September we had a verry remarkable night while working at the Bridge. In the Middle of the night we were all covered with a cloud of locusts that fell two inches thick on the stages and all round the Bridge. The place where they fell was only four or five hundred yards across, and outside of that bounds they had verry few. We found afterwards that they drew towards the lights that we wrought by, as was evidently the case because on the following Night the inhabitants made large fires on different parts of the ramparts and they were entirely surrounded with those aerial Visitors, which expired the instant they reached the Earth. The old people in Givet were of opinion that those strange clouds of Aeriel visitors must be the forerunners of some strange Armies crossing the river at the same place where they first fell.

October 4, 1813.   The newse of this day caused great allarm amongst the inhabitants of the town. The orders were for every man from 16 to 60 that was able to take the field in defence of his own and his Country's cause must turn out immediately and march to assist in protecting the frontiers of the Netherlands against the Numerous Armies of Rusia that spread death and desolation as they passed thro' the different countries where e'er they came and at the present moment were advanced to the banks of the Rhine near Mayence. This was the time to see confusion all thro' the town. The people were running backward and forward wringing their hands and lamenting at the approaching desolation that was hovering over France. Wives lamenting the loss of their dear husbands, Mothers must part with their Son's brothers, and every male that was able to carry Arms was called to Join the levee in Masse and march with all speed to stop the advance of their invadeing victorious foes. Ah, what must be our opinions of the state of France at this present moment! Well I will tell you we were all of the opinion that our welcome day of liberty that we had been so many years looking for with the greatest Anxiety was verry rappidly advanceing triumphant.

October 12.   All the men that were able to carry arms

Marched from Givet towards Liege and left the town in a lamentable state. Nothing but a few Gendarmes and invallides were left in the garrison. On the 1st of November we heard it whisper'd round in the town that the Rusian Army were part of them crossed the Rhine and the French Army was makeing their retreat into the borders of France as quick as possible where they intended to make a most vigourous resistance and in one grand attact put a stop to the advance clouds of Cossaques that spread horror and desolation where e'er they came. Now, says we, it has many years ago been the word amongst the French to say to us. 'Ah, John, me to day, and you tomorrow,' which has every appearance to be verry shortly verrifyed, as our tomorrow is on his way from Mayence as fast as he can get his horses to draw his Sleigh thro' rough rugged hills and vallies cover'd with Snow. Towards the middle of Nov. we had more newse in our favour: the Confederation of the Rhine were all Marching into France, Wellington was on the way to Bayonne, the Austrians were Marching towards Strasbourg with all speed. We hear that their advance guard have already entered France by the ways of Strasbourg, Bale and we shall certainly have to desert our dwelling and leave our University where we have devoted Many years to study, particularily Politicks. Something like the Nuns in France that kept in continual religious ceremonies much against their own inclination, and like us cut off from all intercourse with the world in general.

I shall give a proof of our expected release shortly which was as follows. We met every afternoon with all our Band for the sole purpose of rehearseing and Selecting out tunes such as we intended to make use of as we marched thro' the Country, which was afterwards the case, as will be seen in the following pages. Our Men that were employed at the Bridge had orders to leave off the stone work, and leave the wooden Stages to pass and repass the river, or take them away if it was required to destroy the passage of the river.

December 5, 1813. The Bulletin of the Army was not any longer permitted to be circulated thro the country as it only confused and terrified the whole population at large.

December 19. Ah, what a joyful day to us! Daniel Owlett

the Steward of the depot brought us the glad tidings that we daily were looking for, Orders from the Comissarie de guerre in Paris, to the General and Commandant of the Depot, to have all the British Prisoners of war in readiness to March in an hour's warning and to divide them into eight divisions one party to March each day and also each man to have a Shirt, Shoes, and stockings that was some time due them and laid in the Magazine. Glorious glorious newse! Now, my boys, all hands to work, some makeing gaters bags or knapsacks, some takeing their kitchen ware down to the gate to sell or partly give away for a try to buy a little brandy to drink for joy at such good newse. Thus all hands were in some way of preparation for Marching. All the Men that lived in town returned to the depot to be in readiness when the happy tidings reach'd Givet. We were all muster'd in our Divisions and numbered as first, second, third, fourth, to the eighth division, and the Commandant also made the arrangement so that the Officers, such as Master's Mates, Midshipmen, Gunners, Boatswains, in fine, all the Officers and the Band, were attached to the last division which consisted of nearly three hundred Men. The Commandant's reason for this was that he might have the Music to play each division through the Gates of Givet when they marched away. This we all were quite happy to perform, and so it was afterwards there was no more regular rules observed amongst us. All was bustel & confusion, watching every motion of the Gendarmes, Commandant, Vc. Every time any of them passed the gates we expected to hear the orders for the first Division to March. Christmass at last made its Annual round, but was not respected the same by us as heretofore. Our minds at this critical cricis were engaged entirely on the worldly pleasures we hoped daily to enjoy. However we passed the day quite comfortable and tolerable, peaceable when we consider the unsettled state of the depot. On the 26th, in the Evening, Danl. Howlet came to the gate and gave orders for the 1st division to be all in readiness to march at 8 O Clock in the Morning. 'Now my boys,' says the Steward, 'we are drove out of our boarding house at last, and by all appearance the next lodgers here will be Rusians as their advance posts are within a few days' march of us. Tomorrow morning the first division are to leave Givet, and I give them my friendly advice, that is (as we all are fully assured of the critical situation France is placed in at the present time), let us be cevil and obedient to those that have any command over us and keep still tongues concerning any political affairs. Let all this Sudden overturn in the country pass our British tars the same as many Squalls and thunder storms have done before; this is the way, my Countrymen, for us to be well used and respected like men as we march through the country. Our orders at the present are to march to the City of Blois untill further orders. This my Brothers, is my friendly and Sincere advice to you all. . . .' We all hands gave him three cheers and thanked him for his kind advice. We were dismissed, and then there was fun, one drinking a glass with his old shipmate before they part, another must pass the last night with his Old acquaintance over a good glass of hot Stuff. We mustered our Musicians and rehearsed over the tunes we had selected for the first division's farewell to Givet. This night was kept up all thro' the depot. Sleep was partly banished from every eye and every man was watching with anxiety to see the approach of that blessed day we had so many long nights, weeks, months, and years been looking for, that happy morn that was to break the first link of our Captive chains and restore to us the blessings of that sweet liberty we had so many years been deprived of and not permitted to enjoy.

At last the Gun on Charlemount loudly proclaim'd the approach of the great Jubilee day Dec. 27th 1813. At 8 AM. the word was 'all the first division to muster all ready.' The gates were hove open and they all formed in a line outside the gates, were all present and in readiness. The Band was then desired by the Commandant to form in front and play up a March which we readily obeyed. Then the orders were to March and we struck up 'Over the hills and far away.'

December 27, 1813. The first division of British Prisoners of War Marched from the depot at Givet in France where numbers of them had been confined from ten to Eleven Years and nearly as many more were left behind never More to return. That morning being St. John's day, when all mus-

tered we were 2364 prisoners of War. The first division was
250 men, which left us 2114. However we conducted them
outside the Gates for nearly a mile, surrounded with a great
crowd of the inhabitants. Numbers of them shed tears at
parting after so many years acquaintance. Numbers had
formed such intimate connections that they were parting with
their own children when we took our last farewell of them. For
my own part I must say that my feelings were verry much
hurt when I took my last farewell embrace of Monsieur and
Madam Perriot, their Son John, and some more intimate
friends of mine in town. I say when we parted there was not
one of us could avoid shedding tears, and even looking back
and waving our hands as long as we were in sight of each
other. . . . Therefore it is my opinion many of my fellow
sufferers had the same feeling. We returned back to the depot
pretty well done over, between playing our instruments, and
tasteing a little cogniac at times, to moisten our lips and make
us play with more life, and we spent the remainder of the day
in town, visiting all our most intimate friends and acquaintance. Thus we passed the day. . . . On the 28th the prison was
one continual bustle, selling off such articles as were no longer
of use to us to the market Women and inhabitants of the town.
This day several of the French advance guard (on their retreat
from Rusia) arrived in Givet on their March to Challons,
where it is conjectured there will be a dreadfull contest, as all
the reinforsements in France are to meet at that place of
rendezvous. On the 29th of Dec. the second division marched
with the same ceremonies as the first had done. They were
250 brave fellows, mostly Merchant Seamen. Left us 1864 in
the depot. This day several detatchments from the grand
Army arrived in Givet, on their march to Challons, and on
the 30th the same troops passing in small parties all day.
They appear'd greatly fatigued.

CHAPTER

II

DECEMBER *31, 1813*. The third division left Givet, 250
men, all in great spirits. We paid them the same honour
we had done to the other two that went before them.
One thing was they had some unwelcome company to March
with, the soldiers on their retreat; however they knew perfectly
well that such difficulties were all forerunners of a speedy
release. We shall let them march all this Year, and if all turns
out according to our expectations, we shall follow them on
the ensueing year. We are now 1614 Men.

January 1, 1814. This day we kept as our last New Years
Day in France. We eat, drank, and Made ourselves contented
and happy. On the 2nd the 4th division, 250 Men, Marched,
1364 left. On the 4th the 5th divn., 300 men Marched, 1064
left. On the 6th the 6th div., 350 Men Marched, 714 left. On
the 7th the 7th divn., 350 Men Marched, 364 left. And on the
8th we composed the 8th division, 364 Men. This was the day
I already have mentioned in a former page, when there was
such floods of tears shed when we took our last farewell at
halfway house. The weather was verry Stormy all the Morning;
the roads were verry heavy and what made them still worse
was the baggage, Cannon, artillery, Amunition waggons, and
all the Horse belonging to the first division of the grand Army
in front of us, and they cut up the roads to such an excess that
it was almost impossible to tramp thro' the mud and dirt. They
were verry strict with us and made us walk in the middle of
the road with the troops on each side of us. The General in
Command, an unfeeling tyrant, gave orders to the troops that

if any British prisoner should attempt to leave his ranks or go
off the road without a guard, such man or men were to be shot
as deserters by any French Soldier that might fall in with them.
In this manner we had to march nineteen days successively.
As for my part my fate was not quite so hard as I belonged to
the Band. The Officer that had the command of us was a verry
humane good man and exceeding fond of Music; therefore he
took us to his quarters in Humay and had us to play before
several of the Officers that were attached to the Army, and by
this means we had a good warm room to sleep in. The rest of
our party Slept in the Cells below, and those cells or Cashots
were verry sorry quarters for our partners to lay down in, more
particular as it was the first night, after so many years good
warm lodgings and free from any fatigue whatever. But what
care we for suffering a little while longer we know by the
course of things our sufferings are drawing to a conclusion? We
have various proofs that France is in a tottering state. One
proof is the orders given by the General: not to let any British
prisoner leave his ranks on pain of death (that is to prevent us
from deserting to join the Cossaques) and the second proof is
that all the Army are to encamp on the plains of Challons,
which we are in hopes will be the last push. Therefore the
harder we are used the sooner our hardships will have an end.
When we look round us a moment and consider what a Multitude of Men and horse has to pass the night in this small village
we may be thankful that we have the largest Mansion in Humay
for our nights lodgings. (That was the Gaol.) We played the
band most part of the night and our own officers in company
with the French passed the night in Jovial harmony. On the
following morning we all felt a little heavy headed after our
nights carrouseing.

From Givet to Humay was only 12 Miles and that short
distance harrassed some of our Men to death as one may say,
what thro' drinking with our friends at leaveing Givet, and
then with numbers that accompanied us to the half way house,
carrying our knapsacks and instruments to ease us on our first
day's Journey. We had numbers of both old and young, Men,
Women, and Children, that thought as hard to part with us as
they would have been at parting with their own families. They

most of them took care to have a good pocket pistol with them to moisten the day as we trudged along, linked arms, some with their favourite lass, and Some with their intimate acquaintance and friends, all splashing through the rugged broken path that was all tore up by the heavy Waggons and Artillery that passed in front of us. The troops that were on each side of us stared at the Scene when we took leave of our friends and well wishers on the road, and at the halfway house; Mr. Perriot and his son John would not part with me until we left the halfway house. Then was the time (as I mentioned before) that Manhood forgot itself, and for a little while gave vent to the flowing streams of affection. The tide of affection haveing overflowed its bounds, the sound of 'bonne voyage' was heard from every tongue of the parting crowd, when our trumpets Sounded March, March, away, and the winding of the road soon hid them from our sight. . . . Then we in a short time resumed our former Manhood and to our share of the pleasant long wish'd for walk on the fertile banks of the river Meuse.

We had several Married Women in our Division. Poor souls, their fate was hard, more particular on the first day, first at leaving their parents, their home and friends, and entering into the World to seek their unknown place of rest perhaps never more to return, and another reason was the Season of the Year, where they were exposed to all the severities of a severe Winter Marching in front of a retreating Scatter'd Army. Not even the previledge for them to have a Cart should they be unable to bear the fatigue of an unknown March, as all the Carts and Waggons were employed by the Army. Nevertheless those true hearted Women bore the burthen of the whole Journey by the side of their chosen and dearly beloved Husbands, through all the difficulties and sufferings we had to experience on our long March, of which I have as near as possible endeavoured to give a small sketch of the names of the towns we lodged in every night, their distance from each other in English Miles, our treatment and principal remarks that took place Amongst us, from leaving Givet on the 8th of January untill we embarked in St. Maloes on the 22nd of May.

From Humay to Givet was 12 miles and those 12 miles nearly took twelve hours to march, halt, drink, and answer Muster.

First muster'd on the morning at the gates of the depot, second by the General and Commandant outside the gates, third muster that day at the halfway house. Fourth in the square at Humay, and the fifth by the Gaoler as we passed the gates of his dominions, and the Sixth and last that day was in the cells under the prison at 8 O clock that evening. This made us quite proud to find them so verry careful of us. We ought to think ourselves verry much honoured by so many great donn's speaking to every man and Mentioning all our names. However we got liberty at last to lay down our poor wearied limbs on the lock of wet miserable lous'y Straw.

We that had the good fortune to belong to the band, being 24 in number, fared much better than the rest of our brother Captives. The Captain of the Guard that had the charge of us, being a verry humane Gentleman and a great lover of music, took us up into his appartment to divert him and a number of officers who he had invited to sup with him. We had plenty of the best to eat and drink and remained in the room all night. This made our situation quite different to that of our fellow Prisoners, and on march we used to play on the road. This was pleasant to our people and also to the Soldiers of the Army. Frequently when the weather was bad and the roads verry heavy we Struck up the old air of 'begone dull Care,' or 'o'er the hills and farr away.' Such simple amusement would cheer up many a drooping travailer. Even the poor fatigued Soldiers would take fresh courage at the Warlike sound of Martial Music, and frequently would assist in carrying our bass drum. It was an uncommon large one. We got it made just to answer us in Givet when we performed the Battle of Egypt and several other pieces.

On the 9th of January 1814 in the Morning our trumpets Summoned us to the gates of the Gaol, or town Prison, where our roll was called and all found present. The troops had been marching some time before our orders were to march off. When our Captain had settled his business we marched away from Humay towards Rocroi, 14 Miles. That was a verry cold rainy day and after our night's carrousing with little or no rest, we were a little chilly all the forepart of the day. Nevertheless we soon found a certain cure for that disorder which is reasonable to be true—march 14 Miles in the rain with a knapsack on your back; some tolerable heavy and some rendered light by tasteing another and another drop of the good old Sneek, and some were made quite handy to carry owing to their owners finding it most convenient to put the contents of their knapsacks either in their pockets or convert them into necessary articles for cleaning teeth Vc. With this on your back and a crowd of horse Soldiers or carriages on each side splashing you with good cool mud up to your knees in rugged broken clay cut up by the continual passing of the Army. At times an Officer may pass on horseback; then you are sure to enjoy the pleasure of being christned over again not by the hands of a parson but by the feet of a horse and a shower of Mud in your face and eyes. This we found a perfect cure for a drowsy head.

January 9. We got into Rocroi at 3 in the afternoon and were lodged in the Prison with a great number of troops that were quarter'd there, not haveing room for them in the Barracks nor yet in the dwelling houses; all were full. Our Men were quite comfortable with the troops; they had plenty of hot soup and a good hot fire as much against the Gaoler's will; however the Soldiers bore the sway; they neither heeded the Gaoler nor his Wife. Our Commandant took us to the Hotel where he lodged and gave us plenty of victuals and drink. We played in the large hall until 11 at night then went to rest in a large room with plenty of Straw and blankets where we slept warm and comfortable untill drum beat next morning. Rocroi is a small fortified town on the banks of the Meuse. It has four gates and is surrounded by three Walls with entrenchments one oe'rlooking the other. It is not larger than the Citadella of Vallenciennes and is entirely a Garrison, no place of any Business, only what may arrise from Soldiers and Conscripts. In the morning the drums proclaim'd day and soon the whole garrison was one continual noise and hurry, with troops mustering in every direction in order to march towards Meziers. At 8 AM our commander gave orders for our Trumpets to Sound Muster, As all the troops were nearly gone. At 9 we marched away.

January 10. A fine hard frosty morning; we left Rocroi and made all sail for the city of Mezieres on the banks of the Meuse opposite Charleville, another strong fortified City, the chief town of the department, and the residence of the Comissarie de Guerre General of the district. Its distance from Rocroi is 25 miles. In Mezieres we were quarter'd in the Citadella, pretty good considering the quantity of troops that are in the town. On the 11th we reached the Village of Launcy, 18 Miles, a foggy damp day, the roads verry heavy, and crowded with troops, Artillery, and Military waggons of all description. This day the General gave orders to the troops that if any British Prisoner left his ranks with an intent to go out of the road they should immediately give him 'quatre Sols'; that was the price of a ball cartridge. When at the half way house we wanted a little snack and a drop to drink but the unfeeling Viper gave orders for the Soldiers not to let any of us enter beneath the same roof where his highness took shelter. Then we prayed that his shelter might be beneath the Sheep skin Mantle of an inhumane Cossaque up to his middle in Snow, compelled to eat Snow in order to quench his thirst, which realy was the case.

In Launcy we were drove into an old Church and the National Guard placed round us with strict orders not to let any of us pass the door, nor let any fire be allowed to enter inside, the Sacred abode of Night owls, bats, and verry possibly robbers and murder'rs. We had a trifle of pork and bread allowed us, verry small. The morsel of pork we eat raw, and then laid us down on a lock of rotten Straw, where we verry fervently all made observations concerning the cruel disposition of the Old General. We then concluded with a heavy prayer not entirely for the General's welfare. . . . We then stuck up our band and played 'dull care.' After that went to sleep like hogs in a pen, one on the top of another, all in good spirits, and on the morrow we turned out smokeing like the loaves just from an Oven.

January 12. Our trumpets called us to muster and found all present. We marched over the frozen road with great spirits for Rethel, only 12 Miles. We had one Waggon for our Baggage and Sick. The roads being hard we kept a head of the chief part of the Army. We arrived at noon and were cram'd into cells under ground like as many traitors or Spys, no straw to lay down, our pillow a rock or a large bone. We had some beef and bread with a little soup served us by the Gaoler. We bought a few sheafs of straw from him. He also sold us red herrings at the cheap rate of one hundred pr cent proffit. We also could be furnished with a drop of kill grief at the same rate, and when evening came he told us we might have beds up in the debtors prison at 1 franc each man to sleep 4 in a bed. We laugh'd at his folly and told him to keep his beds ready for the rusinas [Russians]. They were the next visitors he would have, and most likely would sleep in his house on credit. This seemed to hurt this tender man's feelings; however it was all passed away in jest and we struck up a lively Air on the band, out lights and went to rest. . . . We were annoyed much thro' the night by the drops of water falling from the petrified spindles that hung suspended from the roof of our hospitable Mansion. This was only passtime for us; we were certain that a few days longer would terminate our present sufferings. Two days More will take us clear of the Army, then we shall be likely to fare a little better. The Army has all their orders to assemble round Challons there. Bona. intends to risk a battle with Alexander.

January 13. A cold Stormy Morning; the snow fell fast; we Mustered, all present, and off we tramped to the old favourite tune of 'Over the hills and far away' for the City of Rheims, 27 Miles. We had the good fortune to be on the road before the main body of the Army; therefore we let no grass grow under our feet. Haveing the liberty of the road we made good use of it and by 4 in the afternoon we were within the Gates of the City. Our Guard were all well Mounted horsemen and let us hurry as fast as we could. We had two waggons to take up such as were unable to bear the March. In Rheims we were put into a large Cashot below the ramparts; they took out 8 of our men to fetch us Soup, which was just the thing that suited us, good Soup and bread, quite hot. This greatly refreshed us. Our baggage was late before they got in. The Officer of our Guard was a verry good man; he granted us every favour in his power. The sick that came in the Waggons he put up in the Gaoler's room where they had warm soup and a good fire to dry themselves by. They also had comfortable beds to lay their poor wore out limbs to rest. We left 6 of them in the Hospital; poor fellows, we were sorry to part with them but we must submit to the will of providence and live in hopes to meet again in health and prosperity free from the oppressive hand of Tyranny, in that land of freedom where dwells all that is near and dear to us, the hopes of which has caused us to overcome every dificulty that has been daily attacking us in various shapes and ways. As for my own part I can boast that thus far I have never given up the idea, but that I shall live to overcome all my troubles and sufferings in France, and return in triumph to my long absent Nation and my home. This has been and shall be my guide thro' the rough paths of trouble and captivity. I must not forget that we are in a dungeon under ground; the Officer ordered us a sheaf of straw every two Men. We made our beds and went to rest quite comfortable.

January 14. In the morning at break of day we Mustered in the Square, Snow and rain falling quite fast. We had 2 Waggons to attend us. Our Officer being ready gave the word and off we started all in good Spirits for the City of Chaalons [Châlons-sur-Marne], 33 Miles. At 9 in the forenoon the weather cleared off, the Sun broke through the haze, and we had fine weather the remainder of the day. The roads were verry heavy and the artillery and waggons passing all the night had ploughed them up entirely so that it was a great chance to set a foot on solid ground. Therefore we found it was the best plan to drive on thro' thick and thin; we had a great many horse Soldiers in company with us all day, and they are verry unwelcome company where the roads are wet and bad. They Splashed us terribly with Mud and dirt; however we drove along and by 4 in the afternoon got into Chaalons. We left several at the half way house to ride in the Waggons. They were not able to travail any longer. However they all joined us that evening. We were all lodged in a Convent with verry little straw, and that was quite wet and dirty. We had ½lb of bread per man and a small bucket of pease soup for 20 Men. This was the time we had to go thro' our regular platoon exercise, that was to load, fall back, and fire, and so keep your regular rank, advance and retreat in regular order, untill we had conquer'd and entirely plunder'd the citadella of all its Shot and Amunition and then retire to our Guard bed and try to get a little rest before we are again called to arms and March away.

January 14. At Chaalons we hear great whispering amongst the National Guard who are placed round our Castle to protect us from thieves or robbers who they say are overrunning the Low Countries like Swarms of bees. They are called Cossaques, and their whole delight is in fire, Sword, and plunder. This was the tale we were happy to hear and put on a long false face saying the Emperor is only leading the Rusians into France so that he may play them the second Act of Moscow. This would pass off the deception, while we were rejoicing in our hearts to hear that our friends were so Numerous and were so rappidly advanceing into the interior of France. The City of Chaalons is strongly fortified; it is surrounded with Strong walls and entrenchments and stands on a large plain that was then entirely cover'd with troops assembling from all parts of the country with an intent to stop the advance of their foreign invaders. We all were light hearted at the newse and altho' we were Captives in the midst of our Enemies had hope.

January 15. In the morning at break of day our drum gave us the summons to muster in the Yard of our lodging room, which was no unpleasant tidings to us, as we were all desireous to leave this scene of continual bustle and confusion. We were all muster'd and delivered over to the charge of a stern fine old Gentlemen, Captain in the 27th reg. of foot, and a guard of 50 men to conduct us to Vitry, 20 miles. The town being in such a state of bustle and confusion our new Captain thought it would be most prudent to omit the playing of our band untill we had passed the lines or rather the outposts of the Camp and then he said he should be verry glad to have us play at our pleasure because Music would give life and vigour to his men as well as us, and he himself took great delight in music! We had three carts for our baggage and Sick. Being all present the word was given to March, and away we trudged helter Skelter, thro' thick and thin, thro lanes of Soldiers, Artillery Waggons, tents Vc. The fact is the whole of the country round, as far as could be seen, was one entire Mass of Soldiers and the Main road was all day crowded with recruits all Marching (en masse) singing and huzzaing as they went, crowding along past us with some a drum leading the van, and other parties with a bugle or an old fiddle to cheer up their drooping spirits. I well remember that day; the roads were entirely broke up, and made many a stout hearted man almost ready to give up the Ship. We got to the half way house a small village on the way to Vitry and the place was so crowded with recruits (all hurrying to the Slaughter house at Chaalons) that it was some time before, our Commandant could make interest to obtain the liberty of a barn, where we all set down out of the rain to take a little refreshment and rest our poor Mud pelters; our guard were as glad to have a little rest as any of us could be, and what makes me remark this day in particular was a laughable scene we witnessed in the barn yard; there was a whole gang of the recruits that had halted to take a little refreshment, and they had made rather free with poor old cogniac, so that he set them hot for drill. They were all in small parties, in different parts of the yard practiseing their exercise, (raining like fury) some of them had an old Musket wanting the lock, others a Musket without its ramrod, and some with pikes, others with a bayonet stuck on the end of a stick, then again we would see one with an old rusty sword, no scabbard, and a great many with their Staffs, all loading and fireing with as much care and activity as if they had really been embodied and going thro' a field day. Soldiery has for many years been the principal employment of every Male thro France by which constant practice in the use of arms they are all Soldiers before they are Men or even know any other mode of gaining an honest livelihood. What was verry strange to us was to see young boys at the age of fifteen intermingled with Men up to Sixty years of age all Marching to the Slaughter house and appeared in the greatest Spirits; at times we met parties on the road that we heard long before we saw them, all joined in the chorus of some National Patriotic Song with now and then cheering every cottage they passed by. Perhaps they had an old drum that used to take a part of the Oratory. Our Commandant called our band together and he verry kindly requested us if we could make convenient to play a March as we passed thro' the next village (as the rain had somewhat abated), and that little Village was the place where he first drew the breath of life and where at the present time many of his relations and old acquaintance were still living and he was determined to try what they had in their cellars. We informed the Commandant that we were ready at his pleasure to obey him in any thing he requested that we were able to perform. He than called for Serjeant of the Guard and informed him to call his men together and tell them they must all say that we were a party of the Cossaques that they were conducting towards Vitry where we were to be kept in confinement untill further orders and that they were compelled to treat us kindly for fear that we should turn resolute with them and all desert on the road; also that we were verry submissive and obedient when we had plenty to eat and drink and that the band was our greatest delight as it drowned all our cares and roused us from all reflections. This the Commandant contrived so that we might all take some refreshment before we reached Vitry as he was well aware our fare would be verry poor there. As he desired, so he was obey'd; we all halted outside of the Village (its name is St Blanc, 7 miles from the city of Vitry). Our band led the van; the rest all fell into their ranks and the guards on each side. The commandant gave the word to march, we struck up a verry celebrated French rondeau, or quick step, and up we were conducted by the Commandant to the door of the Mayor surrounded by every Soul that levee en Masse had left in the Village. The Mayor was inn keeper of the village, and Brother in law to our Commandant. The orders were to halt and go into a large barn, the guard and band into the Mayor's parlour and lodging room. It was with great dificulty our guard could keep the peasants from crowding in at the doors and windows; they, hearing such horrid tales of the Cossaques, were all anxious to see what sort of wild beasts we were. Many of them that were close to us as we discoursed to each other in English would start and rush back into the crowd exclaiming that they heard us speaking Cossaque and perhaps we were laying some plan to rise and Massacree them all. We soon were served with bread, Cheese and Wine order'd by the Mayor. Our Capt. and his men had their refreshment up Stairs. We all eat and drink hearty for we had realy plenty left; then we play'd a favourite French Air and by this time our baggage joined us. They halted to partake of the good old Mayor's hospitality. We all formed our ranks as before and left room for our Women and sick com'rades that were with the baggage. Made our obedience to the Gentleman the Mayor, struck up our Music and bid good bye to the hospitable little Village of St Blanc. Our Capt. made us laugh all on the road afterwards when he related the story of his Brother and all the poor peasants in the place, how they enquired of him how we had been caught, and if we had committed any depredations since he had been with us, whether or no it was true that we eat those whom we conquer'd and all such simple questions. Our Capt. told them there was no fear of any such outrages being committed as long as we had plenty to eat and drink and if he had his desire, he would chuse to convoy us to Vitry equally as soon as he would so many British Prisoners. And he said on leaving the Village he informed the Mayor what nation we were, and his reason for thus allarming all the old Women in St Blanc. This caused Many a hearty laugh that day on all sides; we then began fast to approach our place of residence for that night. The weather clear'd up and the day being far advanced we were not pester'd with so many troops passing us on the road. We reached Vitry about 5 in the evening. We were put in a small barracks, had plenty of Straw and in a short time were served plenty of good Soup and white bread all hot. All those favours were bestowed upon us thro' the Generous humane intercession of our good Commandant. We had plenty of fire wood and made good fires in the barrack rooms to dry our wet cloathing. Our Baggage arrived about 7 in the evening, all quite comfortable. They were taken care of and we all went to rest.

Next morning Jany. 16th we had orders to halt and wait that day for orders. This was verry good newse and was much needed amongst us, owing to us haveing for several days back had bad weather, heavy roads, and long Marches. This had in a great measure harrassed and partly cut up several of our bravest Men. However thank our good fortune this day's rest, and good warm soup, over a comfortable fire, set most of them on their legs again. We sent three to the hospital. Poor fellows, we are sorry to part with them but it cannot be avoided. (May they and numbers more live to return again to their Native land.) We hear great whispering round that the Austrians have crossed the Rhine into France and that the British have beseiged Bourdeaux. This is all working together for our good; we are sure if all we hear be true France must be in a tottering state and certainly must shortly have a fall. This decessive battle at Chaalons must decide it all.

January 16. Halting in the City of Vitry in a small Barracks entirely for lodging strangers that pass and repass. It is also supported by voluntary contribution, has old people to live and attend as Nurses cooks Vc. (a Noble institution). We had two good Meals pr day, plenty of fire and wholesome warm lodgings, which verry possible was the means of saveing many of our lives. Several of our men began to fail fast owing to the long Marches, bad roads, and continual wet cold weather, miserable lodgings, and Scanty poor rations, and what was a great disadvantage to us was some of our people had been laying upwards of ten years in the depot of Givet and during that period had little or no exercise, then drove as it were from town to town in front of a retreating Army, made our fatigued limbs unable to support our poor feeble bodies thro' every laborious day's work we have to encounter. Should we turn faint hearted and lurk by the way we know what would most certainly be our destiny. That was what the French Soldiers call 'quatre Sol,' the price of their ball and Cartridge, and those orders we knew had been given to all the troops on March but we may hope all our greatest sufferings are past. The Army has halted and we are daily Marching away out of their reach. It is true we are at this verry Moment in a City full of Soldiers but they have no concern with us.

In the evening our Commandant reviewed us in company with the Comissarie de Marine. He then informed us that we were to March in the Morning for Chaumont, and he with his men must return to Chaalons. This part of his story we were verry sorry to hear. He was so kind and attentive to see us well treated as far as it lay in his power, but we must do the best we can and strive to surmount every obstacle we meet with the reviveing hopes that a few days longer will put an end of this wandering unsettled way of regaining our dear purchased freedom.

January 17. A foggy, rainy Morning. At daylight we had hot Soup and at 8 o clock our Captain and an Officer of the Horse Muster'd us, the Captain of Horse took charge of us. Our former Captain spoke greatly in our favour to his brother

officer, he Made a low bow and retired. The General of the
City ordered us two carts and two Waggons to take up any of
our people that could not march. Our Guard of Invincibles,
twenty in number, being ready, off She goes.

We left Vitry and marched across the country to the Village
of St. Dizier, 21 Miles. Rain fell all day and Made the cross
roads horrid dirty and heavy. Our Guard were verry patient
feeling Men. They gave the men every chance to chuse their
footsteps, and made their horses take the worst of the road
or rather foot path. In this kind of Marching we at last reached
the Village of St. Dizier and were locked in a large Tower
formerly some Antient Nobleman's residence. We had a large
room to lodge in and the peasants brought us plenty of Straw,
and Wood, two verry welcome articles, and in a little while
our baggage arrived, then they brought us bread and milk,
Soup, potatoes, and some stewed Mutton, all verry good. We
had some invalides to do duty over us, verry good Men. They
passed the night inside the room with us out of the rain and
cold, and those that were inclined had a plentiful tuck out of
Brandy and Wine which the old Soldiers furnished them with
thro' the night. We got our Stockings pantaloons and even
our Shirts dry haveing plenty of fire all night. Some sat by the
fire all night singing Songs. As for Me I burried Myself in Straw
and slept all night.

January 18.   In the Morning our beugles gave us an invitation to prepare for another day's journey. The weather was
fine but the paths were wet and Muddy. We had two large
waggons to attend us and our Captain must have a tune at
leaveing St. Dizier which was readily granted and we struck
up the quick step in the battle of Marengo. This was the verry
thing that placed us in the highest esteem both by the Captain
and his men. They being all old veteran Soldiers were much
gratified with the complement we had conferred on them. At
the half way house the Captain made interest to get us a snack
of bread and cheese, also each man a dram. We halted an hour
and then started off to the tune of 'Paddy Carey,' the Old
Captain shakeing his sides with laughing when we explained
to him the Name of the tune and part of the words, where it
says:

his brawny shoulders four feet square
his cheeks like thumping red potatoes Vc.

The old captain after this was constantly repeating Poor
Paddy. Vc. This day we kept our baggage in front all the way
and in the evening by Sun set we reached the town of Joinville,
25 Miles from St. Dizier. In this place the Mayor was a great
enemy to the British, so that the good will of our Captain could
render us verry little service. We were put in a large Cashot
under the town's Gaol and in a little while we were served
boiled beans, and one thing I can say of it is a real factorum.
Jack Mclagan tore the top off his loaf and hove it against the
wall of the Dungeon where it stuck fast and there we left it
sticking for a Sign when we left the place in the morning! We
had a little dirty Straw, and with it and our own cloathing we
made out to pass the night tolerable warm and comfortable, no
thanks to Mr. Mayor. At daylight in the Morning the rattling
of keys and creaking of bolts and rusty hinges was our allarm
drum, and then the old Gaoler hoarsly grunted, 'All hands to
muster in the Court of the prison.' The Mayor and several
Gendarmes waited at the door, to take particular care of us,
lest any intruders should (like Paul Pry) pop in and run off with
some or perhaps the whole of us! We may all of us ever thank
those careful keepers for their unlimited care they took of us in
the ever to be esteemed town and Gaol of Joinville, also its
Mayer and Gaoler.

January 19. After being mustered in the court yard of the
prison and found that none of us had either sunk into the rock
or vanished thro' the iron barr'd air holes that shone like two
Stars thro' the vaulted roof of our sleeping room, or rather condemned cell, the place of deposit for Murderers, traitors, and
lice, we were counted through the large iron gate and then verry
carefully turned over to our former Captain and guard. Indeed
we were all of us verry happy to have our old friend once more
to rule over us. 'Come my Sons,' says the Captain. 'Revive us all
with Monsieur Paddy as we leave this depot of Misery. We have
provided three Waggons and they shall keep in front of us so
that those who wish can ride by turns and this I know will
greatly ease any man that feels unwell or any way fatigued.'

The Morning was fine, our Waggons and guard all ready. The Captain took the front of the band, drew his Sword, gave the word, and off we went to his favourite Air, 'Paddy Carey!'

From Joinville to Vignory was 18 Miles; this was only a flea bite! We reached the half way house in good time. The half way house was a blacksmith Shop where we all halted and the Capt. gave each man a dram. We played the old blacksmith and his family a tune. The good woman gave us a large kettle full of boiled potatoes and a bowl of Milk, which was verry kind. Those amongst us that had any Money bought bread butter cheese eggs and herrings so that we all made quite a good dinner. The soldiers gave their horses a small bait, then we again struck up a tune and bid adieu to the jolly old blacksmith. We then met a large reinforsement of horse and foot on their March to Chaalons. They retarded our progress greatly because we had to halt in a field by the wayside nearly two hours so that they might pass undisturbed. We got into the Village of Vignory about five in the evening. The Captain halted us at the entrance of the Village and then he addressed us as follows: 'My Sons, this is a small place and the people are good disposed Christians. The Mayor is a good man and an acquaintance, therefore I shall use my whole authority and interest in your favour. This is not the Mayor of Joinville!' We made our obedience and struck up his favourite Air, Marched up to the door of the Mayor and he appeared and salluted the Capt. They past a few words and we were ordered into a barn, where we soon had plenty of Straw and the peasants prepared some of them Soup, others brought bread, some brought Wine, and some brandy, so that we wanted for nothing they had to spare! In the evening the Capt., Mayor, and several more old gentlemen paid us a visit. They enquired if we had plenty to eat and drink Vc., which we undoubtedly answer'd in the affirmative with respect! The Capt. then said it was the desire of the Mayor and Gentlemen present that we would go into the Mayor's house and play a little while for amusement and to this we readily consented, and muster'd up our tools books Vc., in order to spend the evening. The Mayor also informed all hands that he would have something hot prepared for breakfast before we started in the Morning. We then went to the house where we were treated with every civility.

We had plenty of Wine brandy and cider, bread and Cheese or cold ham at our pleasure, and you may believe me we made that old Mansion tremble that night. We did not break up untill 4 o clock in the Morning; then they made us a field bed in the parlour where we took a short nap untill 8 in the Morning then we were called up to breakfast in the room where we slept. We had hot fricassee Soup and bread.

January 20. A hard frost. We all muster'd to the sound of our beugle, fresh, lively, and ready. We had two large Waggons started in front as before! The word was given to March and the music struck up, 'oer' the hills and farr away,' for the City of Chaumont 23 Miles. We had heard several whisperings amongst the gentry at the ball in Vignory that if our Captain did not look out the Austrian Army would reach Chaumont before we did! This we took as a romance amongst old Soldiers over a glass of Wine. Poor John Mclagan has said two or three times, thro' the course of the Morning, that he hopes the Germans or Cossaques may fall in with us and then perhaps he may get clear of the wearisome Marches that are daily killing him. We often advised him to ride but no! Jack had a heart that would sooner die than shrink. His word always has been that he is a man and never was afraid of any Man; therefore he should scorn to give up marching sooner than any other man.

At 1 P.M. we reached the half way house, halted half an hour, and got a little refreshment. We met the corresponding Gendarmes; they told our Captain that is was in vain to think of going to Chaumont. It would be running into the fire. They told our Captain that the troops had all left the city and marched towards Chaalons and left no other guard in the place than a few invalides, and by some means this newse had reached the vanguard of the Austrians with an account of the weak state this Strong garrison was left in. The Austrians immediately dispatched a division of the Army to take possession of the City and our Captain in his funny manner of discourse Made answer that his orders were to Chaumont and in spite of both Germans and Rusians he would endeavour to fulfill his commands; at least he would try verry hard to do it. 'Never mind, my Men,' says the Capt. to us. 'We have all seen both Germans and Rusians before now; they are only Men and

they know how to treat prisoners of War, particularily you that
are British and their allies! Therefore courage! We will always
hear them before we see them.' We struck up a lively air and
chearfully tript along; about 5 in the evening we entered the
Environs of Chaumont, Marched up to the grand Square and
there we were ordered by prefecture de la police to lodge for
that night in the Citadella and on the morrow they would make
fresh arrangements for us. Up we tramped to our castle, strongly
fortified but weakly inhabited. We lodged in the Barracks. The
Barrack master served us boil'd beans and a Morsel of salt pork
pr man. We had plenty of old straw and with what little wood
we collected round the citadella we rose a tolerable good fire.
Some went to their Irish feather bed and others sat by the fire
reflecting on the curious tales that has been passing all the day.
At last fire wood falling short, and fatigued limbs requireing
natural repose, nearly all hands were lulled in the arms of sleep,
when lo! What allarm! The thundering of Artillery outside the
city walls gave the unwelcome tidings that some strangers on a
visit wished to gain instant admittance into the city! Damn'd
rough visitor! We wished they had kept silence untill daylight,
when a hue and cry ran thro' our part of the old barracks commanding all the British prisoners of war to muster immediately;
then there was hurry skurry, Gendarmes sword in hand driveing
us out of the barracks. They never stopt to count us over, all were
drove out of the citadella at the point of the Sword. They drove
us up to the Gendarmes' horse barracks, where the Gendarmes
Mounted their horses and conducted us out at the West gate
of the city in order to shun the beseigeing army that lay on the
east side of the place. The night was dark and rainy and they
took us across the country over fields and commons, thro'
ploughed fields and broken ground, neither road nor foot path,
nor even light enough to chuse our steps if we had been allowed
time enough to pick our road, because those infernal horse
gendarmes, being well mounted, drove us before them, Sword
in hand, with now and then a horses breast against one or
anothers back followed with a heavey stroke across your back or
shoulders from the Sword of one of those cruel Monsters. . . .
In this inhumane manner they drove us untill daybreak presented to our view a small Village. All the time we heard the

continual roaring of the beseigeing cannon against Chaumont. We got into the Village where we were in hopes to have a little refreshment, but no! Not even a drink of Water. 'Marche buger Marche' was the cry of our tyranical conductors. The people in the place asked what meant that continual rumbling in the air and the old Dutch brigadier told them it was the guns in Chaumont rejoiceing for a Victory gained over the British Army at Bayonne. We got into a country road that led from the little Village we just left to the City of Bar where we were to stop that night. Bar is 27 miles from Chaumont and haveing no Waggon or Cart to help us thro' the fatigues and sufferings of this tortureing Night and day's march, several of our strongest Men began to fail and one in particular that I shall never forget, one of my verry intimate acquaintance while in Givet and on our journey, a brave, brave fellow, a MAN! This was the verry same man that yesterday said if the Rusians or Austrians did not release him the March would soon put a period to his troubles. We had left the Village nearly an hour when we came to a part of the road where on each side lay heaps of stones for the repairs of the roads. John Mclagan chanced to be near Me and kept dropping behind more than he commonly used to do. I in our free way of talk says to him, 'Come Jack, they wont keep us much longer, so cheer up your heart; you heard their guns and almost smelt their powder. Perhaps tonight we may see their faces.' In this manner we used to cheer up each other in Midst of our severest trials. Mclagan says to me, "Wetherell, it is not in my power to walk any further. I am chafed entirely raw and it is death to me every step I take so I will sit down on this heap of stones untill I recover a little.' I begged him to let William Crown and me take hold of his arms and help him along telling him it was only a few Miles more to the town and them savage Gendarmes would most likely beat and ill use him! But no. Every entreaty was in vain, he sat down, and we had to proceed on. We had not left him twenty yards, when up rides one of those butchers, sword in hand. 'Allez chean,' says he to poor Jack, at the same time gave him a heavy blow on the head with the flat of his sword. We all halted to look ... and Mclagan sprang from his seat presenting his naked bosom to his Murderer. The fiend of hell at that instant plunged his weapon in the unfortunate Mclagan's breast and laid him a lifeless corps on the high way. When the rest of the Gendarmes (they were mostly in the rear driveing us along) saw the bloodthirsty deed and we all halting they rode up to us full gallop, Sword in hand and told us that was only a beginning and the first Man that halted again should share the same fate. This was verry galling but what could we do in the Midst of a Squadron of horsemen all well armed, and equal in Number, and us a set of poor moveing Skeletons with no other weapon to defend ourselves that our tongue, and that was of verry little use in supplicating Mercy from a set of inhumane, bloodthirsty Monsters, in humane shape. In short we grinned and bore it, and at last we reached the City of Bar. They drove us up to the Munici-palatie where we were counted and cram'd into a dungeon under ground, with very little dirty straw to keep our wearied bodies from the cold wet stones that composed the bottom of the cell where we were lodged for the night. When we were alone then we had an oportunity to pass our various reflections on the strange overturns that one Night brings forth:

In the first instance we are routed from our confinement by our friends, at the same time they were not aware of us being there. If they had, no doubt we had been all demanded before one single gun had been levelled on the city, or had they had any idea of us being drove out of the place when they first arrived before its walls, one of their out pickets could have secured both us, and our cruel unmerciful bloodthirsty, inhumane, Savage, tyranical cowardly Guards, because experience has taught any Man who has been exposed to the ravages of War, that he is a real coward that will Slay a poor worn down Prisoner of War in cool blood, he not even offering any kind of resistance nor yet has he any means of defence. Let me see that Murderer placed before one of the Germans Hussars that were not far distant at the time; although he be cased in his Steel armour and his sword and pistols about him, his first attempt will be to try if horse flesh cannot make the Hussar run which he is most sure to do, but in what direction? Why, pursueing the Warrior that likes to try his skill in war over an innocent wore out unarmed prisoner of War, a Man that had been Shewn Mercy and quarters already by the Man who first made him Prisoner. That was a Man and Warrior, no cowardly villian that would inhumanely rush upon a vanquished being that was already in his power! Mclagan was captured by Jeromme Bonaparte's Squadron. He was quarter master on board the Hon. East india Company's Ship the Lord Nelson, on her passage from the Indies to England where they defended their ship with the greatest courage against a frigate and a ship of 80 guns untill the rest of the French squadron came up: then, overpower'd by numbers, they were compelled to surrender when nearly two thirds of their men lay dead on the decks. The Nelson Mounted 50 Guns and when she engaged the Squadron had 147 Men all told and when surrendered only 52 souls left alive. Mclagan was one of those Men worthy the title of Men. Haveing described the manner this unfortunate Man first became a captive I shall next hint on the treatment he found on board the Jumbar[1] of 80 Guns after being taken on board as a prisoner of War. The first sight was her decks were all floating with blood and Mangled bodies ocassioned by their determined resistance. Nevertheless the instant they were all on board they had wine bread and Cheese served to those that were able to take any, and those that were wounded were carefully taken down the sick bay and placed amongst the wounded men that had been wounded in the Action, where every possible attention was paid. They had the same attendance as the crew of the Jumbar. The Captain gave strict orders to every officer and man on board the Jumbar to treat the prisoners like Men as they had defended their Ship to the last moment with extroadinary bravery. They were now their captives and had given themselves up to the Mercy of their vanquishers; therefore he considered that the greatest honour that crown'd the head of a conqueror was to conquer and save, and those that were well were distributed amongst the Ship's crew, so many in each Mess, where they were treated like brothers, and no longer considered as Enemies. Those are the Men that I spoke of in the latter page that would have shrunk at the idea of killing a man in cool blood unarmed and wore out with fatigue. This account of the treatment that the

[1] This odd name shows how one Englishman will spell a French name as reported to him by another Englishman. The ship in question is the Jean Bart.

crew of the ship Lord Nelson received on board the French
Ship Jumbar I have heard several times related over by my
own Messmate William Crown. He was Armourer of the Nelson
and slightly wounded in the action.

When I reflect on this and then look at the barbarous Murder
of this brave fellow after being shewn Mercy by the verry Men
he a few Minuites before had been striveing to kill and they to
kill him; but at the moment they struck their ensign as a token
of craveing Mercy, they Mercy craved and Mercy found!
'Quickly Man all your Boats my boys, they are no longer our
foes.' This was the language of that Gallant pillar of France
who had the honour to Command his Majesties Ship the
Jumbar under the flag of Jeromme Bonaparte or rather under
his orders. Napoleon at this time was king in France. William
Crown and me sat most of the night repeating over such
circumstances as those already mentioned.

January 22.   The sound of the Gaoler's key gave us warning
that day had again broke its way thro' the east but not through
the huge rocks which surrounded our cell. The creaking of
the iron doors on their rusty hinges summon'd us forth to the
fresh air, there to answer our muster. Served us a loaf for every
three men, our day's ration, and would not allow us any
Waggon. The morning was rainy and cold; we had a fresh
guard of horse Granadiers and off we started for the Village of
Vendeouvre, only 15 Miles. Our bass drum was the most
troublesome baggage we had, yet we stuck to the old drum
and took our turns two and two to carry it along as we had
done the day before. We got along as well as could be expected
when we consider the Weather, the poor country road, and
worse than all a Surly proud disdainful old Flemish officer.
He was verry strict with us and would not suffer any of us to
leave the middle of the road. This we were no strangers to so
that we gave no cause of any displeasure to our Officer nor
guard. We reached Vendeouvre by two in the afternoon where
we were put in the guard room of the Gaol.

January 22.   In Vendeouvre in the Guardhouse Municipality
town hall Court house and place of safe deposit for Conscripts,
at times a dance house but this day converted into a depot for
prisoners of War, or rather a British barn where Gypsies hold

their nightly Meetings; however we were lodged in this large room within the walls of the Gaol; on the limits poor Jannet Carter was taken quite ill and the Mayor had her and her husband lodged in a room in the Gaoler's house. This good young woman has stood firm thro' all our hardships and always been the first to assist any of us that might be sick, or at different oportunities she has stood Interpreter on the road for the Sick Men in the Waggons. She verry seldom rode but would walk alongside the baggage. She was our trusty guard over any thing we left with the Waggons. Every Man in the division greatly respected her. The Mayor's wife hearing she was sick sent her some warm herb tea and other restoratives necessary for a woman sick with fatigue, and in the Morning she was quite smart again, which we were all glad to hear. That was the only woman we brought from Givet that any of us took any thought or care about.

I shall now turn back to ourselves and try to get something to kill that that surely would soon have killed us. The keeper of the prison had fricasee to sell made of liver, besides a horn of Brandy, but he was Mistaken in his Market because l'Argent was scarce, therefore he made a poor speck of his liver and lights. In the evening the Mayor visited us in our council chamber and he asked us if we had been served any rations. We told him no, but the kind Gaoler had offer'd us fricasee for sale. The Mayor shook his head and said something to a Brigadier of Gendarmes that was with him. The Mayor then asked us if we had got any clean straw; we told him no. Him and the Brigadier left us and presently in steps two men with a large tub full of boild horse beans and a little pork all made into Soup exceeding comfortable and verry acceptable. This was ready on our first entering the place, but the lousey thief of a Gaoler kept it back so that he might make his Market out of us, when we were hungry, with his liver, lights, red herrings, and other trash, such as butter, Cheese, bread, and eau de vie. We eat hearty of our bean Soup. Ah! Hunger is sweet sauce! and after supper the same Brigadier again returned; he took ten of our Men out and in a little while they came back with five large baskets full of good white bread which was divided a loaf to every two Men and one small flat cheese called

frumage de Marolle, verry good with bread. Thus the kind
Gentleman of a Mayor found means to sell us cheaper bread
and Cheese than the thief of a Gaoler. The Mayor entirely
under rated the Monopolizeing Merchant. The Mayor presented us the bread and Cheese as an act of charity; the
bloodsucking imposter sold his trash for the sake of filthy gain.
He kept our allowance of rations from us as long as possible
entirely with an intent to cause us when hungry to buy from
him. We then had a Waggon load of Straw to fetch in and this
finished our Night's adventure. We all went to rest quite
comfortable and after a few remarks on what curious overturns
we had experienced since we left Givet the story of poor J.
Mclagan closed our parliament in the Council Chamber untill
about four O clock in the Morning we were allarmed by the
drums through the town beating to Arms. 'Rouze, My Boys,'
cries Thos. Johnson one of our Men, a Merry Soul, 'Come my
lads, the Germans are haunting us again. Rise and let us clear
out of this. They want this place for their head quarters.' 'Go
to he . . l,' says one, with your newse.' 'Damn you and the
drums too. You wont let a fellow have a wink of Sleep!'
Mumbles out a third, 'God strengthen their Arms. I hope they
wont let us run out at the back door the same as they did at
Chaumont in the middle of the night.'

In a little while all hands were awake. We heard a continual
beating to arms. What can all this mean? No person seems to
interrupt us nor even to come near us. We listned all with
various conjectures till day began to peep in the eastern
windows of our castle. We at last heard footsteps approaching
our door. This proved to be William Carter who had been up
Stairs in the Gaoler's house all night with his wife. He told us
she was much better. Then he told us all the troops, gendarmes,
National guard, and every Man that could carry Arms were
all Marching away to the city of Troyes. An express had arrived
in the course of the night with orders to the Mayor that the
Austrians had taken Chaumont, and were on their March
towards Troyes and he must dispatch every Man that can
make use of arms immediately to the city of Troyes and that
our Guard had gone amongst the rest. Good, good, this was
a pleasant Mornings bitters. Well, let them go. We will follow

them and see that none skulks behind. 'Now boys,' says Jack Waddel, 'We shall have a chance to fall in with the boys that will send us home in short order!' 'Why, you damnd fool,' says Walter Jones, 'they will make you help to fight their great guns!' 'Damn their kindness,' says Charles Jones. 'To hell with them.' Some one opens the door and looks out. 'Whew!' says he. 'What a snow Storm!' And in he pops his head, shuts the door, and again crept into his burrow of warm Straw. 'Let us keep warm when we can,' says he, and down he lays. 'Well, shipmates,' says Carter, 'I will go in and see if Jannet want any thing. The drums are all gone; we no longer hear their warlike sound and the town seems all Silence. He is a good dog that barks when he is told. It is soon enough to rise when we are desired or when we are wanted.' About 8 O clock our friend the Mayor visited us in company with an old officer, an invalide who the Mayor informed us was going with us as a guide to the City of Troyes. We should have soup and soft bread to breakfast, then we should have as many Waggons as we required to help us thro' the Snow. He also recommended us to be cevil and act like men on our March and we would be respected and well treated where'er we went. We eat our breakfast and muster'd at the door. We had five Waggons; two of them we started a head and three in the rear to pick up lame ducks! The Mayor sent Jannet in a carriage after us.

JANUARY *23, 1814.* We left Vendeouvre for Troyes by the Main road, 32 Miles, and by the country road, which is not verry good, only 24 Miles. This we chose. Our waggons being started, the Old Gentleman gave a signal with a twirl of his cane, and to his great astonishment our two beugles struck up a favourite French beugle quick step and the two trumpets took the trumpet part. The old Gentleman halted and shook his sides with laughing, declareing he was never more agreeably Supprised in his life than he was at the present Moment. He was happy to hear that we had such good courage at the first onset in such a heavy Snow Storm. The Mayor sent a boy after the Captain (our Shepherd, as we stiled him); the boy brought him a horse to ride on but he sent the horse back, saying he rather wished to walk and keep in company with the men under his charge. We got along wonderfully. The wind was mostly in the rear so that it helped us along thro' the Snow. The road mostly was clear of Snow as it laid quite above the level of the land on each side, and no fences to stop the wind from blowing all the snow off the road, and as for cold we kept warm with bodily exercise.

About 2 in the Afternoon we came to an old Castle which must have been once in its Splendour the residence of some August family. At present it was the residence of a number of old invalid Soldiers and their families where they lived retired and quite happy. They kept a tavern in one Wing of the building. On our first turning the corner that leads up to the gate of this assylum our Captain smileing said we would allarm the garrison. He desired our beugles would sound a Charge, and we all full of Mischief our beugles readily obey'd! Then believe me if a man had but half life in him he would have laughed then, to see the old fellows hoppling out at the hall door neck over heels with intent to protect their Castle, some of them only one arm, others with wooden legs, then a blind man with his staff of defence, followed by a cripple with his crutches ready for action. Each individual showed fully determined to protect their comfortable habitation. The Captain advanced up to the gate and saluted the person at the bar. He then informed the tavern keeper what we were and the gate was hove open. We were all kindly invited to go in and take share of their little stock which was at that verry time hot and good. What they termed their little Stock was some of their Stock Pork and bean Soup smoaking hot! This was verry wholesome just at that verry Moment. Our Captain took a part in the repast and after that a kan of good wine was handed round. Jannet Carter was taken away by the women and had something comfortable made for her in quick order. We now found we had 9 miles farther to go and it had abated snowing. Our baggage horses had eat their mouthful and it was three O clock, therefore we were determined to please our Jovial friendly old Warriors. We mustered our band privately behind the wall and as soon as the Captain thought of moveing we had a big drum and all ready, and as they wished us a good bye the band struck up 'Mal-Brouk,' a well known French air. The old lads stood some time as in a trance. At last they gave us three cheers and wished us a bonne Voyage. We then placed our drum and instruments in the Waggon again and off we trudged all healthy and Merry! In a little while we saw the lofty towers and steeples of Troyes raiseing their Majestic heads above the white extensive plain that surrounds them. The sight of the towers in our intended port gave us fresh courage and we then put the best leg foremost to try and gain the harbour with daylight, which we did. When within about three miles of the Walls of Troyes we saw numbers of tents and temporary buildings in all directions on the plain round the outside of the walls and centeniels within hail of each other in every direction. When we advanced nearer the lines we were met by a large picket guard and as we were considerably dispersed along the road the officer of the guard desired us to halt, it being his positive orders not to let a Mortal pass untill they gave a satisfactory answer what they were Vc. At this Moment our old Captain came waddleing along. 'What!' says he. 'Have you got some of my Men Prisoners?' With those words he presented our Felle [*feuille*] de Route to the Officer of the Guard! 'There, sir,' says the Capt. 'That will pass my men to the gates of Paris,' and when the officer was satisfied what we were and from whence we came he ordered us to pass. He also sent a Serjeant along with us to the City gates which were Shut. We soon were admitted in thro' the gates.

January 23. We arrived in the City of Troyes and we halted in the Faubourg untill we all had got gathered together, our baggage included; we then were Marched up to the Grand Place. There we got billets to be lodged and victualed on the inhabitants. Verry happy tidings; this was certainly a healing balsam to many of us. The good people of Troyes will never be forgot as long as one of our division draws breath. They nursed us the same as their own relatives, neither spareing time nor trouble to get every thing they thought would nourish us and restore us all to our natural cheerful Spirits. The city was full of troops but they were mostly all quarter'd in the Citadella in barracks and in the Subberbs. After we had got warmed and began to feel good our host, a fine Gentleman who kept two large bakehouses, sat down and called the three of us to take a glass of wine along with him and give him a small idea of our Captivity Vc. We sat down and accompanied our kind host untill we were all called to Supper which was exceeding good. We eat and drank! What more could we require? Well I will tell you. We wanted rest, and that we soon found, good and comfortable. I forgot to mention that when our old Captain served out our billets he requested us to meet in the same Square tomorrow morning at 9 O Clock for further orders. In the Morning we had a good breakfast, then went over to the Square, were Muster'd by the Commissarie de la Ville and Monsieur le Mayor, la Commandant de la place and we then were order'd to our last night's billets as the gentlemen wished us to halt so that we might take some rest and nourishment for a day or two. This was again glorious tidings. Why, it appears almost too good. However we have latterly experienced severe hardships enough, therefore our fortune has taken a contrary turn. We went back to our billets every one praiseing their good treatment. Our orders were Muster toMorrow morning at 9 in the Square. We sent 7 of the sick to the hospital, which is quite moderate after such severe fatigue and sufferings. Our host was happy to see us return. He told the girl to fetch up some Wine and some bread and cheese to take our eleven O clock and sit down by the fire.

January 24. Halting day and very cold. We kept close quarters all day, laid snug in a good harbour where we repaired damages, recruited our Men, Sent our Sick to the hospital, took on board what provisions Wine we could conveniently stow away and made our shatter'd hulks all in readiness for the first fair wind or the first orders from our Commander in Chief.

Our landlord the Baker informs us that the most of the inhabitants would desert the city and leave their all, their houses homes and all they are possessed of in the whole world to fall into the hands of the Austrians. They have left Chaumont and are on the road for this City. 'But why should we leave the home we have to go look for another we know not where? As for me and my family we will stick to our. home untill we are drove away by force. Numbers have shut up their houses and suspended business, terrified out of their senses at the thoughts of the Enemy. They want to abandon the place of Nativity but the orders are proclaimed by the General and Mayor this Morning that not one Soul of the inhabitants shall be allowed to pass the gate of Troyes under its present expectations of a Siege.' The Mayor also advises every person to proceed as usual with their different occupations, as he was well convinced the Austrians were far from distressing the inhabitants of any place. Where e'er they had been they only wanted the command of the Garrison forts and Magazines belonging to the present government of France. This was the most part of the Mayor's proclamation; not one word of defence! Indeed that would be folly and madness. With only troops enough to relieve the posts round the city what could they pretend to do or attempt, offering to stop the advance or even refuse the admittance into the City of an invadeing Army? 'Let them come,' says the Baker. 'I will give them what bread I have to spare and then bake more.' 'This is my creed,' says the baker (takeing a suck of Wine), 'Let who will be ruler of the roast, I must be baker.' We drank round, had a good laugh, and went down to dinner. We had a grand dinner and plenty to drink, which brought on evening. We had several remarks on the wonderful progress the Rusians were makeing; also the British army were Victorious in the South.

Our discourse soon brought bed time. Our host being extroadinary partial to Cogniac and water, I thought perhaps it arose from the dry spark that frequently prevails amongst bakers! However the old lad was quite Merry and was quite hot to hear a Song in our English language before we parted. This was granted and William Crown favoured the Company with Bonaparte's parley with John Bull. After the Song we interpreted the heads of it to the baker and his family. This caused great laughter thro the house and his family. This also brought another round of old Cogniac. One of the Young Men, a baker, favoured us with a voluntary French Song, and this closed the evening. The host was pretty well so, and we had quite plenty, so that we all found bed the best place. made our obedience to the family and crept to our warm nests where we slept till day light shone bright thro' the windows. We rose in order to March away this Morning. Certainly we got a good hot breakfast, then buckled on our knapsacks, took leave of our generous benefactor and family, thanked him for his kind treatment and departed! The old man hollowed after us beseeching us if ever we came that way again to Make our home at the Bakehouse in Troyes.

We all assembled in the Square, were mustered by the Mayor Comissarie, General, and our old Shepherd. They found us all present; the Comissarie then informed us that our Felle de Route mentions four in particular that had been writing in the Bureau at Givet. Those four he wished to see. Accordingly we four were presented to his highness, William Crown, Tho. Johnson, William Aplen, and me; his honour informed us that we all must remain in Troyes this day, and tomorrow morning we were to March to the village of Aix [Aix-en-Othe];

that we should have four Waggons for our accomodations, and
he requested two of the four interpreters to start quite early in
the morning with a passport that he would have ready for them.
This they must present to the Mayor of Aix in order to prepare
billets for the division when they arrived and then the Mayor of
Aix will sign the passport and the other two interpreters can take
their early turn to the next place—only be sure that two remain
with this Gentleman who has verry kindly volunteered his service
to conduct you to the City of Sens as your guide and protector.
We then were dismissed untill 8 tomorrow morning.

January 25. Halted again in Troyes, every man ordered
to return to their former billet and 4 Interpreters to meet at
the Municipalitie at 4 in the afternoon, to get the passport. We
went to the good old father of a baker, who was sitting in his
parlour when we passed his window. He saw us and up he rose,
ran to the door and verry friendly shook hands with us.
'Welcome, Welcome. my Sons. Come in to my house and be
seated.' We followed him in, told him we had one day more to
stop with him. 'Thank god,' said he! 'A little rest will be of
infinite benefit to you all! Catherine,' says the good Man,
'fetch us a cruise of wine and a luncheon of bread and cheese.
Then Make ready a good dinner for my Children.' In fine, we
eat, drank, and Sung untill ten in the evening, except, about
half an hour, when we went to the city hall to obtain our passport. The old man told us he had two sons in the Army, but
had no tidings of them lately; one of them was in Spain last
newse he heard from him, and the other was in the Army of
the north. 'Perhaps,' says the old father, 'they may have been
captured, and may fall into the hands of some humane
Chrisitian that may feel for my poor Boys the same tenderness
I feel for You.' Thus we passed the evening discourseing on the
serious overturn that was likely to take place in France. At last
we felt inclined to take some repose. The old man gave the girl
orders to rise early and prepare some hot breakfast for us in
the Morning before we Marched away. As for William Crown
and Wetherell we had to take the first Morning's early start
for the Village of Aix. We therefore appointed 4 in the Morning
should be the fixed hour for the two that had the turn that day
to go ahead and obtain billets ready for the party when they

arrived. Thus we made our arrangements, the other two Interpreters to remain with the guide and the party so that if any thing strange should take place on the road they would be at hand to speak for any of their comerades should it be required. We all retired to rest for the night where we slept untill 4 in the morning, when to our astonishment the old Gentleman brought us a light, roused Crown and me, telling us that it was Just 4 O clock and the girl had made some hot Coffee. We rose and took our Morning—that was a stiff horn of Cogniac mixed in a bowl of Strong coffee, hot bread, and a hunk of Pellona. That was our Morning's bitters before we left the hospitable Mansion. We left our host with something more than a natural adieu. He shook hands and bid us farewell, wishing his blessings Might restore us safe home to our native Country in health and prosperity. Thus we parted and left him.

January 26. A fine clear frosty morning we passed the gates of Troyes by produceing our passport and there we had a Corporal of the Guard to conduct us to the outer pickets Vc. . . . William Crown observed to me that if we should chance to meet any of the British, Rusian, or German scout parties we must immediately deliver up ourselves to them to remain under their protection. Thus we passed our conjectures as we tripped along untill daylight placed us in the midst of a small village ten Miles from Troyes. We halted here nearly half an hour, then proceeded on our journey and at ten in the forenoon we reached Aix, found the Mayor and presented our Passport to his honour. He perused it over then gave orders to his Secretary to make out the billets for the party immediately in order to have them ready when the Men arrived. As for Crown and myself, the Mayor took us up to his own house and treated us verry politely. In a short time the billets were ready and we took them, went to the entrance of the place where we waited a few minuites. Then we heard our well known beugle sound: 'Fall in!' There was a hill outside the Village which hid them from our Sight. At the Sound of the Beugles and three thundering blows on the big drum, the Villagers flocked round us, all eager to know what was the meaning of all those sounds they had just heard like Martial Music. We smileing told them that a division of British were falling in on the other side of the hill

and would be in Aix directly. Then we had a grin to our own
cheeks when up the hill they marched with the Old Captain
and the band in front, the peasants all standing thunderstruck
as they descended the hill. We addressed the Captain and
presented him the billets. 'Let us proceed,' says the Capt., 'to
the door of the Mayor, so that they may all have a fair chance
to hear what I delight in—Martial Music.' We marched up to
the Mayor's door with a lively French quick step then halted,
and distributed the Men to their respective billets, Jannet
Carter and her husband were taken to the house of a rich lady
where they were well provided for. Tho. Johnson and William
Aplen, also the Captain, all joined us at the Mayor's table.
We eat a good dinner, took a look round the place amongst our
comerades untill night warned every Man to your tents all
Israel! We past the evening quite comfortable, slept in good
beds at night, and gave Henry Alms a hint in the evening that
if they might sound the beugles at Sun rise we would start early
in the morning and get through our day's March in good time.
Aplen and Johnson took their turn at 4 in the Morning. At 7
our beugles gave warning and at 8 we marched with 4 Waggons
in front for the little compact Village of Villenetive [Villeneuve-
sur-Yonne], only 15 Miles. Our band led the Van and although
the weather was verry cold we counted this day's Journey only
a Morning's recreation. We reached the place at noon where
we had a large warm barn for our depot. We deposited our
knapsacks there, then we took a look round the place. Some
that had money purchased victuals in the taverns and others
not overstocked with rhino returned to the depot where they
unexpected were provided with plenty of good soup bread and
meat all hot and ready for their use. The Captain visited us in
our humble habitation to see that we were all satisfied. He told
us that the village was so small we would not have been half
so comfortable at billets as we were in our present habitation.
There was plenty of wood so we kept a roaring fire at one end
of the Chatteau, and we had oceans of Straw to roll amongst.
The poor people also brought us blankets to cover us through
the dreadful cold night as they termed it, but our men all slept
warm and happy. Crown and Me went with Aplen and
Johnson to the tavern to sleep, but we should have fared better

in the company of all our Country men rolled in Straw. For my part I was glad when 4 O clock struck so that I might warm myself with walking which we actually did.

At 7 in the morning we reached a toll bar and a draw bridge with a tavern blacksmith shop. Here we took breakfast and a good dram. Small rain beginning to fall made the roads rather heavy. We rested a while took a draw of the pipe and we took another twist of eau de vie and then mounted shank-naggy and away we went through thick and thin, stopped for nothing (because we had nothing to stop for) untill we ran close on board the city of Sens, 17 miles from Villenetive. We then made our first enquirey where to find the Municipalitie, then we were introduced to the Mayor and the Comissarie general. They looked at our passport, pronounced it good, Signed it, and gave the clerk orders to fill up billets for 343 Men and one woman. (I have neglected to mention the other 6 women that we brought from Givet in my former pages.) We left 2 in Mezieres not verry well and 4 in the city of Rheims to follow us as soon as they were able. . . . We got our own billet which proved to be at the house of a Priest. We went to the Mansion of the holy father in order to wait the arrival of our party. The good old gentleman ordered us plenty of victuals and good Champaign to wash it down. He said he felt sorry for us poor unfortunate young men that had laid so many years confined not even allowed the happy sight of a line from your unhappy parents who perhaps may have entirely given up all hopes of ever seeing you again. 'This present circumstance, My dear Children, is a clear proof to you that we should always have our Anchor fixed on hope, because at the verry last hour there still is hope, and my present hopes are that the Lord may see fit to restore you and all captives safe to your aged parents, your friends, and your Country in Peace to rest your heads at the last moments in the Arms or on the bosoms of those that are near and dear to you. May peace and reconciliation spread their banners o'er the universe and all the inhabitants of the Earth join in one sacred Song of Praise to the great Architecture of the Universe. This, my children, is my wish and earnest desire towards you and all unfortunate captives.' By this time we thought our people would be drawing near the City. We informed our kind host what our business was and took our leave for the present. When we reached the gates of the City we saw no signs of our comerades so we went into a guard house and stood talking with the old gentlemen that kept the gate. In a little while we heard Mount Meg (a name we gave our big drum). They passed the gates and Marched up to the Square, served billets, and conducted 5 of our Men from the baggage waggon to the hospital, an elegant place for them under the superintendance of Sisters or Nuns. We then returned to our fatherly old gentleman's habitation where we were tenderly and kindly treated. The old lady gave each of us a clean Shirt and told the Servant to shew us our room that we might change our linnen. We did all that with pleasure and the servant took our foul linen away. We then were invited to supper, eat a good Supper and after a fatherly blessing went to our comfortable place of repose.

We arose quite early in the morning with intent to March, took some hot breakfast, and got orders to halt that day in Sens, to remain at our former billets. Johnson and Aplen were informed the night before by the Mayor that we should halt one day to refresh our men, therefore they both laid fast in their beds laughing at us. However we passed the day quite comfortable and happy. We had a fine pleasant day which gave us oportunity to walk all round the City. Night at last summoned all Israel to their tents. We partook of our kind host's well provided Supper and after his usual blessings all repaired to our comfortable lodgings. Good night. In the morning Johnson and Aplen started early. We took breakfast and a good hunk of bread and ham in our pouch for the half way house, took leave of our charritable Christian, and away we jogged to the old tune of 'Monsieur de Moulin.' The morning was dull and rainy. Our Old Captain left us and we had two invalid Soldiers, fine old men, as guides. We had two waggons and two carts, and the distance from Sens to Ferrieres is only 15 miles, so that our day's work was soon over. Our two Interpreters Met us at the end of the Village with billets, which were soon distributed and every Man soon found Shelter from the rain. In Ferrieres we found good quarters and plenty, had all our cloathes dried and all quite comfortable and ready for March, and in the morning, being the 30th of January, fine and clear weather, we mustered to the Sound of our well known beugles. We had three Waggons and our two Guides all ready. The Beugle Sounded and away we started for the town of Courtenay, 17 Miles. We then went on ahead of the party and found we had the billets ready in Courtenay equally as well as to start so early, on a cold winters Morning. We therefore after this all left together in the Morning (two men will March a great deal Swifter than a large party). However we drew Billets and met the party on the entrance into the town, marched up to the Hall, served out billets, and discharged our baggage Waggons by 2 PM., got our papers Signed by the Mayor, and had 4 Carts ordered to be in the square at 8 in the Morning, our usual hour to March.

January 31. We left Courtenay, verry cold, and marched to that miserable lousey hole, Montargis, only 15 miles. We counted that only a morning's recreation. On the road we were Passed with Several large Carriages[1] guarded by horse Gendarmes driving in full speed. However on our reaching the town our orders were to take up our quarters in the Gaol as there was some great Personage in the town and the Mayor could not attend us. 'Who the devil can it be,' Says Crown, 'that we must be neglected?' We took possession of this Public hotel and those who had a franc or two in their Pocket were the best provided for. The old rascal of a Gaoler took his oportunity to make hay while the Sun shone. He charged for a bed 1 franc, Supper of fried liver 1 franc, a seven Sol loaf 1 franc, and for a six sol Measure of brandy 1 franc. 'Why, you damn'd old rascal,' says Jack Waddel, 'do you think we are all francs? No Sir! My name you shall know is Jack Waddel and to hell with you and your francs.' At this time our two guides came in and told us the towns people were fetching us bread and Soup or what thay had ready prepared for us to eat. This was a sad disappointment to Mr. Gaoler after all his frankness. He had bought up most of the spare bread in the place, also all the liver and offal to make us a franc feast, but we were so frank, we

---

[1] These carriages contained the Empress Marie Louise, her little son the King of Rome, and their suites, sent from Paris to the Loire to escape capture by the Allies.

kept our francs, and left him verry frankly to try some other method to gain our francs. We also wrote on the Wall (with Charcoal), 'We are not franks but true blooded Johns!' This we wrote large in English and left Belshazzar to send for a Daniel to interpret the writeing on the Wall. Our guides sent us plenty of Straw and the people gave us plenty to eat, and as for drink we could do without. The Mayor Signed our Papers ready for the morning.

February 1. We were not permitted to leave our hotel untill the Company had left the place in their eight Coaches and four horses to each, also two guards to each of the coaches. All we can learn or make out is that they are some characters worth more care than we are. At 9 we were at liberty to proceed. The morning was fine and we had four carts for our Baggage. We left the place with no other Music than a solitary tap on the big drum. This day's march was only 14 Miles. We arrived in the small village of Loreux [Lorris] quite early, drew billets, and were all quite comfortable. We passed the remainder of the day Amongst the Peasants and the Mayor signed our route. Thus we finished the day.

February 2. Weather frosty. We had 3 carts and all Marched together for the City of Chateauneuf, 13 Miles. We reached the place by noon, got our Billets, and spent the remainder of the day looking round this Antient residence and place that gives the title to the Prince of Newcastle or la Prince du Neufchateau![1] Got our pass signed and 4 carts to be ready in the morning.

February 3. Fine weather. We left Chateauneuf for the City of Orleans. Part of this day's March was through the Forrest of Orleans where the people in a small Mill by the road side informed us that they heard this morning by some gendarmes of a body of Cossaques having been seen by several people to enter the forrest yesterday evening, and this we took as a hoax on the poor Miller and his family by the Gendarmes. However we heard afterwards that a party of Cossaques on

---

[1] Wetherell makes a mistake here. The Prince of Neuchâtel (Berthier, Napoleon's famous chief of staff) derived his title from the Neuchâtel which is now in Switzerland—at that time it was a small independent state ruled nominally, until the time of its cession, by the King of Prussia.

that same night plunder'd the Miller's house and Mill, took his Cattle and hogs and what they could not conveniently take with them they destroy'd. They cut the ham strings of two oxen and one horse, ripped open several Sacks of flour and grain, took what they wanted, and left the remainder on the road by the house, set fire to the Mill and disappeared! At that time we must have passed not far distant from Jackey.

We pursued our rout for Orleans and being an ugly cross country road we did not get along verry quick and the distance being 25 Miles caused us to be rather later than usual when we got to the City. We arrived and Marched up to the City hall where we had good warm lodgings ready to go into. This was a Convent and every care possible was given to us by the kind Sisters that had the Superintendance of this Charitable assylum. We had several sick Men in the baggage carts. Those were taken to the Hospital with the greatest care and attention. We had the liberty of the City and were as comfortable as kings. Our orders were to halt next day and take a little nourishment so that we might be better able to reach Blois.

February 5.   We halted and were happy to meet 17 of our old Prison Mates belonging to the other divisions that left Givet before us. They had been left sick in the different hospitals on their March and haveing recovered strength were sent to Orleans in order to join the first Prisoners of War that passed that rout. We learnt by them that they all took a quite different rout from Vitry that we had taken. The seven first divisions were sent to Nancy and Luneville and they also informed us that many of our fellow sufferrers had dropt off in the different hospitals on their March from Givet. We have left in hospitals on our road to this City 21 Sick and 1 Murdered; that leaves 342 arrived in Orleans and those 19 men that has joined us Makes our Number for billets 361 Men and 1 Woman. . . . In this city we enjoyed all the pleasure our hearts could require in our then present circumstances. We had plenty of good victuals, comfortable beds, and each man a new Shirt, Shoes and Stockings. We also were paid up our arrears of Marching Money from leaving Troyes to the present date which amounted to the enormous Sum of 77 Sols pr Man, at that time to us a good round sum! The Comissarie General also appointed another Interpreter to have 5 in case of one being taken ill or unable to attend his duty. He also fixed their daily Pay at 30 Sols each interpreter pr day, so that he might find himself on the way independent of any billets. This Passport was addressed to the Mayor of every town and City where we might have orders to from Paris to lodge or halt in according to the various routes we might be obliged to take at this critical serious instant. Our Passport was delivered to us in the Municipalitie of Orleans Signed by the Prefecture, the Comissarie General, Mayor, Vc., of the City of Orleans, department le Loiret. This ceremony haveing past our next visit was to the Bridge where we saw Jean d'Arc trampling the Soldiers under her feet. We then visited the grand Museum of France where we saw a splendid variety of Curiosities. We also saw le duc. de. Montebello bleeding on the field and the Emperor weeping over him Vc. In the Evening we had an invitation to the Theatre. We went and were verry much gratified with the Music and the performance. We then returned to our Mansion and took share with the rest of our companions in part of a good night's repose. In the morning we all arose and partook of a good breakfast, Milk thickned with flour, and good bread wash'd down with each man a jill of good wine. We had 4 carts and two waggons to help us on our journey after the Mayor had given us his friendly admonition to leave all National politicks entirely on one side, to be cevil Obedient and honest, to fulfille our stations and maintain our character as Prisoners of War. Then let what overturns in France you are likely to find daily be what they will; you will always be protected and respected as prisoners of War. This, my Sons, is my advice to you all! Farewell. We made our obedience to his honour, our Band struck up a lively air, and off we went baggage and all.

February 6. We left Orleans for Beaugency, 21 Miles. The Morning was Mild with a light fall of Snow and at 3 in the Afternoon we were in the Village of Beaugency where our appointed abode was an old Church fitted up entirely for troops or any body of passengers that stopped there during the night. It was on the same principals as our lodgins in Orleans. We wanted for nothing to eat or drink had good field beds. The

Mayor Signed our Papers and appointed 6 carts to be in readiness next morning by 8 O clock.

February 7.   We took our breakfast, started our baggage on before us, then we marched off to the tune 'Paddy Carey' towards the City of Blois, 27 Miles from Beaugency. The weather fine and good road made the March quite light; we halted nearly on hour at a large Castle[1] ten miles from Blois where the English Kings in former days used to reside while on their hunting parties round the borders of the forrest of Orleans. The present duke of Blois was then living there retired from the Court and present administration of Napoleon. We halted at this Antient Structure where we were requested to eat and drink the health of a friend and well wisher to the British, not to mention any names. We had a lunch of Bread and Cheese and several large cruises of wine were handed round by the domestics of the duke untill all had been served. We then Muster'd our band, and play'd 'dull care.' The Duke having been some time in England in his younger days spoke good English and was greatly elevated on hearing his favourite Air. We then struck up 'lee rizs' ['Le Riz'] and away we went. We reached the environs of Blois, before Sun set, where we were met by several British Officers, and amongst them Mr. Pridham, our first lieutenant on board the Hussar. They directed us up to the City hall, where we were directed to a large building called the hotel for strangers; there we lodged our Baggage Vc; being evening we had not an oportunity to have any discourse with our Officers. We therefore attended on the Mayor and had our papers signed; he also gave orders that we should halt next day in order to receive some distributions that was to be served us according to our need of them. We has a good Supper and went to our welcome repose.

February 8, 1814.   Next Morning we all arose in good spirits knowing, in the first instance, that we had a day to rest our

---

[1] This is the Château of Chambord. At this time it was owned by the Marshal Berthier mentioned in the preceding note. Who the 'Duke of Blois' was, with whom Wetherell had converse, it is hard to say. My own guess is that it was none other than Napoleon's brother Joseph, who undoubtedly was somewhere in the neighbourhood, and who, after his abdication of his usurped throne, could well be described as living 'retired from the court' even though he had been given charge of Marie Louise.

wearied bodies and nourish ourselves by the side of a good fire, Secondly we knew the Mayor was going to serve us cloathes, Shoes, Vc., and thirdly we were given to understand last evening by our Officers that they had orders to assist us on our March thro' Blois. By Sun rise Mr. Pridham, Mr. Leftwidge, Mr. Reynolds, Doctor Lawmont, and My friend Mr. Smithson all visited us. They were happy to see us and verry desireous to see all the Hussars we had in our party. We all musterd and made out eleven of the old Ship's crew. We gave them a list of all the Hussars that were left alive when we left Givet, which only Amounted to 95. . . . Mr. Pridham shed tears when he heard so many of that gallant crew had fallen beneath death's fatal sting within the fatal walls of Givet. He then told us that he wanted us all to be present at 2 in the Afternoon as he wanted to see us, his shipmates, in particular, and at 4 he wanted all the rest of the party. They enquired if we were well provided for in our present quarters. We told them we had plenty and good. At ten the Mayor visited us, paid up our arreas, and served each man a pair of woolen Pantaloons, stockings, and Shirt and he then told us we should halt again tomorrow in consequence of the British Officers having to make some arrangements in our favour. We had five of our Men taken with the Ague and they went to the hospital where they would be well taken care of. My Interpreter's business being partly done for a little while, Mr. Smithson, my friend, visited us. He wanted me a little while if I could make convenient to leave My Partners. 'Yes, Sir,' says Crown, 'I will answer for him should he be wanted before he return.' I have neglected to Mention the name of the fifth Interpreter that was appointed by the Prefecture of Orleans. His name was Andrew Smith my young friend and Pupil. I went along with Smithson and took Andrew along with me. We went to a tavern, took a bottle of Wine, and had a great many old stories. He told me how Capt. Alexander shot my old friend lieut. Barker and he also told me that the allied Armies were before Paris, and that the British Army under Wellington were at Burdeaux. Smithson said we might daily expect orders for Morlaix, St Maloes, or some part of the Sea coast to embark for England. He also said Louis was embarking in England to embrace the crown of

France (Louis dix huit). All those tidings we kept privately lock'd up in the secret coffers of our hearts.

The hour of two drawing on, we took our steps towards the camp of our countrymen. We met Crown, Aplen, and Johnson in the street. This caused us to take a small horn. I gave them a hint of what Mr. Smithson had revealed to me, and had we not been required to Meet Mr. Pridham at two O clock, we should have washed that horn down with a second and perhaps a third, on the strength of our welcome tidings, but our time at this moment must be put to a different use. Mr. Pridham and Several Officers passed the door taking the road to our habitation. We followed at a little distance and all met at the Mansion appointed. Pridham desired the Hussars Men to stand together and then addressed the rest of our Men. 'Fellow country men! At 4 O clock I shall be here again and give you what assistance our present funds will allow to help you thro' your toilsome journey, which I have great reason to believe is near an end! God send it May!' We all went down to the British agent's office where each man signed his name and received five French crowns in part of his wages for the Hussar, and one louis d'or per man from Lloyd's coffee house which we also signed for. Mr. Pridham informed us that we were all ordered to Tours to wait there for fresh orders, and they had contrived means to have us all taken down the river Loire to Tours in boats at the rate of two livres per Man, the distance being 39 Miles by the Main road. We then returned to the camp as they had to serve each man a louis d'or. My stars how wonderful rich we all are! Plenty of Money, plenty of cloaths, plenty of victuals, and plenty of rest. All we want is plenty of freedom in our own Native land which we hope will verry soon be our happy fate. We mustered our Band in the evening on the green in centre of the square, where we had all the officers and principal people in the city arround us. We play'd several favourite airs, French and English. Young girls and boys were hopping around the square like as many poppets. The British Officers were verry much gratified to see us so friendly used by the Citizens of Blois. When we left Givet we had 7 new heads in our baggage for our Bass drum, and it happned that Evening, Jack the drummer being a little lively, made rather free with

his 'logger head' as he used to Name his large stick. He drove
in the last head he had left and this put an end to our evening
diversion. Mr. Pridham talked some time with us after we left
off Playing. He was verry happy to find we had devoted our
time in Prison to learning. He was desireous to know in what
manner we first rose money to purchase so many fine Instruments and how we gained our instructions Vc., Vc. When we
told him how we purchased our instruments he smileing said.
'Well you are worthy the title of Musicians, you that can fill
your bellies with Music and sell your rations to purchase
instruments! However in the morning I shall make enquirey
after some new heads for your drum and tambourine.' We
enquired if any of our people had passed thro' Blois lately;
he said three divisions from Givet had passed thro' Blois, since
they had been sent there to inspect the prisoners that passed
through the City on their March towards Tours, where all
the British Prisoners from the North were order'd to Meet and
wait fresh orders. I enquired how many of the Hussar's crew
had passed. He said he believed about 27 but if I called at the
Bureau in the morning I should have all their names and what
day they left Givet Vc. We then took our leave and away to
our tents where we slept without rocking all night, and haveing
got permission from the Mayor to halt another day, and then
Make two days' stages in one, by going down the Loire to
Tours in boats we would fill our regular stages as specified on
our felle de route from Orleans. On this account we took our
time to rise in the Morning.

February 9. A fine hard clear day. We visited our sick
comrades in the Hospital. They really looked like other men;
they looked clean, lively, and contented, and they said that
place was a heaven on Earth, it was enough to bring a dead man
to life. In short they were all on the road to recovery. We told
them to make haste after us to Tours, where we were to lay
some time, shook hands, and parted. We then went to the
Bureau and got a list of the Hussar's crew that had passed Blois.
Mr. Pridham sent Mr. Sutton the Midshipman to our encamp-
ment in search of Jack Leversedge the drummer. Jack was soon
at his side and he went to the Bureau where they furnished him
with half a dozen new heads, an Apron, and a Pair of new

gloves, with a Crown to drink the health of the Merchant that presented the heads to us. He was a leather dealer in Blois, verry partial to the British. We got our drum rigged again and that evening we gave them a real round turn after dark. The young women began to muster, and the British Officers haveing after so many years confinement in France become quite fameliar with the French mode of Waltzing joined in with those lovely creatures that were left (as in other parts of France) without one single young man to join them in their simple exercise of Waltzing. We play'd untill 12 at midnight, then broke up the ball and all Israel to their tents. We went to our Mansion and soon were lulled to sweet repose, where all care was entirely forgot, and the business of the day was left untill we saw the light of another day or sun rise next Morning.

February 10, 1814. Fine warm clear weather. This morning we were all bustle prepareing for our grand expedition down the Loire. Mr. Pridham had already engaged 20 boats to carry from 18 to 20 men each at the rate of 2 francs each man from Blois down the river to Tours. Our detachment at this time amounted to 356 Men and our only young Nurse Jannet Carter. She stuck true to us! Never was seen nor even heard in the greatest of our sufferings, to murmer or in the least to reflect on her rash step she took in marrying a Prisoner of War. She was beloved by every one and often would drive away Melancholy reflections from any of us that appeared to be low in Spirits. At 9 A.M. we embarked. The key or quay was crowded with People and our officers were all present. We embarked the band in the two first Boats, to lead the van. All hands embarked. We gave three cheers, which was answer'd from the shore. Our Band Struck up 'O'er the hills and farr away.' We had a fine breeze down the river and the strong current in our favour soon wafted us out of the sight of friendly spectators. We had a fine passage down the Loire. Had it been in the Summer season the beautiful villas and seats on the banks of this large river must have presented to us a beautiful romantic landscape. . . .

February 10. At 4 P.M. we arrived at the large quay, near the bridge in Tours where we met numbers of our countrymen ready to direct us to the Citadella, where the Secretary of the

Mayor attended in the Bureau. William Crown and Johnson went to the Bureau and presented our felle de route. They returned with orders to proceed to the citadella where they would find barracks all ready for us. We discharged the Boats and proceeded up to the dwelling appointed and placed 20 in each room. In this place we had the happiness to meet many of our Shipmates, Prison Mates, and Countrymen flocking round us, all happy to have the Band join them again. We found our Seventh division had been in Tours ten days. They were taken a quite different rout to that we took, from Vitry. They had left a great many brave fellows in the different hospitals on their rout. They mentioned several of the first divisions that left Givet had [word missing] thro' fatigue and perished with cold in the Miserable cold cashots where they were drove for security thro' the night. All those sufferings we were no strangers to; dear experience had made them known to us. We had every thing comfortable, both victuals and lodgings, also liberty in the City from 8 in the morning till 8 in in the evening. The draw Bridges were drawn up all round the City at gunfire, 8 O clock, and opened in the morning at 8. We sent 12 men to the Hospital, none of them seriously ill, but fatigued, and severe colds were most of their ailments. This reduced our party to 344 Men. On the third day after our arrival we were joined by a detachment from Bitche consisting partly of those men that were sent there from the different depots in France for Punishment, desertion and being taken again. Amongst them were many of our old companions in Givet, and Particularly their Interpreter, no other Person than Robert Smith my old messmate and Andrew's brother, and with him his wife the late Madam Gammant. Young Andrew was happy to meet his brother. Madam Smith was also verry glad to see us both in good health and Spirits. The Bitche division were 273 strong. Their route was from the city of Chateauroux to the city of Angers, in Maine et Loire, so that they only halted with us one day, got some refreshment and proceeded their March towards Angers, that evening being the 14th of February, Valentine's day! And my day! The Mayor sent for the Interpreters of the 8th division Prisoners of War British from Givet to Tours. The five of us attended his worship the Mayor at the

Bureau where he presented us our felle de rout for the city of
Richelieu to march on the succeeding day; also three other
detachments were ordered to the towns of Chinon, L'Isle
Bouchard, and Loudun, all in the same direction with Richelieu. We warned our party and on the following Morning we
had two carts and after being Muster'd by the Comissarie de
Marine, Mayor, Vc., we Marched from Tours on the 15th of
Feb., 344 men, for the Village of Axay [Azay-le-Rideau], 18
miles. The cross roads were frozen hard so that we soon performed this day's journey. We had a large room in the town hall
to lodge in and seven Sols pr Man paid us by the Mayor to find
our own rations. This village afforded plenty of Bread Milk
cheese eggs, also excellent cider. This suited us. We had plenty
of Straw allowed for those who chose to sleep in the camp and
those who chose to hire lodgings had beds at 6 sols each man.

February 16. Fine weather. The Mayor had two carts prepared for us. He signed our rout and we took our departure
for Chinon, 17 miles, which was only makeing game of us. By
the time our joints got limber we were in Chinon, drew billets,
and all quartered safe by two in the Afternoon. Next Morning
we met and the Mayor had three carts ready. He signed our
rout and we have made a general rule that where the Mayor
acts like a gentleman and gives us billets, we always give them
a tune on leaveing the place. We therefore Mustered to the
call of our beugles.

February 17. We travailed to L'Isle Bouchard, only 14 miles.
Our band in front by turns did play 'March on my boys make
no delay.'

At 12 noon we landed on the Island. The river Vienne runs
on each side of this curious little town. Rain began to fall
shortly after our arriveing. We drew billets for 344 men, served
them round, and all took shelter from the storm. In this place
we lived on fish, a rare treat. The people were remarkable
clever liberal folks. They kept us employed relateing old Sea-
fareing adventures in which they greatly delighted. They
reckoned themselves partly sailors as they lived by fishing
although they had never seen the Sea Shore perhaps in their life
time. We had plenty of Wine at 3 sols pr bottle and other things
cheap in proportion. We slept well that night and on the 18th

of February we had 4 carts and Marched early the Morning. Being fine we gave them a tune and took the Woods leading to Richelieu.

February 18, 1814. At 3 in the afternoon we arrived in Richelieu about half an hour before the party reached the gates, William Crown, Andrew, and your humble Servant. We went to the Mayor in the Municipalitie, presented our felle de rout. He looked at it and smiling said to some of the Gentlemen sitting at the desk, 'We are going to be honoured with a party of foreign visitors. They intend to stop some little time with us. They are near the gates at this present time and request our advice to find them lodgings. Those three Gentlemen are their interpreters. What must we do in this case? Shall I give them billets or what do you prefer or wish me to do?' 'What Nation are they?' says an elderly Gentleman. 'British Prisoners of War,' answered the Mayor. 'How many of them are comeing to visit Richelieu?' says Monsieur. 'The Felle de rout says 344 Men and one woman,' answered the Mayor. 'Well then, let us divide them amongst us and our friends through the City. As for me I should like to have 8 or ten,' says Monsieur. 'Well,' says the Mayor, 'I should like to have the like number,' and a third Gentleman says, 'If you begin to take so many you will not leave any for those that are not present! Numbers of our friends that perhaps might have a desire to share their generosity with that of their fellow citizens on poor captive prisoners of war will be disappointed. Therefore my advise is to let them all march up to the square; then we can divide them thro' the city to those that are able to use them like Men and Brothers!' As he finished his decision, we heard three strokes of the big Drum. . . . 'Hallo! What is that?' says the Mayor in amazement. 'That, Sir, is our big Drum, warning us that our party are at the gates of your city' was our reply to the Mayor. 'Go, go quick,' says the Mayor, 'and conduct your brothers up to the Square.' We were leaveing the room when old Monsieur says to us, 'Please to favour the citizens of Richelieu with your Music on entering our small but humane city.' We made a bow and parted and went to the gate, the Mayor in company with us. Our Men were all ready; we gave the signal and in one moment the streets of Richelieu were throng'd with astonished spectators. Our band had a grand effect in the street. We made the Windows and doors all rattle, at every stroke on the big Drum. The air was a trumpet tune, with a trumpet Solo, which had a grand effect. We then changed to a French Rondeau with a beugle solo; this was grand! The Mayor and several gentlemen Marching in front, we got into the Square, halted, and then we were surrounded with gentlemen. Some took 8, some 6, others 4, and so on, untill the square was entirely clear of our folks. As for us five interpreters we were taken to the house of the Mayor's Brother, at the Prefecture of the city, named Monsieur Blanchard, a fine young Gentlemen, and a great Musician. We had clean stockings and slippers first thing, and then the Servant conducted us to a large room where we left our knapsacks, and instruments. We then were invited to take some refreshment. After a while we walked out to see the place. We found Leversedge, and Henry Conolly our octave flute player, Frederick Taylor the band Master and Henry Alms the first trumpeter, were all at the Mayor's house. In fine, we soon found all our comerades well taken care of. The whole of our Men all declared that this place ought to be called Paradise, and no longer have the name of Richelieu. Aplen said if it was possible for happiness to be found on earth that was the place!

FEBRUARY *19, 1814.* Richelieu. Rain and cold in the Morning. We all kept close quarters this day, repairing damages. On the 20th, fine weather, we began like snails to creep out of our nests and look round our city of Paradise. We also visited the Antient castle of the renowned Cardinal Richelieu. Four of our men were sick and went to the hospital. Many of our people were so contented that they kept close quarters to their houses, and as for Jannet and her husband they were at the house of Monsieur Beaumont, a verry rich respectable Gentleman, where the old lady treated Jannet the same as her own daughter. In the afternoon Monsieur Blanchard would have us sit down and give him some information, how we were captured and how we were used in France, Vc. We had wine, cakes, and fruit in abundance. We gave him the outlines of the loss of the Hussar, our sufferings in the Boats, and we also gave him a sketch of our March from Brest, our Sufferings in Givet upwards of ten years, our March from Givet in front of the Army, and several trials we have gone thro' to our arrival in Richelieu. Those heads or outlines were the subject of his discourse whenever we sat down on an afternoon or evening, which gave him great satisfaction to understand the whole of our Narative. In the evening he brought out an elegant Clarinet to hear what we thought of it. Crown took it and play'd 'Monsieur de moulin' in style. He looked and smileing said, 'If I mistake not Sir, you play on the horn when you arrived in Richelieu.' Crown told him he play'd any Instrument that he fell in with occasionly. He then took the Clarinet and play'd a Waltz verry Masterly. He desired us to muster our Instruments and try out one of our tunes. He should like to accompany us which he did and in a short time he could run over our Music quite correct, and Made his large front room the Band room and invited all our Musicians to Meet there every afternoon and rehearse. We had ten or twelve Gentlemen belonging the city Joined us, and attended regular every afternoon. Our host Mr. Blanchard kept the decanter always ready to wet the Instruments; in fact we had far too much wine. One or the other continually were haveing us at their houses. The Mayor and several other Gentlemen requested us to play a little while every evening (when the weather was fine) in the grand Square. This greatly amused the inhabitants. They Made it their business every evening to meet in the square and pass an hour in Mirth and friendship. We became so far acquainted with the young ladies that we gave them a ball every Sunday evening on the green outside the gates. We were also invited to play in the Theatre and we had our fishing, shooting, and all sorts of simple Amusement with the gentlemen of the city. We got so habituated to them that we could go out to the field or the Vineyard as regular as any old farmers and assist in what ever was doing. The word would be, 'Where are you going tomorrow?' and the Answer, 'To our farm or our Vineyard to work.' What ever was the property of our host was ours. Monsieur Blanchard would say to us, 'My children, we will visit our farm, or our Vineyard tomorrow.'

This was the manner we amused ourselves daily. We constantly found some diversion or exercise so that the time passed away like a dream. We have even gone over to Isle Bouchard on visits to our countrymen that were quartered there. We also heard various reports such as the Rusians were at Paris, the Germans at Fontainbleu, the Prusians at St Dennis and the British at Bordeaux, but we left them to settle all disputes. We gave up the notion of troubleing our heads with National Politicks and diverted that part of our leisure hours in the lovely company of our female companions, where we found more comfort in the tender tales of love in one evening, yes, more than we could, or had found, in ten years debateing on Politicks. Mr. and Mrs. Blanchard called us their Children and treated us the same. We were counted as their own family in regard to washing, victuals, or any thing that was to be done in or out of the house. We had three of our Men went into the hospital during our stay and four on our arrival. One of them named Henry Stevens, formerly of the Lord Nelson Indiaman, died, and we burried him with all the honours our circumstances would afford. We had no other Misfortunes worth relating; all was friendship and harmony with us in Richelieu.

The Month of February stole away. March crept along unnoticed, except on a Saturday afternoon we used to go out to the brooks and pick watercresse. This warned us that Spring was hasteing towards us with rappid speed. We used to say that when Spring came we would do this thing, and when Summer came we would do the other thing, but no more of that building castles in the air; the scene is changed. Preparations are makeing to restore us to our own Nation, but by a long tedious round about turn. Such strange overturns took place in the administration that our happiness began to tremble. The shatter'd government contrived a plan. In order to keep us from falling into the hands of any invading Enemies they gave orders to have all the British Prisoners of War in France Marched with all speed to the south clear of all the allied armies. The Mayor got some hint of this but not any particular account nor yet any orders in Particular. In the latter end of March, Monsieur Blanchard, at the Prefecture, our generous land lord (or supporter) desired us to write him the Music of some favourite English pieces that he had taken a great fancy to. At the same time he observed he was rather suspicious that the Minister of War was inclined to drive all the unfortunate prisoners of War into some remote place of security, to prevent their falling into the power of the Enemies of France, and we amongst the rest would be tore from our friends and well wishers to wander and suffer every sort of hardships that some tyranical, inhumane rulers art verry apt to inflict, on a poor unfortunate prisoner of War. And afterwards boast of their brave exploits when o'er their cups, thinking it does them great honour to say, 'I have had my Satisfaction out of such a Nation, I made their prisoners remember me, when I had them under my jurisdiction Vc. I took my revenge out of them, by confinement, starvation, beating them, defrauding them of their rations, and confineing them in the cells of a dungeon, to sleep on the bare ground without any straw or covering.' Perhaps he can boast that he ran one or two of those poor unarmed captives thro' with his own hand or gave orders to some of his followers to shoot that damn'd Englishman if he dont march quick Vc! or keep the middle of the road, or keep his place, or something to find a reason for their barbarity. This is the treatment that has been, and I am afraid will again be given to prisoners of War when under the tyranical government of such inhumane unfeeling Monsters!

This was the character that this worthy Gentleman gave of his own country-men. He observed he was sorry to have such a character to give his own Nation, but all those acts of cruelty and oppression that he had just mentioned he heard his own dear Father say, that he in the time of the tyrant Robespierre was a Soldier in the army and had seen all those acts of tyranical cruelty put in execution both on French men prisoners and also other Nations that fell beneath his displeasure. 'However,' continued Monsieur Blanchard, 'we will not point this out to be so, only it has been so. I hope and pray your fortune may be quite reverse to what we have conjectured. It is the humble request of all the Citizens in this our small city that you may remain with us untill some arrangements are made to restore you all home to those that are near, and dear to you. Therefore hope for the best, keep up your spirits, and like Men undertake and perform the Second part of your long fatigueing pilgrimage. Come, my Sons, take a glass of cogniac. Then we will have a tune and drive all care away.' We play'd a while and then took our evening's walk, each to their choice, some to see their heart's delights, others to join in a song, or a dance. I shaped my course to the Mansion of Pierre Collordo the Vintner. That was my usual retreat; on any evening there was a loadstone under his roof that had verry great attraction over me, and frequently caused me to make Night, day, and day, Night. I told the old gentleman what was the apprehensions of Monsieur Blanchard, but the old gentleman would not hear a word of our leaveing Richelieu untill the orders were for us to March to the sea coast in full express to embark for our native country. On the 28th of March three of our men came out of the hospital, quite smart.

On the 30th of March the ladies gave a grand ball. This ball was in the city hall, and our band was invited to attend and take parts in the Music in concert with the violins. They had some verry grand performers on that Instrument, all of them gentlemen of the city. The house was verry much crowded and the evening was passed in friendship and good order. The gentlemen that frequently played along with us would come and relieve one or the other of us so that we all had an oportunity to take a few round turns round the room with our little loadstones that had been all invited to attend, and when the Gentry and their ladies had danced then the Master of the ceremonies called the young men and young women to fall in and go round with a dance. We had a variety of dainties both to eat and drink and kept up the sport untill past two in the Morning, when we closed the ball with an English hornpipe danced by young Andrew Smith. We left our Instruments in the Orchestra untill next morning, and all retired home to rest.

On the following Morning, March 31, we mustered and collected our instruments, went thro' our rehearsal in the Theatre, then to the Music room in our house (as we then termed the house of our host Mr. Blanchard). When our band were all present, French and English, playing some of the favourite marches Rondeaus or Waltzs the city of Richelieu would echo from corner to corner. Our band consisted of 24 Men and we mostly had from twelve to twenty French, mostly performers on the Clarinette and horn. We now consider'd our selves in perfect paradise! But stop! Look to the first of April. What fools! The sudden change that this fools' day made with the young girls that had been danceing to our Music the night before. They were heard in various parts of the city performing Music of their own composition which had an entire different effect on both the hearer, and the performer. The Solos were pensive and solemn. The Chorus or forte parts were like the dead march in 'Saul,' and those active limbs that had so gracefully beat time to the music were seen trembling beneath the heavy load of grief. Even those enchanting eyes that had been an illumination to the room where they shone were like stars shrouded in a cloud which turns into rain. Those bright orbs were also shrouded with sadness and bathed in tears, and that Member of the body that expresses the Sentiments of the heart and by the least turn can give ease or pain, joy or grief, was by this sudden stroke of unexpected seperation entirely for some time deprived of its usual utterance, only able to vent its grief by sobbing, sighing, and inward lamentations. This was the effect this grievous first day of April had amongst the young females in this blessed assylum for the unfortunate Captives, that had the fortunate change from hunger and cruelties, into the hands of good humane friendly affectionate Christians.

I shall endeavour to explain the cause of this sudden revolution that took place amongst us in Richelieu on April fool day. William Crown and Myself were bussyly employed in the Music room writeing out a book of Marches from various selections that we had collected in Givet, which we intended for Monsieur Blanchard, when we heard a noise in the street, looked out at the window, and saw a horse Gendarme in great haste, ride up to the Municipalitie. We left our music, being jealous that this Messenger bore some orders concerning the Prisoners of War. Numbers like ourselves crowded round the square, both citizens and prisoners, all desireous to hear what hasty tidings this Messenger bore to Richelieu! We were however soon given to understand his Mission. The Mayor sent for the British Interpreters; we answer'd his call. He desired us to let our Beugles call all our Men to muster immediately; he also said the Messenger was the bearer of dispatches from the Comissarie General in Tours, Signed by Orders of his highness Monsieur le duc de Feltre, Minister of War in Paris, to March all the Prisoners of War under his orders in Richelieu from that place on the third of April. That he had also received a felle de rout of every day's stage we had to Make from Richelieu to Orillac on the borders of the Pyrennees, ready to fill up with our names. He therefore desired all the men to Muster in the square and give them timely notice. We immediately went to our trumpeters; they took their Beugles and sounded the old call to muster. That was the time, and that the verry cause of the sudden change that took place amongst the young girls, and, I Must tell the truth, many of our own young countrymen. However all hands were mustered and warned to make themselves in readiness to leave Richelieu on the third of the month. This caused a great bustle with all those who thought to fulfill the scripture, by leaving tomorrow to provide for itself. Many were sorry to leave their only comfort behind, but the orders are given and we must obey. We went home and found Mr. Blanchard, his Wife, and his aged Father, all quite down cast at the newse of our haveing to leave them and March such a long distance entirely from the sea shore. Madam Blanchard provided each of us with a new Shirt, new Stockings, and Shoes. Mr. Blanchard made each of us a present of a Jacket and Pantaloons and the Old Father presented us each a louis d'Or to help us on our journey. On the 2nd of April in the Morning we made a general Muster to see that all the names were correct in the new felle de rout, or, in English, the list of the towns we had to pass thro' and the day of the Month we had to sleep in each town, also to have our rout signed by the Mayors of such certain places on such particular dates, and that we are to victualed and lodged on the Inhabitants of the towns appointed on our route to sleep in. The next thing we had to know what was to be done with our six men in the hospital. We visited them and found them all willing to join us as they were quite smart. We have lost one Man by the fever and ague which leaves us at present including the 6 in the hospital 343 Men on the list and one female. We have lived in paradise upwards of 6 weeks where we have become robust healthy looking men and make a quite different appearance to that we made the day we arrived. In the evening I visited my happy retreat and passed part of the Night in the charming embraces of one that proved faithful and true, as will be found in the following numbers. I took a little rest towards morning and then arose in order to attend my business in leaving Richelieu at 8 in the Morning as proposed the night before. We had 4 waggons and two cover'd Carts to attend us to Loudun, 17 Miles. The Morning was very heavy rain which made the March quite unpleasant, yet we got all ready to start and were detained some time in the

square by our friends and well wishers pouring their blessings
and good wishes on us.

Shakeing hands, embracing, taking a farewell glance across
the square at the lovely beauty that waves her handkerchief
for the last time and retires leaning on the assisting arm of an
elder sister. At that moment we gave the Signal, and our large
drum Made the Square echo with three thundering strokes.
Mr. Blanchard, and the Mayor, and the Old father's last
request of me was to be sure and write on the first opportunity.
They bowed their heads and drew back. Our band then
struck up the French farewell quick-step, 'Farewell Sweet
Maid'! And away we Marched crowded on both sides of our
friends, one carrying our knapsack, another with a bottle of
kill grief. All this time the rain fell in torrents. Nevertheless we
had both good inside and outside lineing to defend us from the
severity of the weather. We got clear of the city by ten O Clock,
kept slowly pursueing our journey, and by twelve we had
nearly parted with all our company. We secured our drum in
the cart appointed for the band and thus proceeded along.

April 3. Marched from Richelieu for Loudun where we
arrived about 4 P.M., still raining. We had sent Andrew Smith
and Aplen in front to prepare billets for the Party. They had
our billets all ready when we arrived so that we soon all
found Shelter from the rain. We were verry kindly treated by
the inhabitants. Several of them had frequently visited our
happy residence on business. The Mayor was a kind old
Gentleman where we, the five Interpreters, lodged. He was a
great friend of our protector Mr. Blanchard in Richelieu. We
were in discourse concerning our next day's March and,
looking over our felle de Route, our next day's March was to
Argenton [Argenton-Château], in the departement of Deux
Sevres, 19 Miles. The Mayor was signing our Route when a
rap came at the hall door. The door was answered and found
the visitor to be a courier from Tours with orders from the
Comissarie to alter our route from Richelieu to Chatellerault
and Poitiers on the Main road to Niort. This caused us to
return back to Richelieu next day. For my own part I should
rather have proceeded our route to Argenton than to have
another parting with Richelieu. Still at the same time there

was a sort of wavering in my unsettled mind that almost
caused me to think I should like to have one more glance at
my greatest treasure. Morning came; still rain falling inces-
santly, but the idea of returning home drowned and oercame
every obstacle either in regard of rain or roads with the greatest
part of our company. We had the same Waggons and Carts
back again. We took breakfast and then left the town of
Loudon April 4th. At 3 P.M. we entered the Western gates of
Richelieu. We dispersed as quick as the Mayor could reach
us, every Man to his former home! We five were welcomely
received by our worthy Benefactor, had our linen changed,
took a little refreshment, then took two of our men to the
hospital. They had taken severe colds thro' being wet the two
days following; we then had a long talk with Monsieur Blanchard. He said he was certain that our confinement in France
would not be long, owing to the tottering state the country
was placed in at this present Moment, entirely thro' Ambition. He said France was entirely overrun by her Enemies and
their determination was to reinstate the Bourbons on the
throne of France, Louis the 18th. 'Therefore make the best
shift you possibly can a little while longer; a few more weeks
will restore you all to your Native country. Therefore, my
Children, bear your hardships a little longer with manly
courage and you will find my words verrified, then you will
remember that those were the predictions of your old father
Pierre Blanchard.' We then began to make a move to our
seperate parts of the city where we had to enjoy the pleasure of
one more evening's company with those that made our Captivity the happiest part of our lives. As for my Part I visited
my Old Father the Vintner. He always saluted me. He was
very happy to see me returned once more to his house and the
sound of a favourite voice soon was answered from the room
above with the enchanting words of 'Father, is that my dear.'
The Old gentleman kindly answers, 'Yes, my Child. Come
down and make him welcome and happy and drive away
your Melancholy sadness. Be cheerful and let us pass one
more happy evening together in the same manner that we
have passed numbers before.' There certainly was something
whispered in each fluttering heart that whisper'd, 'We will

never be parted.' We were at last aroused from a lovely trance by the Oldest Sister entering the room. 'There, Louisa,' said the Father, 'I have the happiness to see Mary once more roused from her Melancholy dream.' Louisa was verry happy to have the pleasure of saluteing her favourite Lincolnshire hero, and once more the house of sadness was by chance transformed into the abode of Momentary gladness and chearful smileing faces once more enlivened the aged spirits of the Affectionate Father, Pierre Collardo.

We sat, loveing and beloved, repeating our little tales concerning our various changes thro' life and the old father was at last inclined to go to his bed. He wished us all a good night and shakeing the hand of his young English Son says, 'Ah, my Child, would to God you were a Christian. You should not leave my Daughter in Richelieu to Mourn your absence and never more to behold your presence.' 'Father,' answered Louisa, 'John is a good Christian.' 'Yes Father,' says Mary, 'he is no heretic like the other English men. We can soon instruct him in our mode of worship.' 'Ah, my child, the laws and rules of our Church will not grant you permission to stray beyond the bounds of your holy Church by joineing hands with any Man unless he be baptised in the faith of our holy Virgin.' He then retired to his bed.

Mary smileing says, 'Well, Louisa, you are much older than me. Can you advise me what is the best course to take, because I am convinced that I cannot live if my dear boy must be tore from my Arms never more to enjoy his lovely presence?' 'I can tell you, Sister,' says Louisa, 'what my advice is. Take part of your cloaths in a handkerchief and I will assist you to leave Richelieu early in the Morning. Take the road to Chatellereault and boldly venture to try your fortune with the only man you adore.' 'What say you Brother?' says Louisa. 'Wont that be the best way Mary can do?' My answer might easy be known, it was sure to be, 'Yes, and we will be married the verry first oportunity. We cannot be separated. Yesterday I suffered more than my tongue can express, and if I have again to part with my lovely Mary I might as well part with my life, because death is far preferable to a life of Misery and woe. I will protect her by Night and by day. I will travail by her side and make the fatigues of March slide softly away by my presence and affectionate conduct.' 'Yes, my dear,' says Mary. 'I will take the advice of my Sister, and trust myself under your loveing protection. We will enter into the World together and when that happy day does arrive that you are restored to your Native country I shall also be restored to you. Your happiness will be mine, your parents will be mine and you shall be mine untill separated by death, our fortune shall be the same.' 'Sister,' says Louisa, 'let us begin to prepare your articles most required on a journey. Father is fast asleep, therefore we have nothing to fear, and we must leave this house before daylight so that the neighbours may have no suspicious thoughts.' Being all prepared for our elopement the clock struck five, Louisa and Mary both took their bundles and as old Father never rose early they were not under any apprehension that he would find out our departure untill we were some miles from Richelieu.

When we left the house Mary and her Sister passed out at the North gate and walked round to the road that leads to Chatellereault where they were to join us at the half way house, and our hero took the road to his lodgings to prepare himself for the bold stroke for a Wife. Crown rose on my entering the room and we awoke our other three partners. I informed them that we had a frosty Morning to start this time from our homes, therefore we would be better able to perform our day's work of 23 Miles than we had been to perform yesterday's that was only 17. Daylight began to make its appearance thro the windows so we got our traps all ready and in a little while Henry Alms saluted us with the old Mornings bitters on his beugle which said, 'Rise and march away.' We left our noble Benefactor's dwelling, haveing before observed that we would not disturb the family again to take our leave; once was enough.

April 5. Being all present in the square we counted over and made 341 Men all included and 2 left sick in the hospital made the old complement 343. We now waited for his honour the Mayor to see the Men counted over and to Sign and Make a little alteration in our Felle de Route. He soon was with us and in a little while was satisfied with the number of

Men, went to the Bureau corrected our papers and with our
6 Carriages in front we again took our last farewell of that
heavenly abode of humanity Charity and true Christianity.
Our band Played up a fresh quick step called 'My honour calls
me from thee,' and for the last time passed the gates of Richelieu. We were again crowded with our friends and acquaintance. Several of our boys had heavy heads all this day's
march; our day's march being 23 miles caused our company
to part with us soon so that we might proceed on our journey.
They gave us three Cheers at parting, which we answered
with three times three and three rolls of the big drum: we
then marched on all in good spirits and William Crown,
Andrew Smith, and his honour . . . went ahead as usual to
have the billets ready for the party on their arrival. The
ground was hard and we let no grass grow under our feet.
They had no idea that I was in chase of a beautiful French
frigate, but believe me every corner we passed and every
movement I saw on the road I thought was the prize I looked
after. We reached a small Village 12 miles from Richelieu;
we called at a tavern and took a Mouthful of bread and cheese,
a bottle of Wine and off we tramped. We had many little
rigs on each other on account of the girls in Richelieu. Crown
was resolved in his mind that if peace took place and he was
released he would shape his course direct for Richelieu (which
he realy performed). Aplen said (as we heard at Chatel-
lerealt) that the three of us had gone back to Richelieu after
our Girls. However they found the contrary on their arrival in
Chatellereault, because Crown and Andrew met them with
the billets. For my part I went in search of my only treasure,
and not more than two minutes after I left them with a pretence to find out what sort of a billet we had allotted us I
heard a tap at a window, looked round and there stood the
two young adventurers. I rushed into the house perhaps a
little bewilder'd. However they told me I never spoke untill I
had taken a bite at each of their faces. We then sat down and
discoursed a little while Mary told me she had taken a cart at
the half way Village; her bundle was too heavy for her and
her Sister, and they gave 5 francs for a Carriage; that was the
reason we could not fall in with them on the road. Louisa says,

'Brother, where do you sleep to night?' I answer'd, 'At my billet most likely.' 'Well,' she said, 'that will be best. This lady of the house has promised Mary and me lodgings for the night and I shall want to see you early in the Morning as I am going back with the same carriage we came in.' 'Why, Sister,' says Mary, 'Father will be sure you have been with me.' 'Yes, I shall tell him I have been striveing to take you back, but finding my entreaties were all in vain, I was under the necessity of returning without you, and by that time you will be far distant from Richelieu. You know what I did when I married Francois. Father would not hear a word of my leaving home to travail with my darling husband, to join the Army in Germany but all his talk was mere folly. I mounted the baggage and like a brave Amazonian followed my heart's delight in troubles. I comforted him in sickness, I lulled his poor aching head in my bosom, and on that unfortunate day he fell at the battle of Wagram I bathed his dear bleeding wounds with my tears. And then I for the first time felt what it was to be robbed of my heart's delight, I returned home with the wounded or at least I came with the waggons to Strasbourg and then travailed home to my father. Mother was no more. Father had only you, My dear Mary, left to comfort him; you were then young and found the loss of our dear Mother. I returned to my Father and he was happy to see his lost Louisa return, and he oftimes has said he believed nothing except Death could prevent a woman from following the Man she has placed her affections upon. This, my dear Brother and Sister, is the reason of my trying every effort to have you both made happy. I have seen and am fully convinced that you dearly love each other, and with my consent you shall never more be parted. God bless you both,' kissing us while the tears ran plenteously over her downcast cheeks; poor Louisa Francois. . . .

We were in a neat little Parlour. I called the lady of the house to know if she would provide dinner or supper which we may please to name it. She said, 'Certainly, with pleasure.' I called for two glasses of Ratafia for the ladies and a horn of Cogniac to my own cheek. Then I went to our billet which was near at hand and found all my Messmates at dinner.

'Where the Devil have you been?' says Johnson. 'We thought you were in Richelieu by this time,' says Aplen! 'Ah,' says Crown, 'I rather think he has been looking out for another sweetheart on purpose to kill the thoughts of his Mary in Richelieu in the Wine house.' We had our jokes all pass in friendship. I made an excuse that I fell in with a man that was a Soldier sick in the hospital at Givet the same time that I was nurse in the 4th Ward and that he was a tanner and lived in the environs of the City Vc. This proves that a lover is never without an excuse. I sat down and took a glass and made excuse as to eating, because I had promised to take supper with my particular friend, the tanner (but that friend was Mary). Supper being over we then went to the Mayor after our papers and to hear the orders for Morning, how many Waggons Vc. Our next day's march was to Poitiers, 25 Mile, and to have 4 carts. We got our papers and returned to our lodgings where I left them in order to fulfill my engagement to sup with a particular friend. I was soon in the Arms of that particular friend. Supper being ready we sat down and enjoyed it with comfort. I repeated over their different joaks and my story of the tanner which made a hearty laugh and kept us cheerful all the evening after Supper. Mary begged her sister to excuse her a few minuites as she wanted to speak to me. . . . We went into the yard and my lovely Girl gave me a small locket containing ten Louis'd'or.

'This locket and its contents, my dear John, was presented to me by my poor Mother on her death bed and I present it to you as a sure pledge of my love and faithfulness towards you. From this Moment I willingly leave myself entirely under your protection. I give myself up to your advice and directions as to what you may imagine for both our welfare and by this embrace! I will never leave you nor forsake you in whatever situation you may be placed, but will in trouble be your comforter and in sickness I will heal you with tenderness and affection, and should we live to reach your native land your Mother I will love as my own, your friends shall be mine and when death calls us to leave this world and fly to the realms of bliss may we go hand in hand, loveing and beloved.' My reply was verry easy made and easy signed and sealed with the impression of her sweet ruby lips, and one moment of silence lock'd in each other's arms signed our definitive treaty for life!! We then returned to Sister Louisa; she was uneasy at our long absence, but we told here what was our real business. She rose and embraced us both, saying she was now contented and could return home with pleasure being fully convinced of our regard for each other.

The evening was farr advanced and I must repair to my billet and take some rest so as to be ready to start early in the Morning for Poitiers; therefore it was propper for me to provide conveyance for my sweet Girl to Poitiers. She proposed to walk! 'No, no! That wont do. I will find a Carriage in a little while.' I called the man of the house and told him I wanted a Carriage in the Morning to take that Lady to Poitiers. His answer was that his horse and light covered Waggon was at liberty. If that would do we could have that, and his boy to drive, for the sum of ten francs. I sealed the bargain and was quite contented. I then addressed Louisa, desireing to know how I might address my letters to her. This I soon understood. Next was to know what time she intended to return back in the morning. She said the cart would be ready at 7 O Clock, therefore she wished to see me by 6 if possible, unless I could make arrangements to stay with them all night, but this would not be prudent at present, therefore I thought best to retire, I took my leave of my charmer and Louisa and then made all sail for my destined port. I arrived in time. My Messmates were all quite merry over a game at cards. They had two or three bottles of wine to come in, and we sat chattering with the Old Landlord, a Butcher by trade, a great royalist. At last the clock struck twelve and all hands immediately fled to their nests. We had good beds but sleep was farr from me. My thoughts on what steps I had already taken and what I was about to undertake occupied my mind untill I heard the clock strike five. I rose and drest, walked the room a few minuites, then called on Andrew, my only confidental friend. He soon dressed himself. We left the house; Andrew wanted to know where I was going so early and I soon convinced him. On entering the Mansion where all my comfort lay, Mary was the lovely Porter. Andrew drew back. Mary flew to my Arms and with her lively turn says, 'What, Mr. Smith, are you affraid of me? You were not so in Richelieu.' He then enter'd and saw Louisa. They as usual salluted him. He then turns round to me. Louisa and me made our excuse for a little while and left Mary to unfold the whole secret to Andrew. Louisa advised me to get married in Poitiers as there was a Protestant Church and ministers established in that city since the reign of Edward the black Prince who lays burried in the Church.[1]

April 6. Louisa also requested me to write her word from Poitiers how circumstances were with us and every particular that might occur, to direct to Louisa Francois; her father would not know any thing of it, untill his pursuit would be vain. She also made me promise if ever we got our liberty that Mary and me should pay them a visit in Richelieu, all which I sealed on her lips with a faithfull promise to perform, and at parting her last request was not be ungenerous to Mary nor act beyond the bounds of honour untill the laws of God and Man had united us together in lawful wedlock which she hoped another night's sleeping apart would terminate. I faithfully promised Louisa to take her kind advice; we then entered the room where Mary and Andrew were verry busy, Mary relateing our intentions, and he listening. 'Come, Wetherell,' says Andrew, 'we must go. Our beugles sounded some time ago.' I advised Mary not to start untill after breakfast with the waggon, so that she might overtake us at the half way house.

We took our farewell of poor Louisa never more to behold her lovely grief worn face. Tears fell on all sides; I took my leave of my young adventurer and we parted. We went to the Square where our Men were nearly all present. The morning was quite hazy and soon turned into a rainy day. Never Mind; the two Sisters have each a covered carriage, and as for me I can back off a little Moisture. The Mayor saw us count the men and all being correct signed our papers and off we started with our four baggage carts in front. The rain prevented the band playing but our beugles made a verry good change, and

[1] The Black Prince lies buried in Canterbury Cathedral, although he won the most famous of his victories at Poitiers. Many of his ancestors, however, those of Angevin origin, have their tombs there.

took us clear of Chatellereault. William Crown and Johnson took their turn to start ahead. We all proceeded on with speed. Owing to the rain nothing particular took place untill we were close up to the halting place, a beautiful little village. I began to look back for my young adventurer and on entering the Village I, being nearly the headmost man, heard some one call my name. Looking round saw a Waggon driveing up towards me with a horse Gendarme on one side, and an old Gentleman rideing on the other side. Ah, I was thunder struck!! All the fiends from the infernal regions could not have struck me with such unexpected terror as those unwelcome visitors at that present moment! I stood, my heart flutter'd within me! I gazed, and Oh, cruel fortune; what was worse than a dagger pierceing my breast. I beheld what nearly deprived me of my reason—My dear Mary waveing her white handkerchief to me and beckoning me to go to them. I was young and robust and in fact could bear more than the general run of young men. They stopped the Waggon and the two horseman sat by it. I plucked up every grain of Courage that was to be found in my possession. Towards them I went, casting a side glance at the fountain of my joy, or Grief. She was bathed in tears. Father Collardo rode up to me; he looked sorrowful at me. At last he says, 'My Son, give me your hand,' which he held fast in his. 'Be not the least daunted my Child. I lay nothing to your charge, nor yet to my own Child. She has already confessed to me that she followed you entirely for the love she has for you and that you did not delude her away from her home with any carnal intentions. Things appear to me that you do love each other but you must be parted at present. Perhaps,' continued the Father, 'the day is not far distant when you will have free liberty to return to Richelieu where you shall both be united in one and untill that time you must be parted. My daughter must return with me to Richelieu and you must pursue your journey. This, my dear young man, is the only advice I can give you. Wait with patience, be true to your country, and perseverance may restore my daughter lawfully to your arms once more. This is all the chance you can have to gain your prize. Therefore we must return. The rain is too heavy to delay. If you wish to speak to her and take your leave I will wait with the greatest pleasure.' He rode on one side and I flew to the arms of my lovely Angel. His utterance was nearly past comprehension owing to her sobs and sighs. 'Ah, my dear John, this will soon terminate my existence. I shall never live to see you again! Let me feast my eyes on you for the last time. My dear John, my last request is keep my Medal and what it contains, and when you look at it think of your faithful Mary, and she will always love and pray for you. Farewell, my darling boy, farewell.'

I descended from the waggon; the old Man took my hand, shook it, and put five crowns into it. 'There, My Son, take that and my blessing, farewell. . . .' They turned round their horses and back they drove and left me standing a living Statute, worse than I should have felt had I fallen into the hands of some Banditte of robbers that took from me all the treasure I had in the world, then strip't me of all my apparrel and left me like Adam naked; I stood and gazed after them reflecting on cruel fortune Vc. They vanished from my sight. 'She has gone. My all, my only hope is tore from me; what shall I do? It is folly to pursue her, she is safe guarded and cannot be regained, God bless her, I will follow my companions; their lively romances and cheerful discourse perhaps may drive away part of my ponderous burden of trouble and sorrow.' My young companion Andrew waited on the road for me; he joined me, and he himself was very much hurt with the unfortunate circumstance. Him and Mary were always great friends in Richelieu. We waited a little while in the village, took each a little Brandy and water, and so proceeded on to Poitiers. We had a heavy shower of rain as we drew near the city, went into a tavern in the environs of the city, waited near half an hour until the rain abated and we entered the gates of Poitiers.

I felt a little apprehnsive that Crown or Aplen might have some hint of my disappointment but they had not taken any notice of my being called and stopping behind. I put the best leg foremost as we passed thro' the streets. We soon Met Crown, Aplen, and Johnson. They took notice of me not being so cheerful as usual. Andrew said I had felt a little unwell and he staid by me in a tavern on the road till I felt a little better.

Aplen said yes, he supposed I was fretting about the girl in Richelieu. I utterly denied that story, being certain she was a considerable distance from Richelieu. However when supper was over my only study was to get to my bed, which I had a good oportunity to do. My Messmates all went out to see fashions. I embraced the oportunity and off I went to bed where I lay meditateing on the sad reverses of fortune that had that unfortunate day tore from my Arms, my sweet lovely Mary. I slept a little towards Morning and that greatly refreshed me. I considered that she was gone, and were I to give vent to grief I should make myself continually unhappy all to no purpose. It would not bring back my lost treasure nor do me any good whatever. I therefore determined to form a resolution and drive all Melancholy thoughts out of my Mind. In the Morning I arrose, took a walk on the ramparts and being warned the night before that we were to halt that day in Poitiers I did not return home untill breakfast was over. The good lady of the house made me a bowl of strong coffee which gave me great relief. I had been verry sick all the morning oweing to my not eating any thing since the morning before when I took a cup of Coffee at Chatellereault at 12 noon. We mustered in the grand Place and were all called over by the Comissarie Mayor, Vc. We were all correct according to our Felle de Route, 341 Men and 1 Woman. 2 Men went to the hospital left us 339 Men. The day was fine and clear. We were greatly amused, looking round the antient works and curiosities that were once the pride and dwellings of the King of Great Britain.

At 4 P.M. the beugles sounded to muster, which was answered. The Mayor's secretary brought orders from the Bureau that the Comissarie and Mayor thought propper for us to halt again tomorrow as the roads between Poitiers and Louisgnan [Lusignan] were verry bad owing to the late heavy rains. This Muster was soon over. We had nothing to do, only eat, drink, and Sleep. Crown, Andrew, and myself took a walk round the Subberbs of the city and returned home owing to some Snow beginning to fall. We passed the evening with our landlord; he was a Doctor, a fine Old fellow, one of Louis's party. He made himself certain that before another week passed round Louis 18th would be king of France; he also told us that Paris was taken by the Allied Armies and Bonaparte was made prisoner by his own Officers. This all helped to cheer our spirits, and give us fresh courage to continue our March a few days longer. He then caused us to wash this down with good Cogniac.

We passed the remainder of the evening in discourse on various subjects. The Old Gentleman spoke his mind freely as to his opinion regarding the present state of France and its Imperial Government. I begged to be excused from the company owing to not having much sleep the night before, neither did I at that time feel verry smart. My absence was granted, and bed was my most agreeable company at that time. I retired to my room and when alone by myself my past disappointments began to crowd on my mind; nevertheless I diverted trouble with the conquering delusions of Sleep and it was daylight next morning before any thing troubled me, excepting silly foolish dreams. I found myself greatly refreshed after my good night's rest, got up, went down to breakfast, eat quite hearty then we all took a walk round the ramparts. We visited the English Church (the Church that was to have sealed all my joys) and we also were admitted into the Burrying place of the English Kings that in former days were laid within the vaulted walls of that Antient Mass of Magnificent Architecture. We also took a turn round the Grand horse barracks and should have visited many other curiosities in this Antient City, but a heavy fall of rain caused us to repair home and take shelter under the doctor's roof, where we passed the remainder of the day. In the evening Aplen went up to the Bureau for the Mayor's Orders, Our Route was signed, Waggons ordered, and all ready to March at 8 in the Morning. He returned with his message and we all went to rest early, that we might rise early.

On the following Morning, April the 9th, we rose early in the morning and found the ground all covered with Snow. We should have chose to be excused starting that Morning, but the decree was passed and we must proceed; we all met in the square, were muster'd by the Secretary, had two large covered Waggons, secured our Drum and Instruments with our Baggage, Mounted Jannet as a guard in one of the Waggons, and Marched 339 Men for Lousignan, 18 Miles, snow falling lightly all day. However the wind blew quite fresh, which kept the roads pretty well clear of Snow. We got to the town of Lousignan about 2 PM. and met Crown and Johnson on our entering the town. They had no billets but what we found afterwards was equally as good: we were quartered in a Church that had been converted into a sort of hospital or assylum, for those that passed thro the place. We arrived at the appointed place, and found every thing clean and comfortable, cradles with straw beds and two good blankets for every two men, a large fire at each end of the ward, and several Women to attend and prepare Victuals which we soon had the oportunity of tasteing, because they served us Soup and bread, for eight in a Mess, then beef and potatoes, Vc . . . all good and clean. We got our route from the Mayor and went to rest early (no brandy enters those doors).

April 10. The Morning was quite mild, made the roads a little sloppy under foot, but we were all pretty well shod, and met, all present, had three carts, and started, for the Village of St. Maixent, 19 Miles. We soon got through this day's journey, arrived, were billeted, and all to our quarters by three in the afternoon (fine people in this little place).

April 11. A fine warm clear Morning. We mustered early and had our Route signed. We had one Waggon and three carts, 339 all present. We made the happy little village all ring when Leversedge gave his arm a swing. We gave them a parting tune and by the good character they had given us of Niort and the newse we had on the road we were all eager to get there. The roads were good and we had 25 miles to March. Aplen and Johnson were left with the party while Crown, Andrew, and his honour, Made the best of our way ahead, to get the orders ready when the party came up to the City!

On our way we met several Peasants, some of them quite Mellow, waveing their hats and shouting, 'Vive Louis dix huit!' Crown first took notice of what they said. He turned round to us took off his hat and cheered danced and caper'd round like a mad man. I stared at him. The Peasants began to draw near us; we then heard them distinctly proclaiming Louis the eighteenth king of France!! What glorious tidings! 'This cannot be true,' says Andrew. 'The newse is too good!' By this time the smock frocks were up to us. 'Vive Louis dix huit,' says a Merry old farmer. 'What are you?' says another. We answered them that we were British Prisoners of War. 'No, no,' says the old Grasscomber, at the same time tugging out a bottle that he carried in the bosom of his frock. 'Come my friends, drink, long live Louis the 18th. You are no longer Prisoners. You are our friends and brothers! your liberty is restored and Louis is Proclaimed king of France, this day in Niort. Napoleon is dethroned and Peace is once more restored to our distressed and depopulated country. Come, Sons, take another swig, and we will make our village ring with the happy tidings we are bearing to our families and friends. Adieu my Brothers! Vive Louis dix huit,' says the hearty old cock, and away they trudged towards their homes, and we towards Niort: it is easy to think what effect those glad tidings had amongst us. One moment we thought it could only be a delusion and perhaps what was the desire of the Peasants. On the other hand we said it was possible enough as we had been frequently told by People that were the most experienced and able to form some idea of the state their country was in. We kept wandering along as quickly as we possibly could to be convinced whether or no; we soon came near the Gates of the City and seeing nothing more than usual we began again to be doubtful but this silly notion was soon banished. On entering the city some of the Soldiers in the Guardhouse between the Walls fired a Musket out at the Window and displayed a large white Flag with the following inscription on it: 'Vive Louis dix huit.' Now what ought we to say? Thank kind fortune this must be true.

We had not gone many steps farther before an elderly lady looked out at a window, 'Stop, young men,' says she. 'You look like strangers. Step in a moment!' We did; it was a large Gentleman's house. The Lady enquired our Nation, what we were, and she then made us welcome to what we pleased, to drink the health of Louis. She also gave us each a white ribbond for our hats, informing us that we were no longer Prisoners! Our captive chains were burst asunder that Moment Louis was proclaim'd king.

CHAPTER

14

APRIL *15, 1814.* A Snowey Morning. At 7 A.M. our beugles
sounded, 'Up and march away.' We Muster'd in the
Square at 8. The Mayor and Comissarie were present;
our number was 332 present (and 7 in the hospital). Jannet
Carter had been so much kept among the ladies of the city that
I have not had a sight of her in Niort until this morning. Poor
girl, she has been verry kindly treated by the ladies. They have
furnished her with a verry handsome new cloth habit, laced
boots and every thing comfortable for the road. Jannet was as
usual ready to take charge of the Baggage but the lady of the
house where she had been liveing in sent her chair and horse
with a servant to drive it and requested the little heroine to be
seated in the chair; that his orders were to take her to Melle.
Away goes Jannet. The Mayor presented us the felle de route,
and we started. Aplen and Johnson off to Melle mounted on
two Mules to have our billets ready on our arrival. All being
ready the word was given to proceed, and Leversedge set all
hands in motion by a stroke on his drum. Our Band struck up
the favourite old air of 'Brittons strike home.' Thus we left the
city of Niort.

April 15. We marched from Niort to Melle, a double stage
27 Miles. Light snow fell most of the day. Our party towards
the latter part of the day must look something like a gang of
Gypsies changeing their abode. In one place there was a horse
or mule with two or three Quixottes mounted waddling thro'
the snow; in another place one mounted, another leading the
poor creature by the bridle, dragging him along with his head

and neck stretched out in a direct line, and three or four dodgeing along under his lee, and as for the Waggons they were the head quarters and towards the latter end of the day's march well manner both within and outside under their lee.

We reached the Village of Melle about 4 P.M. Our Partners had Billets ready on our arrival. We took our Baggage from the Waggons and to our quarters with all haste out of the snow. We had verry good billets in this small place amongst the farmers. Milk and eggs were chief of our diet, then to bed, as it was the best place after our fatigueing day's journey.

April 22. A fine dry morning; we left the City of Limoges for the Village of Pierre Buffierre, 18 miles. Aplen and Johnson went a head. Crown Andrew and me remained with the party. We passed along quite cheerfully nearly half way, with many of us wearing the white cockade, when on turning a corner of the road we saw a whole body of Soldiers meeting us. At this place the road was cut thro' a hill and the foot path led above on each side the road. Crown was driveing a head, never took any thought about his white cockade, nor did he notice their tricoloured flag on their helmets. One of the Officers rode up to him and gave him a blow with his Sword and iron scabbard that laid poor Crown sprawling on the grass. 'There you English rascal. Take that, and strike your white cockade in a Moment or I will sever your head from your body.' At the same time two or three soldiers dismounted and ran up to Crown tore the cockade off his hat and they all danced on it exclaiming, 'Down with the Bourbons and long live Napoleon!' We that were behind and saw how the game went had our colours struck in an instant. They left Crown and passed thro' the midst of us looking for more game but we took the hint on the first onset and untill they had all gone past put on quite serious tricoloured face but still kept a heart as pure as a lilley shelter'd by a British rose.

As we passed those ill minded fellows they passed a great many malicious threats on us. We were this, that, and the other, and if they had their will they would send us where they had lately sent some of our countrymen at Toulouse (that was to grass with our mouth downwards). We made no reply but proceeded our route. We then came up with Crown. He was verry angry at the mean spirited fellow that struck him in such a cowardly manner. We proceeded on towards our destined Village. When we got there our two comerades gave us the hint that those were not our kind of folks. We therefore halted on the entrance of the place, served out billets, took each man his baggage and to our quarters. Those who had not enough to eat and drink contrived to buy what they needed and we passed the evening and night as well as we could. We learnt also that those troops we had passed were part of the Army that Wellington had beat near Toulouse thro' their not acknowledgeing Louis as their King. They held the city in the name of Napoleon untill they were compelled to surrender after a horrid slaughter when the British took the city in the name of Louis the 18th.

April 23. A fine hard morning. We had 3 carts, got our papers signed, and marched thro the place with the March. Played 'Louis Returned.' Outside the place we made the best of our way to St Germain, 16 Miles, and got there quite early. Our boys were ready for us. Andrew and Johnson preferred the task to go a head and draw billets, which I cared verry little about. I mostly remained with the party and Andrew being the fifth Interpreter mostly took my turn to start ahead. They gave us to know that we were all right. We soon awoke all the children in the Village with a volley or two from our travailing two gun'd battery. We entered the village and set their windows all danceing to our electrical instruments. At the Mayor's door we saluted the old gentleman with three rolls and then served out billets and dispersed every thing good, and free, in this little paradise. Next Morning it rained hard, however, we all met at the Mayor's door, had 4 Carts, and on the 24th of April we marched for Uzerche, 23 Miles. We had a sorry day of it; however we got through and arrived, got billets and took shelter.

April 24. We anchored in Uzerche after a verry disagreeable day's journey, eat our victuals and soon looked for bed. Hung our wet things in the corner and started to our rest. The Mayor was a horse so we let him rest in the Stable. He is three colours and might kick, so we leave him and start away in Search of the Mayor of Tuolle [Tulle], only 18 miles. We had 4 Carts and a fine morning to March through Uzerche to the rap, tap, rap, pap, tap, dumb March. We soon reached Tulle April the 25th; 325 Men. My friend William Crown was quite out of order all the day yesterday and this day he gave up, unable to proceed any further on foot. At the half way house we fixed him quite comfortable in a coverd baggage cart in the charge of our trusty young Nurse Jannett. We reached Tulle and were directed to a Convent, a real fine place, an Assylum for travellers. Here is also an hospital on the same principals, attended entirely by the ladies of the Veil. We had every thing good, clean, and plenty: clean linen for every man and good comfortable beds. We lodged Crown by his own request in the hospital or rather in the Nursery.

The Mayor visited us and told us to ask for any thing we wanted, and the ladies would get it for us. He also told us that we must halt in Tulle tomorrow and those who wanted shoes should have them on the new constitution in the name of Louis the 18th. This was happy tidings to us haveing to halt tomorrow amongst our friends where we can speak our mind without deception, nor false faces. We took a look round this beautiful city, and at Sunset our band play'd a tune in the yard fronting our Castle. We passed the evening verry comfortable and on the 26th in the morning, fine weather, we took a tour round the Market. We then attended breakfast. After this was over the Mayor sent word that he wished to see the Interpreters at the Bureau by ten O clock. We attended his honour, and his request was for our people to Muster and be at the Bureau by 2 in the afternoon. This was also done, and all who were badly shod, got new Shoes and Stockings. Then we got an order to admit 2 More of our men that were taken verry ill to the hospital. This was granted and we returned to our castle well shod.

We then took our sick to the hospital and saw Crown. He was rather low. We did not trouble him much but passed on. The ladies said he required to be kept as still as possible in his present situation. We left them and called at the Bureau. The Mayor expressed a great desire to have our Music Play in the Square that evening at 6 O clock. We told him that the Musicians were dispersed all round the city and the only way to gather them together was to let our Beugles Sound a general

THE *Adventures* OF JOHN WETHERELL

Muster, then all hands could be counted over and the band have their notice to attend in the Square, and thus dismiss again. This was his wish; we therefore sent Young Andrew to look for Alms or Mr. McNally, the two leaders of the Beugles, and warn them to sound General Muster. It was not long ere we heard our Beugles rattle thro' the Streets in all directions. The Mayor attended the Muster. We counted heads and Made 322 Men, gave the band their orders and broke up; at 6 we met in the square where all the heads of the city were met to hear a specimen of our Abilities.

April 26. This evening we played two hours in the square, then we were sent to the Hotel de la Ville where we had what ever we chose to drink and 5 francs each man a present from the ladies of the city. We play'd them the new rondeau, 'Louis's return,' and returned to our Castle.

May 1. Marched from Aurillac and left Tho. Johnson and Andrew Smith with the party. Aplen and me, haveing fine weather and, more than that, light hearts, were wide awake this day. We came to the first Village on our way, took a little refreshment, and away we tramped for the next place to halt in. We reached that village at the same time some of the British Officers entered the place, being some of the Officers belonging the British troops that were on their March to Aurillac. Some of them halted at the small tavern where we were. They seemed not to take any particular notice of us, as we were in our French dress and were speaking French to the landlord; however one of the the young fellows, I suppose a Captain, steps up to the landlord. 'Well, my old daddy,' says he, 'have you any cogniac brandy?' 'Oui Monsieur,' says the landlord. He presents the Officer a bottle and a glass, as customary in that part. 'No, no, old man, I dont want this thing, give me a tumbler and some water.' The old man shook his head, not understanding what he said. Aplen and me sat by the window grinning to see the farce.

One of the Officers that stood near the door says, 'Come Captain, I believe the Old Gentleman and you are makeing that grog,' 'Why damn it, I am waiting for a tumbler.' Aplen spoke to the Old Man and told their wants; and he gave them a tumbler and a jog of water. The Captain then looked round at us. 'What? Do you understand English?' 'Yes, Sir,' said I, smileing, 'I ought to.' 'Why, what the devil are you, in that gaol bird's dress?' 'We are English Men and have suffered nearly eleven years confinement in the cause of our country.' He looked in amazement at us. 'My God,' he exclaimed. 'Gentlemen, look this way,' says he to his brother Officers. They all gather'd round. 'Here is two of our Countrymen that has been confined all the war in this country by that infernal Bonaparte and his cursed crew.' Then was the time that I wanted half a score tongues to answer each person's questions. They wanted to know the whole history of our Captivity at once; however we gave them to understand our present business. Then we must drink and eat and talk all at one breath. They wanted ham and eggs, but for want of time had to put off with bread and cheese. They said their Men were two leagues behind, and we calculated our party about the same distance. They asked us how the Bonaparte's followers used us since Louis was proclaimed king. We mentioned the affair of the Officer that struck Crown and trampled on the white cockade and how they made us all strike our white colours, threat'ning us what they would do. 'Stop!' says the Captain. 'What was their number?' 'They were the 7th regt. of Invincible guards,' says Aplen, 'on their march to Fontenay in La Vendee.' 'Damn me!' says the Captain. 'Those were the verry same fellows stopped our baggage Guard on the road from Niort to Limoges. They made all the guard halt in a small village and ordered them to strike their white ribbons that they wore in their button hole. The Serjeant answer'd them that the Men in that little village had just given them the white cockades to wear as the Emblems of Louis the 18th. This Serjeant of ours is a Guernsey Man and spoke French fluently. His name is John Bray. He knew that our Men were close at hand—so they were; however this valient Egyptian hero, as they stile the invincibles that were in Egypt, he ordered them to strike their white colours; if not he would be at the trouble to do it for them. "Well Sir," says Bray, "and supposeing we were to strike the colours of Louis the 18th, what will be the consequence? By whose authority am I to inform my General that I was ordered to do so? Certainly when we arrive at our place of destination my officers will require an account for such cowardly conduct as this will be, if I were to do it, to strike the colours that we are sworn to defend, and not know who it is we have struck them to, nor by what authority you have given those orders." "I tell you, Sir, I order you and your Men to strike them in the name of our Emperor Napoleon." "Ah, ah, ah," says Bray, "now you Mention your Master, I shall have to consider a moment. Pray, Sir, have you seen your Emperor lately to give you those orders?" The great and valliant hero drew his Sword, and swore if he was not obeyed instantly his men should obey him and use such means as he would not wish to do, but as words appeared to be useless he should try what the Sword could do. "Now Sir," says Serjt. Bray, "you are jesting. I know you are more of a Gentleman than to use any rash means on such a silly affair. We are only eleven men and you are a regiment strong, as appears by your Men that are comeing up. Suppose you take us back to the next Village; there you can lodge our two waggons and I shall save my character. There in presence of the Mayor I give you my honour we all will strike." But Serjeant Bray knew the detachment of his division was near at hand; this was the Mayor he meant. "Well then return back before us," Says Monsieur Steel Jacket. So Bray and his small party, with their two heavy waggons turned about, and like a decoy duck, let Monsieur into such a snare that he would have given all the tricolour'd cockades in his regiment to have passed Bray; and as he could not bear the sight of the Bourbon cockade, he might have shut his eyes and rode along. But to return to Serjeant Bray: He, and his few men countermarched the road about a mile, when turning round a corner of a Wood, that lay on the side of the road, there the whole body of the British troops were close at hand. Bray proceeded on towards them.

'Monsieur looked, then halted, then conversed with some of the Officers, then halted the regiment. He was struck with astonishment. "What shall I say to those fellows when they enquire My reason for insulting one of their Officers and makeing prisoners of their guard and baggage?" By this time the party were up with Bray. "What the devil is the matter now, Bray?" says the Lieut. Colonel. Bray, smileing, repeated

the business in a few words. He told the Colonel that he came
back to strike Louis's colours, as he made sure they could not
be verry far in the rear and the Man of Steel was there waiting
to see him fulfill his verbal treaty. "Yes," says the Colonel,
"you shall strike and that damn'd hard." He then halted the
whole division, formed 8 deep and then advanced with the
drums and fifes playing "Louis's return." Monsieur sent 6 or
8 of the Steel Jackets a head to hear what newse. They were
rideing past verry cevil, but Bray, by the Colonel's orders,
commanded them in French to halt. They obey'd. He then
ordered them to strike to the honourable flag of Louis the 18th
by order of his highness the Duke of Wellington, commander
in Chief of the British forces in France. "Strike immediately
that tri-colour'd cockade from your helmets or they will be
immediately struck for you." The Col. order'd the 12 Men to
advance up to them with charged bayonets but not to touch
one of them. The moment this was done, Bray, being the
Interpreter, asked them if they were going to strike the tri-
colour'd cockade. They looked round to their Commandant
(he was observing their motions at a distance). "Well," says
the Serjeant, "it is useless to resist any longer," so he very
tenderly took his blue, white, and red from his helmet and the
others followed his example. Serjt. Bray stept up and took the
Serjeant's cockade, hove it on the ground and set his foot on it.
"There Monsieur," says Bray, "I told you I would strike when
we got to the Village, but we have not reached it yet, therefore
you have to strike to me for not takeing me there undisturbed."
The Col. then told Bray to tell them they might pursue their
journey, and the Colonel advised them not to interfere any more
with any British Subjects on their travails through the country.
They passed on and the British Marched on towards the
Commandant and his men of Steel. They remained in their
position the same as at first only with this exception: they had
every Man taken off their cockades. We marched past them
with the same tune as before "Louis's return." When we passed
their Commandant, Bray saluted him with "vive Louis dix
huit," and in this Manner we left them.'

This tale took our time nearly an hour, which made both us
and the Officers think about moveing. We took our road

towards Argental and they towards Aurillac. We hurried along nearly 4 or 5 miles when we met all the troops and their baggage. We spoke to several Officers who enquired what we were and where we were going and many other questions. We answer'd them all as quick as we could with civility and respect and kept on our journey untill we had seen the rear of them. Then our discourse was entirely about those lousy invincibles and poor Bill Crown untill we reached the town of Argental, went to the Mayor, got our Billets, and met our Men in good time at the entrance of the town. Served the billets and Marched up to the square to that verry hateful tune (to those folks) 'Louis's return.' We dismissed to our quarters, small rain beginning to fall quite fast.

May 3. Hazy weather. Took breakfast and made ready to start. Crown came danceing in and halloo'd out for something to eat and drink We then met together in the square. Had 4 Waggons, started them off under the charge of our female guard. His honour the Mayor visited us and bade us a long adieu. We then started the waggon with 'o'er the hills and far away,' and on passing the gates struck up 'Louis' return.' Johnson and Smith took their turn to provide lodgings at night. Crown, Aplen and his honour remained with the party. After we had got well started we began to have a little pastime with Crown about the length of the steel Jackets Sword and how heavy he thought it was. 'Well, Crown,' says Aplen, 'Wetherell and me can tell you a little ditty that will make you treat at the half way house,' 'You can?' says Crown. 'Well then, go on with it and we will leave it to the opinion of Wetherell who shall pay the piper.' All agreed. Aplen related over the tale of Bray and the Man in Steel. He got to where Bray turned back to see the Mayor before he liked to strike his white cockade. 'There, there,' says Crown, 'it is my treat.' 'Wait a moment,' says Aplen, 'till you hear how he struck.' 'Well, proceed,' says Crown. He then got to where they met the whole division of British that Bray was attached to, and indeed them he was looking for. Crown was fully satisfied, but when he heard how Bray took their three stripes and stamped his foot on them and the Commandant with all his invincibles had to dowse their stripes, Crown leaped and halloe'd like a wild man.

'Now,' says he, 'I will treat twenty times at such a curious way as this is to hear how things will round. Makes the French word prove true that says "never mind, John, your day to day and mine to morrow." Now I am contented,' says Crown, 'and freely forgive the fellow that took such a pleasure in laying a snare to take himself.' We arrived at the half way house, took our treat and then travailed on for Uzerche, only 18 miles, a light days Journey. We are in no great hurry to this three coloured Mayor. We know him before; however in our present circumstances we regard him no farther than in civility. We reached the town, got our Billets, Marched in to the tune of 'Louis's return'd,' discharged our baggage, and to our billets, much of the miserable (says poor Thomas Crisp). However we made crooked places straight and brought morning.

On the 7th of May we left Limoges for the Village of Bellac, 26 Miles. This was only a morning's promenade for us. We were at the Village in a jiffey. In this small place we all turned farmers, eat fat bacon and beans. We also drank small wine by the jug full as a substitute for tea or coffee. Some of our men were billeted, they said, three miles from the Village. Aplen, Crown, Andrew, and me were at the Mayor's house, a good mile across the ploughed fields from the Main road.

It was in this Village that we took possession of a farm house from the whole family merely through harmless passtime. Crown and Me took our Bassons along with us into a cottage near the Mayor's house. Our errand was to look for a drop of Brandy, which we found. We sat down talking to each other in English. The Old Man, the Old Woman, their Son and Daughter all stared at us! 'What are they saying?' says the Son. Aplen winked at us. 'Now,' says he, 'we will have a little fun.' He turns to the Master of the house and says in French, 'What nation do you think we belong?' The poor Man shook his head and said he could not tell unless we were English or Germans. 'No, no,' says Aplen. The Son steps to where we had set the two Bassoons. Takeing up one of them he says to Aplen, 'What is this thing to do?' Bill starts at the poor fellow. 'Oh, my God, take care—you will kill some person. She is loaded.' 'What!' exclaimed the old father. 'Loaded, is it a gun?' 'Set it down, Louey, set it down and go away from such dangerous engines as them. You might have blown the house and all of us in it into the Air had not this good gentleman been fortunate enough to have noticed you in time. He most likely has saved all our lives.' 'Yes,' says the Old Woman, 'I have often cautioned you, Louey, not to meddle with things that did not belong to you. A pretty story would have been to tell. Perhaps you might have shot Me, or your father, or even your dear Sister, with your curiosity. Do, my good Gentlemen, put them instruments of death in the barn, where they will be quite safe untill you go away.' 'Now you shall see some sport,' says Bill. 'No, Madam, says he, running to the Bassons and took up one of them holding it out towards the Son and Snapping one of the long brass keys, 'we are Cossaques.' The Son set up a roar and fled into the barn, where his Sister was already concealed. The Old woman fell speechless across the table; the Old man down on his marrow bones, praying us not to take their lives nor terrify them out of their Senses and we should have the best of all he had in the house. Aplen returned his gun into the Corner and told the Man we wanted some bread and Milk made hot. 'Yes Sir, yes Sir,' says the old Man, 'in a minute, in a minute.' The good old dame arose from her dream and tottled across the room to a large Chair in the corner. She looked verry hard at the two guns, then at us. At last the old man came puffing in from the milk room with a large brass kettle full of Milk. He soon made it hot and put plenty of bread in it, then set it on the table, gave us bowls and spoons, and at it we went, more for the sake of deviltry than for the want of bread and milk. When we were engaged with the bread and milk the good Man enquired of Aplen if we were the Cossaques that kill people and eat them and destroy every thing they fall in with. We now thought we had carried the joke far enough and must wind up a little; 'No, no, Sir,' answered Aplen, 'we are quite a different Nation. Our greatest pleasure is to prevent the shedding of humane blood and this is our Motto—we conquer to save—so that you nor your family has the least cause to be any ways jealous of us. I suppose,' says Aplen, 'you know that your neighbour the Mayor directed us to your cottage? 'Yes Sir,' answered the peasant. 'We always lodge the people that are billeted on the

Mayor; he has a large family and no room for Strangers Vc.
I suppose he informed you that my beds were straw but clean,
and clean warm bed cloaths to cover you. This is what we give
all our own troops that pass and repass thro' Bellac.'

Night drawing on we went to bed quite comfortable and in
the morning quite early the Old Man and woman were up
they had a good fire and another kettle of Milk hot ready for
us. We arose, took our poultice as the doctor had prepared it,
and Mounted our knapsacks, shoulder'd our Muskets and just
as we gained the top of a little hill outside of the barn Aplen
looked back and saw the farmer's Son and Daughter peering
out at the barn door. Aplen snatched my Bassoon and pointed
it at the two poor terrified Prisoners; they quickly hid themselves again by slamming to the door. Again we made a start
across the wearisome ploughed fields; the morning was
charming and the small birds salluted us from each bush as we
passed along. Our Beugles also invited us to pay our Morning
visit to the rest of our countrymen who were mustering together
from all direction. We being all ready and three waggons for
our baggage, made Sail for the Village of Lusac, all in great
spirits Vc., distance, 34 Miles.

May 8. After a long day's journey we arrived at Lusac,
got our billets and found all things plentiful and good, went
early to bed, and took our rest Vc.

On the 9th of May all met quite early to start off for Poitiers,
29 Miles. Fine Morning and 4 Carts to attend us. We gave the
Mayor (a fine young Gentleman) three rounds from our two
gun'd battery, and a taste of 'Louis's return' Vc., then steer
away for the City of Poitiers. We got there by 4 in the afternoon, Johnson and Smith met us with the Billets. They found
a new Mayor in the city, a good sort of a man. We served our
billets and repaired to our various lodgings. after we got
settled and took our dinner, Aplen went to the hospital with
2 of our Men that were Sick, and brought back the two that
we left on our March to the South; I went along with my
bosom friend Andrew and took a look at the English Church
that was once to crown all my happiness . . . but, no, it was
not to be, therefore I must take my farewell of both the Church
and the treasure that it was to have bequeathed to me. However

I can yet have a glimerring spark of comfort, that is of fulfilling her last request—that was, to write every oportunity! Accordingly we went to our lodgings and I took my pen and wrote in my usual Style. I addressed old Pierre Collardo as Father, and Louise, as Sister Vc., and as for the grand address! That is left to myself. I told them I should write again on my Arrival in St. Maloes which would be in about 12 days' time and to be sure and have a letter ready for me when I get there. I gave them My address Vc., to be left in the Post office untill call'd for yours Vc., J P W. I then took it to the Post Office and finished my day's work, went to bed not to Sleep but lay and think what to do.

May 10. Fine morning, We had 3 carts and marched to Marebari, 25 Miles. we had good billets and on the 11th of May we had 4 Carts and travailed to Airvault, 33 Miles. Fine weather good billets, and on the 12th of May rainy Vc., we arrived in Chatillon [Châtillon-sur-Sèvre], 31 Miles, had grand usuage and plenty. On the 13th we reached the Village of Mortagne [Mortagne-sur-Sèvre], 18 Miles, good lodgings Vc. Next day the 14th we got into the City of Nantes, 29 miles, good quarters, left 3 in the hospital, and on the 15th of May we Marched to Blain, 17 Miles. Poor billets, left Johnson Sick. May 17th we reached BALM [Bain-de-Bretagne?], 34 Miles, good billets, and on the 17th we arrive in Rennes, 29 Miles. We had a large room in the City hall and plenty of everything. On the 18th we halted to have our Arrears paid up, and new Shoes Vc. May 18th we were paid 12 francs, each man had shoes where they were wanting, put 3 Men in the hospital, and on the 19th, fine morning, Aplen, Andrew and Myself left Crown with the party, and at 4 in the morning we left Rennes and walked to Becherel, 27 Miles. By ten O clock took some refreshment and walked to Combourg 17 Miles by 3 in the afternoon halted at the Mayors left our orders and made the last Push.—to St. Survey [St. Servan], 23 Miles, where we took lodging in a tavern for that night. Now my boys we once more beheld the Salt water and Vessels Vc. We were determin'd to call this a day's March, only 67 Miles.

We being at last arrived on the Sea coast, it was time to leave off keepping any more journal of our land travails. I therefore took an oportunity at the time my Messmates were sleeping I was employed writeing a few incorrect lines that chanced to strike my intention at that present time therefore I sat down in the bed chamber and wrote as follows:

> each day we various scenes behold
> at night in cells we sleep
> should all prove true that we are told
> France for thy children weep.
>
> No more beneath th'oppressive hand
> of tyrany we groan
> but March to join that happy land
> which freedom calls her own.   J P W

*   *   *

*H*ere *is a fitting place to end Wetherell's account of his adventures. He still had to wander for some time and in the end it was an American girl from Connecticut who secured him in matrimony. Wetherell subsequently became a Captain, and then migrated to New York, where he endeavoured to establish himself in a shore job as a ship fitter and rigger. This was when he married, but hard times frequently drove him to sea again to earn his living, even before the mast, and he suffered more than one shipwreck while engaged in the West Indian trade. For a time he had a home in Rahway, New Jersey, and he lived, and made his fair copy of his diary, in Chrystie Street, New York City. His later notes have not the interest of the earlier ones, and there is a bitter flavour to them, the result of hardship and disappointment, which is notably absent from the passages selected. It is best to leave him here in his new freedom.*